CRITICAL INSIGHTS

Fahrenheit 451

CRITICAL INSIGHTS

INSIGHTS

Fahrenheit 451
Ray Bradbury

Editor
Rafeeq O. McGiveron
Lansing Community College

SALEM PRESS
A Division of EBSCO Information Services, Inc.
Ipswich, Massachusetts

GREY HOUSE PUBLISHING

Library of Congress Cataloging-in-Publication Data

Fahrenheit 451 / editor, Rafeeq O. McGiveron. -- [1st ed.].
    p. : ill. ; cm. -- (Critical insights)
Includes bibliographical references and index.
ISBN: 978-1-61925-224-0
1. Bradbury, Ray, 1920-2012. Fahrenheit 451.   2. Book burning in literature.   3. Censorship in literature.   4. Science fiction, American--History and criticism. I. McGiveron, Rafeeq O. II. Series: Critical insights.

PS3503.R167 F363 2013
813/.54

Contents _____

Resources

About This Volume

Rafeeq O. McGiveron

Critical Insights: Fahrenheit 451 explores Ray Bradbury's most famous and most influential work of literature in a variety of contexts and from a number of different critical perspectives and intellectual foci. It is a cliché of the worst sort, of course, to observe that Bradbury's evocative, swiftly moving little novel is *more important now than ever*…and yet Del Rey editors of the 1990s did not hesitate, emblazoning the phrase upon the very cover of the book, so perhaps the editor of this volume could indulge as well. The statement is true, after all.

Yes, in *Fahrenheit 451*, we may catch the unmistakable, bygone flavor of the 1950s: the growing popularity of television in sensible little suburban houses, where cheery middle-class housewives pop Miltowns while looking ahead to the evening's cocktail party, the threat of atomic war never forgotten and yet never truly evaluated, and the McCarthyite climate of fear underlying it all. Even in a future of jet cars and motorcycle-helicopters and roboticized gizmos that butter the morning toast, still we recognize the quaintness of our long-vanished past. Readers once could only imagine ear-bud radios and four-wall televisions, but now we can truly *feel* the utter interconnectedness of the internet and ubiquitous smartphones and social media updated—and checked—around the clock.

Certainly, in our present world of fact, books in general are not banned, nor do the hoses of fire crews spew kerosene rather than water. The true future thus apparently is far, far different from Bradbury's cautionary nightmare, is it not? Why, we are not enslaved to our technology-enabled pleasures, are we? No, and our political parties are not merely the Ins and Outs, nor are our national elections only half a notch elevated from mere beauty contests. And in twenty-first-century America, our reading habits are not scrutinized by vast bureaucracies, nor can the publicly smiling agents of a seemingly beneficent government kick down citizens' doors to ransack their possessions, their rights, their very thoughts. Or— Hmmm…

Clearly, then, *Fahrenheit 451* is a work still worthy not only of wide readership but also of the scholarly investigation we do here. This volume is divided into four main sections. In the introductory section, I will discuss Bradbury's influential novel in broad terms—rather more experiential than thematic, actually—while Garyn G. Roberts gives a biography of the man behind the literature. The book's concluding section contains helpful resources such as a brief chronology of Bradbury's life for quick reference, a list of his major works, a bibliography of critical essays and books for further study, and an index of key terms used within this text. Bracketed between the opening and closing apparatus is the "meat" of this project: one section of critical context to help inform and set up readers' understanding of *Fahrenheit 451* and one section of critical readings exploring many various facets of the novel.

Garyn G. Roberts begins our critical context by discussing the cultural and historical milieu of Bradbury's now-famous book. Using the influences of Bradbury's childhood in the 1920s—small-town Midwestern life, literature from L. Frank Baum and Edgar Rice Burroughs,*Buck Rogers*, and *Flash Gordon* comics to "classics" by Victor Hugo, Alexander Dumas, and Fyodor Dostoyesky, and even films such as *The Hunchback of Notre Dame* and *King Kong*—Roberts discusses the role of Nazi book-burning, McCarthyism, the Cold War, and campaigns against comic books in shaping Bradbury's art. These personal, cultural, and historical elements affected the author and his work, and as new generations read the novel, this art in turn becomes part of our personal experience, our cultural inheritance, our historical milieu.

Robin Anne Reid then provides a nuanced overview of the way our fellow critics have responded to *Fahrenheit 451* in its first 60 years. First anchoring the novel as a work recognized not just as part of the genre of science fiction but also as a true literary classic, she surveys over 40 pieces of scholarship from the 1960s until almost the date of our own text's publication, grouping the works into six broad categories. In addition to providing full bibliographic information for this great range of criticism in English, Reid also identifies a number of recent resources in other languages as well.

After this, Joseph Michael Sommers gives a reading of the novel informed by the dialogic theories of M.M. Bakhtin. Despite the book's various didactic monologues—think, for example, of Fire Chief Beatty, Professor Faber, and book-memorizing Granger—Sommers notes as well the interplay of many voices (polyglossia), and even different kinds of voices (heteroglossia), that go into making the discourse of the novel. The writer, then, as Sommers puts it, is the funnel, who directs these various streams of voices to the reader, often with delicious and ironic inversion, creating paradoxes that further open up the conversation between author and readers.

I wrap up our context section by examining *Fahrenheit 451* in comparison to Bradbury's other book that ends in atomic fire and yet also the hope for rebirth, *The Martian Chronicles*. While Bradbury in *Fahrenheit 451* does step back from the notion of near-complete nuclear annihilation, the latter novel's treatment of humanity is much more pessimistic. In *The Martian Chronicles*, after all, despite occasional bad apples, people in general are presented more as being caught up in irresistible forces beyond their control, but in *Fahrenheit 451* it is the mass of the populace itself that is blamed for the decay of society.

Starting our section of critical readings is Jonathan R. Eller with a richly enlightening explanation of Bradbury's path from his various short-story starts to the novel itself. Most readers, presumably, are familiar with Bradbury's 1950 dime-per-hour marathon typing session in the basement of the UCLA library. This chapter, however, takes the tale back much farther, using both broad strokes and meticulous, telling detail to follow the fascinating false starts, revisions, side tracks, and tributaries to what became *Fahrenheit 451*.

Phil Nichols then approaches Bradbury's work from the perspective of adaptation studies, which takes into account, and even celebrates, the way adapting art from one medium to others entails responding to the source work in interesting, sometimes unexpected ways. Whereas some bibliophiles resist, say, the great differences between the novel and François Truffaut's 1966 film, Nichols reminds us that Bradbury himself was no stranger to adaptation, for he adapted *Fahrenheit 451* into a play, and even reimagined certain aspects in light of Truffaut's reimagining. This chapter examines the reworking of Bradbury's classic novel as a radio play, film, and stage play: the differences, the challenges to the interpreting artists, and the enrichment for audiences.

Wolf Forrest, in a wide-ranging study, situates Bradbury in the utopian/dystopian tradition, ranging from Thomas More's 1516 *Utopia* to the works of nineteenth- and twentieth-century authors and filmmakers. Looking at the works of many different artists and time periods, Forrest thus traces the interrelation of psychological matters. This includes the notion of *doppelgängers*, religion and humanism, and the longing for a return to Eden; the brainwashing from the tortures of Orwell's Room 101, Huxley's hypnopaedia, and the constant television and radio jingles of *Fahrenheit 451*; and the threats of widespread drug use, censorship, and war.

Andrea Krafft notes that Bradbury's bleak future burns not only the houses of people possessing books but also the very concept of *home* itself. Technology in this consumer's paradise has undermined domesticity of all sorts, so has the mass-culture pursuit of pleasure, and so have the government schools that indoctrinate children at ever-younger ages. The firehouse, for example, is described in images of hardness and coldness, reflecting the disintegration of what once was a place of warmth and brotherhood, and just as the "firemen" are, essentially, grown juvenile delinquents reveling in burning, the average youngster now revels in violence and mayhem. And marriage, the source of those children, has grown loveless, anesthetized, and atomistic.

Timothy E. Kelley then focuses specifically on love and the women of *Fahrenheit 451*. While previous critics have discussed the novel's diametrically opposed female characters in terms of the ideologies they represent, or of the catalytic effect of Clarisse McClellan on the wavering Montag, Kelley examines the subtleties of the ill-defined love between the imaginative teenager and the book-burner. I happen to know from personal experience that certain students—reading too much into the text, obviously—sometimes mistakenly hypothesize an illicit sexual affair between the two. Yet,

Kelley is right to point out that, while Montag feels at times like a father to the girl and at times like a best friend, he also feels a very deep and heartfelt—and scarcely explored—connection that he no longer has even with his own wife.

Imola Bulgozdi investigates gender issues as well, namely Bradbury's treatment of masculinity, maturity, and knowledge in a society that has forgotten what humanity really is. Montag's identity comes from his respected male profession of fireman, but in a way, Montag and his colleagues are not really *men*—they are simply overgrown boys, unable to reach maturity without the guidance of caring senior mentors. In addition to following Montag's progress from brash, self-centered hero to true adult, Bulgozdi also points out in the novel other roles, such as the Hunter, the Manipulator, and the Magician, concluding that these archetypes can be the fundamental blueprints to being human.

In the view of Guido Laino, *Fahrenheit 451* is almost less a novel in the utopian/dystopian tradition than the dream or nightmare of a true bibliophile: sketchy in its description of the workings of this future, while always looking nostalgically to the past. The novel's hopeful nod to the future is vague, for as Laino observes, the struggle here is philosophical, even metaphysical, rather than merely political. In this conception, therefore, Montag is a postmodern Don Quixote who uses literature and memory to write his own reality against an intolerable world.

Although the society of *Fahrenheit 451* bans books because they can bring thought and unhappiness, Anna McHugh points out that books also are a type of memory, and memory is subtly forbidden as well. History as traditionally defined has been lost, of course, but so has the individual's history, whether remembrance of where one first met one's spouse or even of how many sleeping pills one took that night. Drawing on sources from Classical notions since the time of Cicero to modern theories of pedagogy and neuroscience, McHugh then further explores Bradbury's portrayal of the uses and misuses of memory in the development of a rational, moral human being.

Aaron Barlow very innovatively looks at issues of intellectual property that previously have lain unnoticed. Literature in this novel is banned because of the ideas it contains, while comic books remain—of course, for *content* is more important than the physical artifact itself. Yet Barlow points out that this gets to the heart of issues of intellectual property that scarcely existed before the technology for truly widespread photo-mechanical—and finally electronic—reproduction of literary art. When Bradbury's intellectuals memorize word-for-word the works of dead authors, this is laudable…but what does current copyright law say about reproducing them technologically? What is the difference between piracy and the cultural commons of a society? Barlow's arguments are intriguing.

Ádám T. Bogár and Rebeka Sára Szigethy close our section of critical essays by looking from the world of *Fahrenheit 451*, where reading is forbidden, to our wide-open world of the present, and into the future as well. Networked reading among groups of people and near-infinite searchability linked out from electronic texts themselves offer interesting new possibilities for personal and social enrichment. Still, as Bogár and Szigethy note, in a world where every file looks like every other until opened, a stubborn few of us nevertheless will prefer physical books that "smell like nutmeg or some spice from a foreign land… "

THE BOOK
AND
AUTHOR

On *Fahrenheit 451*

Rafeeq O. McGiveron

In the grand scheme of things—of readership, of authorship, of popular culture, of the intellectual development of not just another half century but more—*Fahrenheit 451* seems likely to remain Ray Bradbury's most influential and longest-lived work. *The Martian Chronicles* may have brought Bradbury to prominence[1] and enchanted with its lyrical retelling of American frontier myths on an ochre backdrop only faintly tinged with even Lowellian planetology. *Dandelion Wine* may be his heartfelt opus to youth and to the Midwestern small town of hazy decades past, but it is *Fahrenheit 451* that truly speaks, calls, shouts to so many readers of different backgrounds and different ages, across the years and across the continents. Out of all of Bradbury's works, this novel's title alone is inscribed on the author's gravestone, and the book contains ideas, situations, and images, which admiring readers will carry with them to their graves.

Yet why is this so? Why have millions read this slim novel, often again and again? Why is the book placed on assigned reading lists in countless classes in both high school and college? Why is it a cultural touchstone, its themes nearly as widely known as the now-ubiquitous title of George Orwell's *1984*? And why are critics still compelled to write about it? The answer, of course, is that *Fahrenheit 451* is a very fine, very approachable, very meaningful work. The book is not flawless, naturally—perhaps no piece of literature is—and one may quibble here and there about the depth of it, the occasional over-exuberance of Bradbury's style, or other comparatively minor matters. None of this detracts from the monumental significance of Bradbury's work, however. *Fahrenheit 451* calls to us because it is a profoundly moving artistic and intellectual experience. Its plotting is deft, its language haunting, its themes frighteningly relevant.

Kingsley Amis famously termed *Fahrenheit 451* "a fast and scaring narrative" (109). The evaluation is memorable and fitting, and apparently, Ballantine editors of the 1960s thought so, too, for they put that line upon the cover, above even the novel's title. And fast and scaring it is, indeed. At only about 50,000 words, the book is comparatively brief, but of course even the shortest novel can be deathly plodding if not handled with imagination and skill. *Fahrenheit 451*, however, definitely does not plod. While much of the speed of the narrative is the result of Bradbury's style—to which we will attend shortly—structural choices play a significant part as well. The book has no chapters as such, after all, no natural stopping places beyond the divisions of the its three "Parts," titled "The Hearth and the Salamander," "The Sieve and the Sand," and "Burning Bright." Instead, each section is merely divided into scenes separated not by a chapter break but only by a single blank line. The first scene, for example, is not even a full page, the second scene is around six pages, the third a page and a half, and the fourth not quite four pages. Such is representative of the way the book as a whole is set up: easily digestible scenes, whether of action, of characterization, of philosophy, leading easily from one to another. Once captivated, the reader encounters something of a narrative slippery slope effect.

And captivated the reader is, from the very first line: "It was a pleasure to burn" (3). Ah, now that's a hook. Presuming that we have not already, like young Amis of the 1930s with the Woolworth's bin of tentacle- and cleavage-adorned science fiction pulp magazines, been drawn inexorably in by the early Joe Mugnaini impressionistic cover art, with its sorrowful newspaper-clad figure standing amid flame, or by the 1970s Barron Storey portrayal of beautiful red-and-gold destruction, or by the more restrained 1990s Donna Diamond cover with its half-consumed classics on a featureless black background, surely this first line sells us. The novel begins in medias res, in the purposeful midnight burning of some unknown victim's house. And as the man with the "stolid head" and blithely unthinking grin exults in his "symphon[y] of blazing and burning" (3), the reader simply *must* know where it all started and, just as important, where it will lead.

This amiably whistling fellow, this uniformed arsonist, this Montag, is a fireman. He works in a firehouse, after all. In fact, the *where* of Guy Montag's work is named a good 500 words before the *what* of it specifically is, and this—the stretching out of the reader's curiosity and the parceling out of tantalizing clues—is indicative of Bradbury's plotting. Once Montag's new neighbor, Clarisse McClellan, out for a socially frowned-upon stroll and perhaps a serendipitous meeting with the kerosene-smelling object of her insatiable inquisitiveness, voices the potent word *fireman*, there pass another 300 words before she tells us that many of the public may fear such a man. And there are nearly another 200 before the text finally reveals what, so far, only the novel's back cover has: reading books is illegal, while burning them—and any houses hiding them— is unquestioned law. When Clarisse asks, perhaps a bit probingly, if firemen once stopped fires instead of starting them, the blue-jowled professional dismisses such seeming nonsense with grand tolerance. When she persists, he simply laughs (6-8).

Why is this the state of things? How did it start? Clarisse's quiet suggestion of the fright of "many" notwithstanding, what does the public at large think? The reader, at this stage, does not know, and although the enigmatic Captain Beatty—Montag's as yet unglimpsed superior—later will give a history lesson spanning ten pages, that will not happen until near the end of the first third of the book. The pattern of hint-tease-delay is seen, too, in the skillfully piecemeal revelation of Guy's relationship with this wife Mildred. Clarisse's parting words, tossed off apparently by afterthought as she heads back into the house where her anachronistic family converses late into the night rather than let the multi-wall television yammer at them, are to ask whether Montag is happy (10). The question is rather impertinent, really, and it is unexpected, not just to the surprised fireman but to the reader. It is, however, spot-on, the perfect hint with which to begin the exposition of the man's marriage, his wife's personality, and hence the society she represents.

Montag's response then is the perfect tease:
"Happy! Of all the nonsense."
He stopped laughing. (10)

Of course he stops laughing. The vapid Mildred, overly made up and under-stimulated by anything except mass-market electronic slush, speaks in clichés and snappy one-liners and lives for her soap operas, begging like a child for the fourth and final wall of her living room to be replaced with a gigantic television screen. Her nights, spent in a separate bed, are soothed with Seashell radios tamped in both ears and with sleeping pills consumed with disturbing carelessness. She cannot remember where or when she first met her husband, and after ten years of marriage the couple has no children. Mildred is, Guy realizes later, a "silly empty woman" (47), and in the end, she loves her mindless utopia of consumerism and conformity, along with the broad-brush television characters she calls her "family," more than she does her own husband.

Again, however, it is later that Montag puts the pieces together. The author will hint with Clarisse's question, then tease with the fireman's reflexive dismissal—and drop a separate cryptic hint about the ventilator grill in his hallway at home that will be not be clarified for another sixty pages, plus one about the mentor who will not be revealed for ten more pages after that—but Bradbury on each point, very skillfully, will delay and thus pique curiosity. Here, after Clarisse's exit, he spends roughly 300 words of narrative for Montag, in an almost giddy wonderment, to consider the import of his meeting with the impish neighbor girl, and only then does the man enter the "mausoleum" of his cold and lonely bedroom (12). Back and forth, Bradbury alternates the short scenes, touching on one topic, hinting at another, and always pushing the true revelations farther into the future: the horrifying discovery of Mildred's overdose and her little less horrifying stomach pumping and almost vampiristic blood replacement by the impassive technicians "with the cigarettes in their straight-lined mouths" (16), Guy's confused listening at the McClellans' old-fashioned conversation next door, the inconclusive talk at cross purposes over a machine-prepared breakfast the next morning, Clarisse's divination-by-dandelion showing that Montag is not in love, the introduction of the sinister Mechanical Hound, and the eerily all-knowing Captain Beatty. The jet bombers go over "one two, one two, one two, six of them, nine of them, twelve of them"

(14), the raindrops fall "One, two, three, four, five" (19), the days pass "One two three four five six seven" (29), and the scenes are interspersed like the cards being shuffled in one of the interminable late-night poker games at the fire station.

And, of course, it is the high priest of that firehouse, Captain Beatty, who provides, after all the hints and bits of evidence gleaned here and there from Mildred's behavior and Clarisse's observations, an explanation for the violence and unhappiness and emptiness of society, and who also gives the novel some of its most exquisitely tense and, to use Amis's term, "scaring" scenes. As Donald Watt notes, Beatty and Dr. Faber catalog and explain the ideas by which Mildred and Clarisse live (197). And although Montag later pays a call to learn from the "very fragile and very much afraid" (Bradbury 87) old professor, whom he suspected of heterodoxy but never turned in, it is Captain Beatty who first pays a call on the wavering fireman's sickbed, where, deeply shaken by the death of the woman who burns herself rather than leave her precious library, he cannot bring himself to rise for work. The enigmatic Beatty's studiedly casual history lecture to Montag is the novel's clearest account of how books—and, essentially, thought—came to be banned; even Faber, later, agrees with his adversary's understanding of how it happened. Yet just as memorable as the intellectual discussion is the exquisite tension of the scene.

Beatty is avuncular and deceptively easygoing, and yet we can never forget that he is the enforcer of government repression, ebon-shirted like Hitler's Schutzstaffel or Mussolini's Blackshirts, able to send his enemies either to a Soviet-style psychiatric prison or to death. Walking in, he "look[s] around at everything except Montag and his wife," and his first words are not a greeting but a command to silence the banal racket of the television (56). The effect is ominous. When he settles himself into a chair and lights his pipe with great ceremony, however, the man's face is placid, his smile candy-bright, his demeanor oh-so understanding. The Fire Captain knows, he explains tolerantly, the psychic shock that occurs when a fireman first chances to think. He has "seen it all," he assures Montag chummily, and can "let [him] in on it" (57). Yes, and as cheery amid his swirling clouds of tobacco smoke as a character from a Norman Rockwell painting, Beatty is more than happy to explain why society has fled the bane of "conflicting theory and thought" (66). Diversions, pleasures, entertainments from sports to sex to television to drugs—these, he croons, are what people crave.[2] And if, as may happen, Beatty allows with a seeming worldly shrug, a fireman "gets an itch" to see what is inside one of those books he burns, why, of course there is no harm in that…so long, naturally, as within twenty-four hours he brings the book to the fire station for its proper burning (66-67).

Though honestly curious and asking a number of questions that are, essentially, put forward on behalf of the reader, Montag is nervous, too, and guilty; he has lost his faith, after all, in what Beatty, with great irony, terms "our happy world" (66), and for a man who has seen what happens to secret freethinkers and who has helped mete out their punishments, that is not good. And of course…well, we should not forget the forbidden book stashed beneath Montag's pillow either, should we? Certainly Montag cannot. He has others in the air duct of his hallway, but Bradbury, though having hinted earlier, will not reveal this until several pages later. The particular book in this nerve-wracking scene, however, seems as important as all the rest of his hoard together. Taken by scarcely understood compulsion during the midnight raid upon the woman whose charred remains now smolder along with the ruins of her house, the book under his pillow represents thought, questioning, rebellion, and—Montag realizes now for the first time—a human life. Not only has an author recorded a lifetime of learning and wisdom and wonder on that ink-stamped wood pulp, a reader has died for that freedom of thought, too.

To exacerbate Guy's stress, Bradbury has Mildred fidget and putter in housewifely fashion, straightening objects, smoothing the covers of his bed, attempting to fluff his pillow. The narrative cuts back and forth between Mrs. Montag's efforts at normalcy and the lecture of the Fire Captain, before whom it seems at any moment she will reveal her husband's secret. From where she first "pat[s] his pillow" (59), the peril is stretched over an almost unendurable 200 words of text, the stability of the situation seeming to worsen as the lines of the three characters' dialog alternate ever more rapidly:

"Let me fix your pillow," said Mildred.
"No!" whispered Montag.
"The zipper displaces the button and a man lacks just that much time to think while dressing at dawn, a philosophical hour, and hence a melancholy hour."
Mildred said, "Here."
"Get away," said Montag.
"Life becomes one big pratfall, Montag; everything bang, boff, and wow!"
"Wow," said Mildred, yanking at the pillow.
"For God's sake, let me be!" cried Montag passionately.
Beatty opened his eyes wide. (59-60)

Of course, miraculously—yet inevitably, for we are still only one-third of the way through the novel, after all—when Mildred reaches under the pillow and discerns the shape of the book, and then "almost with delight," as if perhaps, childlike, she imagines the rectilinear thing might be some present for her, she asks, "What's this? .... What's this here?" the inscrutable Beatty simply continues with his lesson "as if nothing ha[s] happened" (60).

Much later, near the end of the novel's second section, Bradbury brings back Beatty as the lead figure in another scene of masterful tension, the one that provides the unforgettable cliffhanger before the aptly titled "Burning Bright" conclusion. The emotional intensity of that episode, however, is heightened by the action, which immediately precedes it: when the enraged Montag, infuriated by the mindlessness, superficiality, and, essentially, inhumanity of his wife's visiting friends, flourishes a book, telling the shocked women that it is not "fireman theory," as one innocently supposes, but poetry (106). Again Bradbury cuts swiftly back and forth among Guy's ravings, the visiting women's uneasy reactions, Mildred's surprisingly quick-witted attempts to play his actions off as a form of lawfully sanctioned educational outreach to show "how silly it all was" in "the old days" (107), and the whispering voice of Faber pleading through the tiny two-way radio in his ear the same advice.

Even after his reading of Matthew Arnold's "Dover Beach" has upset the guests so deeply, Montag's dutiful dropping of the book in the wall slot leading to the incinerator could have preserved the fiction of orthodoxy, but instead he turns on one of the women with a cathartic savagery that delights readers as much as it frightens the guests:

> "Go home." Montag fixed his eyes upon her, quietly. "Go home and think of your first husband divorced and your second husband killed in a jet and your third husband blowing his brains out, go home and think of the dozen abortions you've had, go home and think of that and your damned Caesarian sections, too, and your children who hate your guts! Go home and think how it all happened and what did you ever do to stop it? Go home, go home!" he yelled. "Before I knock you down and kick you out the door!" (110)

Despite the magnitude of "his terrible error" (111), Bradbury then lets Montag almost forget how dangerous his outburst truly was. The back-and-forth pattern of tension and relaxation is better that way, after all.

Later that night in the firehouse, however, rather than blandly ignoring all the clues, the Fire Captain this time is tauntingly superior, missing nothing in a cat-and-mouse game of delicious intensity. After accepting the forbidden book from Montag for destruction without looking at it, the smiling Beatty proceeds to tease Montag even while he purports to welcome the man back "to the fold"—for "We're all sheep who have strayed at times," the Chief adds unctuously (115). Over the card table Beatty tosses out literary references in profusion, superficially playful but deeply meaningful jabs from which even Faber's secret voice cannot fully protect Montag. The guilty fireman fidgets, he blushes, he bites his lip, he washes his hands and then hides them, but Beatty is calm, so calm that when the fire alarm rings, after strolling to the teletype with "exaggerated slowness" and "glanc[ing] perfunctorily" at the address to be burned, he is ready to finish out that hand of cards first (118). Montag agonizes on the ride over to the offender's house, wondering how he ever can force himself to do his job again, but as they slam to a stop at last, Bradbury keeps Montag's eyes downcast on the railing of the fire engine. That way, therefore, when the introspective fireman finally raises his head, the author has set himself up, at least semi-plausibly, for perhaps the best line in the entire novel: "'Why,' said Montag slowly, 'we've stopped in front of *my* house'" (120).

The fugitive Montag squeaks through one dramatic tight spot after another: the flamethrower killing of the hollowly jesting Beatty; a semi-paralyzed escape from the hideous eight-legged Mechanical Hound; the near-miss of the murderous teenagers who try to run down this rare pedestrian in their car; the nightmarish sprint to escape into the rather conveniently near wilderness before the populace, in unison, steps outside to spot the running man. The driving swiftness and life-and-death import of the adventure make for an unforgettable read. Yet so, too, does the very language with which Bradbury builds his narrative. Really, the style of *Fahrenheit 451* is not easily characterized. As Robert Reilly observes, "Bradbury's style is like a great organ" (73). Occasionally here it is delightfully ironic, often brimming over with imagery, sometimes adjective-heavy, now and then terse or even artfully monosyllabic; sometimes Bradbury philosophizes or drops in a sizeable aside, for as he puts it in the Author's Afterword, later called the Coda, "digression is the soul of wit" (183); often a third person limited point of view delves into Montag's thoughts and feelings, while at other times, a third person dramatic point of view keeps a scene taut and swift. Despite occasional tics or heavy-handedness, the mix is entertaining and effective.

Bradbury's use of irony can be as subtle as a faintly arched eyebrow or as obvious as a guffaw. For the opening scene to describe the burning of a home as pleasurable, for example, is arresting indeed, while to juxtapose with grand attitudinal irony the imagery of serpents and venom with that of a musical concert is slyly disquieting (3). Of course, the central irony of the book is that of Montag's job, for in an era before such gender-neutral terms as *firefighter* or *mail carrier* or *congressperson*, Bradbury can use the linguistic ambiguity of the term *fireman* to transform a profession once considered perhaps the most unambiguous force for good into one sinister and threatening. Beatty's ironic description of the novel's violent, manically hedonistic society as "our happy world" (66) is particularly memorable, though lesser examples abound as well.

Donald Watt has discussed in detail the complex imagery of fire in *Fahrenheit 451*, and he and others have looked at Bradbury's nature imagery as well.[3] Eric S. Rabkin, in writing about *The Martian Chronicles*, has noted Bradbury's use of such elements of "fairy tale" writing as the "crystalline description" (111), and we see much of this incongruous, but memorable, language in *Fahrenheit 451*, too. For example, the container for Mildred's sleeping pills is called a "crystal bottle" (Bradbury 14), while the Mechanical Hound is described not only in terms of modern materials, like steel and nylon and rubber, but also with the fairytale trappings of brass and copper and "ruby glass" (26), with this pinnacle of robotic science giving both an "electrical sizzle" and a primitive "scraping of metal, a turning of cogs that [seem] rusty and ancient with suspicion" (27). The firehouse pole, now automated like a hand-grippable elevator, is still made of brass, while the kerosene in the fire engine sloshes in a "glittery brass tank," and even the numbers on the vehicle are made of brass (119). The ubiquitous television walls are described as a "crystal barrier" (49) and "a gigantic crystal bowl of hysterical fish" (102), and even in this age of atom bombs and shrieking jet bombers and the mysterious "enemy disks" in the sky (99), Faber's electronics workshop still contains crystals for radio work (98).

Bradbury's sentences alternate among those that are fairly unremarkable, those that stretch grammar or sense with a gusto— often successfully, though occasionally less so—and those that hustle the reader through with either crisp brevity or with a string of irresistible monosyllables. When Montag thinks of the catalytic Clarisse immediately after their first meeting, his mind's exuberance seems to run away with itself:

> She had a very thin face like the dial of a small clock seen faintly in a dark room in the middle of a night when you waken to see the time

and see the clock telling you the hour and the minute and the second, with a white silence and a glowing, all certainty and knowing what it has to tell of the night passing swiftly on toward further darkness, but moving also toward a new sun.

"What?" asked Montag of that other self, the subconscious idiot that ran babbling at times, quite independent of will, habit, and conscience. (11)

Despite the protagonist's sheepishness, the "babbling" works, at least in moderation. Yet John Huntington is not unjustified in finding that occasionally "purple prose obscures true perception" (137-38), nor is Kingsley Amis in complaining, in Bradbury's works in general, of "dime-a-dozen sensitivity" (106); the passage in this novel that always strikes me as an unfortunate gush occurs during Montag's escape into the wilderness when in the fragrant night darkness he "put[s] down his hand" and feels a licorice-smelling "weed rise up like a child brushing him" (156-57). To borrow the words of Damon Knight, writing of the author's other works, the simile "slops over into sentimentality" (111). On the other hand, in great contrast are times, perhaps a bit gimmicky yet on the whole enjoyable, when Bradbury employs a verbal accelerator such as in Beatty's "*Click, Pic, Look, Eye, Now, Flick, Here, There*" speech (59; italics Bradbury's) or the characteristic trick of counting, such as "One two three for five six seven days" (29).

Bradbury moderates his narrative's point of view in similar fashion. Through most of the novel the point of view is third person limited, with Montag's thoughts and feelings revealed to the reader. When Guy finds Mildred glassy-eyed and unconscious from an overdose of sleeping pills, for example, as the black-painted jet bombers scream overhead "Montag [is] cut in half. He [feels] his chest being chopped down and split apart" (14). When Clarisse questions him about his profession, suggesting that it does not seem to fit him anymore, there is a subtler type of chopping or division: "He felt his body divide itself into a hotness and a coldness, a softness and a hardness, a trembling and a not trembling, the two halves grinding upon one another" (25). At other times, the disturbed fireman thinks of his now-unsettled future, his empty marriage, the joys and the sadness of his childhood.

Occasionally, however, Bradbury shifts point of view to third person dramatic; this not only speeds the action but also heightens tension by hiding Montag's inner responses and making the reader guess at them solely from the few to nonexistent external clues, just as another character would have to do. The cat-and-mouse scene of Beatty's history lecture at the sickbed, for example, is painfully spare due to the prevailing third person dramatic point of view. This is perhaps most evident when Beatty comments that Clarisse, apparently run over in the streets, is "better off dead," and the replying line is only "Yes, dead" (64). We see this skillful withholding of interiority as well when Montag asks his superior what would happen in an oh-so hypothetical situation:

> "Well, then, what if a fireman accidentally, really not intending anything, takes a book home with him?"
> Montag twitched. The open door looked at him with its great vacant eye.
> "A natural error. Curiosity alone," said Beatty. "We don't get overanxious or mad. We let the fireman keep the book twenty-four hours. If he hasn't burned it by then, we simply come burn it for him"
> Of course." Montag's mouth was dry. (66-67)

Montag's inner turmoil is nearly unimaginable in its intensity, but the only crack in POV which Bradbury allows is his dry mouth, which then leads to Montag's thought—the first revealed in a good 800 words, actually—that he will never go to work again. The dynamic is exquisite. Bradbury is indeed, as Willis E. McNelly notes, "a careful craftsman, an ardent wordsmith" (23).

Finally, of course, it is the ideas of Fahrenheit, which ensure that the novel lives on. The most eloquently written book will be forgotten if it is trite and unimaginative, and the most brilliant intellectual exercise will never be read again if it is dull; Bradbury, however, has combined the aesthetic and the philosophical in a passionate work of art that will be enjoyed, pondered, discussed for generations to come. Really, having touched upon certain of the affective characteristics of the book in some detail, regarding its themes, I for now will conclude simply with the reminder that *Fahrenheit 451*, with its plea for curiosity and expression and humanity, is relevant. It was in the McCarthy era. It remained so in the time of Valium and full-color variety television shows, and in future, it will continue to be. Whether the political parties are the Ins and the Outs or something else, and whether analgesic pablum of the various entertainment media comes via flickering cathode ray tube, via portable palm-sized screen and tamped-tight ear buds, or via direct beaming to the cerebral cortex, Ray Bradbury's masterful little novel will, to paraphrase the master, still whisper, as the parade of consumerism and conformity roars down the avenue: "Remember, reader, thou art mortal."

Notes

1. See, for example, the praise of Isherwood.
2. For an investigation of the "technology, mass exploitation, and minority pressure" that Beatty cites as the driving forces (58), see McGiveron "What 'Carried the Trick'?" For a pooh-hooing of Bradbury's treatment of the masses, see Zipes.
3. For the use of nature, see, for example, Huntington 137-38, Watt 199 and 209-10, and McGiveron "Hercules and Antaeus."

Works Cited

Amis, Kingsley. *New Maps of Hell: A Survey of Science Fiction*. 1960. New York: Arno, 1975.

Bradbury, Ray. *Fahrenheit 451*. 1953. New York: Del Rey, 1980.

Huntington, John. "Utopian and Anti-Utopian Logic: H.G. Wells and His Successors." *Science-Fiction Studies* 9 (1982): 122-46.

Isherwood, Christopher. *Rev. of The Martian Chronicles*, by Ray Bradbury. *Tomorrow* Oct. (1950): 56-58.

Knight, Damon. *In Search of Wonder: Essays on Modern Science Fiction*, 2nd ed. 1956. Chicago: Advent, 1971.

McGiveron, Rafeeq O. "'Do You Know the Legend of Hercules and Antaeus?' The Wilderness in Ray Bradbury's *Fahrenheit 451*." *Extrapolation* 38 (1997): 102-9.

_____. "What 'Carried the Trick'? Mass Exploitation and the Decline of Thought in Ray Bradbury's *Fahrenheit 451*." *Extrapolation* 37 (1996): 245-56.

McNelly, Willis E. "*Ray Bradbury*—Past, Present, and Future." Ray Bradbury. Ed. Martin Harry Greenberg and Joseph D. Olander.. New York: Taplinger, 1980. 17-24. Writers of the 21st Century Ser.

Rabkin, Eric S. "To Fairyland by Rocket: Bradbury's *The Martian Chronicles*." *Ray Bradbury*. Ed. Martin Harry Greenberg and Joseph D. Olander. New York: Taplinger, 1980. 110-126. Writers of the 21st Century Ser.

Reilly, Robert. "The Artistry of Ray Bradbury." *Extrapolation* 13 (1971): 64-74.

Watt, Donald. "Burning Bright: *Fahrenheit 451* as Symbolic Dystopia." *Ray Bradbury*. Ed. Martin Harry Greenberg and Joseph D. Olander. New York: Taplinger, 1980. 195-213. Writers of the 12st Century Ser.

Zipes, Jack. "Mass Degradation of Humanity and Massive Contradictions in Bradbury's Vision of Humanity in *Fahrenheit 451*." *No Place Else: Explorations in Utopian and Dystopian Fiction.* Ed. Eric S. Rabkin, Martin H. Greenberg, and Joseph D. Olander. Carbondale: Southern IL UP, 1983. 182-98. Alternatives Ser.

Biography of Ray Bradbury

Garyn G. Roberts

When asked how he would like to be remembered by future generations, Ray Douglas Bradbury once replied, "As a magician of ideas and words." Indeed, Bradbury was such a magician, and he was one of the twentieth century and early twenty-first century's most important storytellers and allegorists. An author who wrote from personal experience and cultural inheritance, who relied on the history of ideas and free word association and who threw his first million words away, Bradbury proved himself a master of words and a teller of universal tales that incorporate myths, theologies, beliefs, themes, rituals, motifs, and character types that define both American and world cultures.

Ray Douglas Bradbury was born 22 August 1920 in Waukegan, IL, the town north of Chicago on the southwest edge of Lake Michigan and just south of Kenosha, Racine, and Milwaukee, WI. In the midst of the Great Depression, Bradbury's father moved the family west, first to Arizona and then to the greater Los Angeles area, in quest of work—much in the fashion of the Joad family in John Steinbeck's *The Grapes of Wrath* (1939). However, Waukegan would become the model of Bradbury's oft-used fictional story setting of "Green Town, Illinois." Ray's father, Leonard Spaulding Bradbury, was a telephone line repairman, and it is interesting that Russell Johnson (b. 1924), best recognized as the Professor from *Gilligan's Island*, plays a telephone lineman in the movie *It Came From Outer Space!* (1953), written by Ray.

Ray Bradbury graduated from Los Angeles High School in 1938, was a newsboy from about 1940 to 1943, and married Marguerite Susan McClure in 1947. They had four daughters and were married until her death in 2003; Ray's older brother, Leonard "Skip" Bradbury, died a few months later in 2004.

Starting in 1939, Bradbury was writer, editor, and publisher for a short-lived yet famous semi-professional fanzine called *Futuria*

Fantasia. Early entrants into what would later be deemed the "Golden Age of Science Fiction" appeared in *Futuria Fantasia.* Among these young talents was Robert A. Heinlein.

The author's first professional sale, entitled "Pendulum," was co-authored with Henry Hasse and appeared in the November 1941 issue of Frederik Pohl's *Super Science Stories* magazine. However, Bradbury had had a variety of short stories and commentaries published in fantasy and science fiction fanzines as early as January 1938. By the mid 1940s, Bradbury's work was appearing regularly in several pulp magazines, including *Weird Tales, Thrilling Wonder Stories, Planet Stories, Detective Tales, Dime Mystery,* and *New Detective.* He also had occasional publications in *Super Science Stories, Astounding,* and *Captain Future.*

Bradbury's first publication in the legendary and most famous fantasy periodical of all time, *Weird Tales,* was "The Candle." This early work was partially ghost written by Henry Kuttner and appeared in the November 1942 issue. Some of his early contributions to *Weird Tales* were the beginnings of his first major story type and thematic device. These were stories of the "Dark Carnival," in which Bradbury used the travelling carnival as a metaphor for life. His first published book was a short story collection entitled *Dark Carnival,* published by August Derleth's Arkham House in 1947. This volume was significantly revised and reappeared in 1955 as *The October Country.* By 1962, several of the themes and ideas from the Dark Carnival stories were adapted, synthesized, and expanded into the episodic novel *Something Wicked This Way Comes.* Ultimately, four Bradbury short-story collections were framed by the Dark Carnival Mythos. Between and beyond *The Dark Carnival* and *The October Country,* there were *The Illustrated Man* (1951) and *The Small Assassin* (1962). Bradbury published a second Dark Carnival novel, *Death is a Lonely Business,* in 1985.

The genres and related story types that Ray Bradbury created and contributed to those early "pulp" days are numerous. A representative list includes the Dark Carnival stories, Gothic tales, weird tales, dark fantasy, weird menace, detective fiction, fantasy, and science fiction. Bradbury not only wrote genre fiction but crossed between genres, and even ignored such categorization all together. For example, *Fahrenheit 451* (1953) and *Dandelion Wine* (1957) fall neatly into no specific genres. *Fahrenheit 451*, a stern warning of potential, near-future apocalypse if we do not change our ways, is a futuristic novel not dependent on science fiction, science fact, or horror for its ultimate message. It is influenced by George Orwell's *1984* (1949) but is uniquely Bradbury. Its author claimed that like Orwell's novel, *Fahrenheit 451* was designed to prevent a potential future, not predict one. *Dandelion Wine* and its sequel, *Farewell Summer* (2006), are similarly beautiful, brilliant episodic novels that really defy genre classification.

The subjects and social issues addressed in the fiction of Ray Bradbury are some of the most poignant and profound of the human experience. Here are found detailed discussions of religions and theologies of various sorts: youth, adolescence, and older age; death and dying; nature and the environment; family and friends; race and ethnicity; gender; love, sex, and Eros; the rural community and a variety of geographical locales; and much, much more. The episodic novel *The Martian Chronicles* (1950), among other things, is best appreciated as an environmental allegory. In the early 1940s and early 1950s, Bradbury was writing intelligent, insightful stories about ethnicity and race relations and about issues of gender long before such stories became fashionable. Stories like "The Big Black and White Game" and "The Other Foot" told more about racial harmony than many works before or since; stories like "I'll Not Look for Wine" and "Cora and the Great Wide World" featured women with great stamina and independence and individual identities.

Bradbury's short stories, novels, stage plays, screenplays, poems, radio plays, teleplays, and drawings appeal to all ages, making his storytelling significant and meaningful to a wide-ranging public. A visionary who was sensitive to the emotions and idiosyncrasies and wonders that comprise the human experience, Ray Bradbury always drew heavily from his personal experience, making autobiography the most important and largest overriding thematic elements of and input to his work. If, at times, the logic of his stories is suspect, his ability to solve the human equation makes these errors insignificant.

In the early 1950s, Bradbury began having his stories adapted for comic books and for movies. As early as 1951 and 1952, Entertaining Comics' William Gaines began using the author's previously published stories (mostly *Weird Tales* and similar stories) in his horror, science fiction, and fantasy comic book lines. The story of how this all came about is legendary. Ultimately, Bradbury had a couple dozen of his stories interpreted by renowned comic book artists of the day, including Wally Wood, Al Williamson, and Frank Frazetta, for Gaines' E.C. The comic book titles that featured Bradbury's stories included *Weird Science*, *Weird Fantasy*, *Tales from the Crypt*, *Crime SuspenStories*, *Shock SuspenStories*, *Vault of Horror*, *Haunt of Fear*, and *Weird Science-Fantasy*.

While a range of Ray Bradbury's stories and novels would be adapted for motion pictures in the second half of the twentieth and early years of the twenty-first centuries (most notably *Fahrenheit 451*, *The Illustrated Man,* and *Something Wicked This Way Comes*), the then-thirty-year-old author scripted some films that are best described as contributions to the Science Fiction Invasion craze of the 1950s. The most famous of these were *It Came from Outer Space!* and *The Beast from 20,000 Fathoms*, both released in 1953. Bradbury's best and most important motion picture script was his adaptation of Herman Melville's *Moby Dick*. Produced and directed by the legendary John Huston and starring the equally legendary Gregory Peck, this movie and script remain the most definitive interpretation of Melville's novel yet done. The story of how this movie, filmed in Ireland and released between 1956 and 1957, came to be is chronicled in *Green Shadows, White Whale* (1992), a fictionalized, autobiographical episodic novel that recounts Bradbury's experiences with that eclectic group of people and archetypal motion picture.

Ray Bradbury's short story book collections of the 1950s and 1960s are legendary. Like the master, Picasso, the author entered a new phase in his art. Personal experience and cultural inheritance were still central to these stories. A literary maturity evolved for Bradbury, and he became a regular contributor to upscale "slick" magazines and higher paying markets such as *The Saturday Evening Post*, *Collier's*, and *Playboy*. *Fahrenheit 451* was serialized in the second, third, and fourth issues of *Playboy*, and publisher Hugh Heffner claimed that Bradbury's work in those early issues was responsible for much of the success of the magazine as it was getting started. Some of Bradbury's landmark collections from the 1950s and 1960s include *The Golden Apples of the Sun* (1953—same year as *Fahrenheit 451*), *A Medicine for Melancholy* (1959), *The Day It Rained Forever* (1959), *R is for Rocket* (1962), *The Machineries of Joy* (1964), *S is for Space* (1966), and *I Sing the Body Electric!* (1969).

The 1950s and 1960s also saw Bradbury deliver his stories in other media. A variety of stage plays were written, developed and produced that would later become collected—in part—in book collections. The most famous of these stage play collections were *The Anthem Sprinters and Other Antics* (1963), *Pillar of Fire and Other Plays* (1975) and *The Wonderful Ice Cream Suit* (1972). In 1991, a collection of some of these plays was assembled in *Ray Bradbury on Stage: A Chrestomathy of Plays*.

Ray Bradbury created original dramas, short stories, and plays for radio. Some of his previously published short stories were adapted for radio by others. NBC radio adapted a few dozen of Ray Bradbury's stories—especially installments from *The Martian Chronicles* that had tremendous appeal in 1950s Cold War America—for its *Dimension X* and *X Minus One* series. His stories appeared as installments for other various ongoing radio drama serials. These included *Escape*, *Lights Out!*, *Suspense*, and others.

Television's *Alfred Hitchcock Presents*, *The Alfred Hitchcock Hour*, and a range of other programs adapted Bradbury stories. "I Sing the Body Electric!" premiered 18 May 1962 on Rod Serling's *Twilight Zone*. Bradbury wrote original stories for television, while *The Ray Bradbury Theater* (HBO 1985-6; USA 1988-92) featured stories the author adapted and revised from his earlier published work.

By the 1970s and 1980s, Bradbury the storyteller continued to diversify. By this time, he had created more stage plays and screenplays, radio dramas and television plays, and much more. He wrote new short stories and a new novel or two, and he started to publish his poetry in hardcover collections. Bradbury published five major volumes of poetry and a range of small press booklets and chapbooks, often paying tribute to poets and other literary figures that preceded him, including Walt Whitman, Emily Dickinson, and others. The five major collections were *When Elephants Last in the Dooryard Bloomed* (1973), *Where Robot Mice and Robot Men Run Round in Robot Towns* (1977), *The Haunted Computer and the Android Pope* (1981), *The Complete Poems of Ray Bradbury (1981),* and (2002). Two celebrated children's books appeared, first in 1955 and then 1972: *Switch on the Night* and *The Halloween Tree*, respectively. Others followed.

More short story collections appeared in the 1970s and 1980s, including *Long After Midnight* (1976). The first of two 100-story Ray Bradbury collections, a large hardcover titled *The Stories of Ray Bradbury*, which went through multiple printings, debuted in 1980. *A Memory of Murder* (1984) collected, in paperback form only, most of the short detective fiction and "weird menace" the author had written for the pulps in the 1940s. The stories are wonderfully satisfying, though Bradbury notes, in his introduction to the volume, that Dashiell Hammett and Raymond Chandler need not fear competition from him. Ray Bradbury's short story collection, *The Toynbee Convector*, was first in print in hardcover in 1988.

In the 1990s and early 2000s, the author, now in his 70s and 80s, began to experience some health issues that would plague him off and on through the remainder of his life. But story quality continued to be topnotch, and original stories, though maybe not as prolific in number, also continued. This was a time in the author's life when he became intro- and retrospective regarding his own life, and he continued to produce new material and revise and re-present older works—some previously uncollected or even unpublished.

A second, distinct 100-story Bradbury omnibus debuted in 2003, titled simply *Bradbury Stories*. *Quicker than the Eye* appeared in 1996 and *Driving Blind* in 1997; both were literary events. Two celebrated short story collections appeared in years following: *One More for the Road* (2002) and *We'll Always Have Paris* (2009).

Two especially noteworthy short story collections from the early twenty-first century are *The Cat's Pajamas* (2004), which features previously published and unpublished Bradbury stories that span most of his lifetime, and *Summer Morning, Summer Night* (2007), a collection of previously published and unpublished stories set in the worlds of *Dandelion Wine* and *Farewell Summer*—Green Town, IL. Like the novel *Farewell Summer*, these collections are wonderfully nostalgic and reflective.

Perhaps due, in part, to the 50th anniversary of *Fahrenheit 451* (1953-2003), and a nationwide celebration of the anniversary in a variety of school and library "Community Reads Programs," Ray Bradbury shared with us some of the stories and situations that led to his novel, *Fahrenheit 451*. A limited edition collectable hardcover, *Match to Flame* (2007), collected a kaleidoscope of stories from the author's previous work that influenced his writing of *Fahrenheit 451*. This collection was followed by the somewhat shorter and further revised mass-market hardcover, *A Pleasure to Burn* (2010). Ray Bradbury also shared his craft, art, and insights in *Zen and the Art of Writing* (1990, a book expanded from an earlier paperbound chapbook) and *Yestermorrow: Obvious Answers to Impossible Tomorrows* (1991).

It should be noted that Bradbury's best novels are episodic (i.e., they are carefully woven series of short stories). It also should be noted that Bradbury's stories and publication of the same, remained, by and large, consistently excellent throughout his writing career. Many authors cannot boast this legacy. Bradbury earned a range of national and international awards—most very prestigious, like his 2004 National Medal of Arts, presented to him by then-President George W. Bush and First Lady Laura Bush.

When Ray died on 5 June 2012, he was just short of his ninety-second birthday. One of the twentieth century's great visionaries, allegorists, and magicians had made his almost inhumanly wonderful contribution to us. Ray was a kind, loving, and good man, and he was human. He had emphatic opinions; he could be romantic and, especially later in life, at times unrealistic, and sometimes outright cranky. But he was most often right, being more accurate than most all of us. Ray loved life, and he loved people. Anything that compromised or hurt either one was a target for one our greatest humanists of all time. Mostly, Ray celebrated all the good things in life as these things are found in people. He often said that he liked books because behind every book there is a person.

Bradbury's pseudonyms: "D.R. Banat," "William Elliott," "Leonard Douglas," "Douglas Spaulding," "Leonard Spaulding," "Brett Sterling."

CRITICAL
CONTEXTS

Some Social and Cultural Context for Ray Bradbury's *Fahrenheit 451*

Garyn G. Roberts

Ray Bradbury lived in a golden age—a time that was uniquely rich in history and popular cultural advancement. From his earliest days of cognition, young Bradbury was able to effectively tie his personal experiences both with the cultural inheritance that his family provided him and with the burgeoning society around him. The result was that the young dreamer and author found and exploited a combined source of subject matters and atmospheres that framed his stories. In the process, he was able to connect with an extensive audience that could relate to what he felt and recorded in stories, plays, poems, and other art. There is so much to admire in the life, mindset, and creative art of Ray Bradbury, but if this were to be distilled into one explanation for his success, it would be that the author, from the start, brilliantly drew from his personal experience and cultural inheritance as the basis for his storytelling. By doing so, Bradbury was able to hit an incredible "responsive chord" in his vast international audience. His personal realism and romances alike were, and are, the stories of his audiences.

In the last couple of decades, the very best scholars of the life and work of Ray Bradbury have reviewed and scrutinized the personal and cultural contexts of the author's life, and—using this method of inquiry—have endeavored to analyze evenhandedly what transpires in the creative work of the master. Nowhere is this form of analysis more appropriate and effective than in considering the social, cultural, and historical contexts that explain *Fahrenheit 451*.

Throughout his life, Ray Bradbury often claimed that he had very detailed, if not perfect, recall of the events of his life—even in uterus. While such claims are incredibly fantastic on the face of them, and perhaps not entirely humanly possible, there was some significant truth to this assertion. Bradbury proved time and again that he had extraordinary recall, and his art reflects at times memory large and small, personal and cultural.

Ray Bradbury was born to a lower middle-class family in Waukegan, IL. (Geographically, the town is located north of Chicago, on Lake Michigan, just south of the Wisconsin border. It is a very different, urbanized community today.) At the time, Waukegan, much like its fictional counterpart, "Green Town, Illinois," was a frontier town in its waning days. The industrial revolution was catching up with Waukegan in the 1920s, and there was a massive paradigm shift—a big change. Much of this change is chronicled in Bradbury's novel, *Dandelion Wine* (1957), wherein, among other things, a few Civil War veterans still linger in their twilight years, while trolley cars are replaced by buses and more modern forms of mass transit.

Change is not always good in the world of Ray Bradbury, or in the world of Guy Montag's *Fahrenheit 451*. In both worlds, there is a very appealing call for romance, for how life used to be. Montag opines on several occasions throughout the novel that he needs to catch up with the memories of the past. And there is beauty in simplicity. In the not-so-distant-future world of Montag, old and abandoned railroad tracks are the last vestiges of, and fleeting connections back to, a frontier past. Now overgrown with plant life and strewn with rubble, these tracks remind of us of a time that was—or, perhaps, that never really was, but which we wanted it to be.

Perhaps the most insidious and threatening technological advance of Montag's world is the Mechanical Hound, the invention that first terrorizes, then spies on, and finally hunts Montag, intent on his extermination. By its very nature, the Hound is devoid of human compassion and reason, for it is programmed by the firemen, the gatekeepers of morality, to seek out and destroy—much like the Daleks of *Dr. Who*. The mechanical dog in *Fahrenheit 451* is a perverse modernization of the old firehouse dog. Its menacing presence in the story, with its aggression and death-dealing poison, is highly effective as a vehicle that condemns future advances. It is technology that has gone wrong, like advanced forms of weaponry in the 1950s. Junior United States Senator Joseph McCarthy might very well have liked to have had this Mechanical Hound at his disposal during his administration.

Throughout his fictional yet highly autobiographical accounts of life in the 1920s, Ray Bradbury reminisces about his extended family that lived in an old Victorian-type house complete with ornate fringes, gingerbread, and cupolas. The Bradbury family came from Protestant theology, though the family and Ray found God in a vast array of places. Bradbury's childhood is a maze of nuclear and extended family members and friends. Residents and frequent visitors of the home included grandparents, aunts and uncles, cousins, siblings, and Mom and Dad. People rocked in rockers and swings on cool autumn evenings, and everyone knew everyone. All of this is antithetical to the world of Montag, wherein Bradbury uses his own personal experience and cultural inheritance as a counterpoint to the story.

As *Fahrenheit 451* unfolds, Guy Montag increasingly discovers the depths of his living nightmare. He has no extended family, and his own wife, Mildred, is a monster of banality: cold, unfeeling, and consciously and unconsciously blissfully uninformed. She is a spouse in name only and is not even a distant friend, much less sensual lover. In Montag's world, no one is allowed to walk outside under the stars, or swing on swings or rock on rockers. People stay indoors, in small, cold, barren structures. The only practiced religion is the religion of the State—a theology of ultimate compromise, cold stasis, and the lowest common denominator.

In his early years, Ray Bradbury discovered and embraced the popular culture of the day. At this time in the 1920s, young Ray had a treasured aunt named "Neva." In later years, Bradbury recounted on numerous occasions how important his Aunt Neva had been to him. It was she who introduced him to and nurtured his love for literature, silent film, newspaper comic strips, and much, much more. For young Ray, there were picnics by the water, adventures in the woods, extemporaneous plays and other imaginative exploits that seemed to come straight from the life of Tom Sawyer. There was opportunity seemingly everywhere, if one just looked for it.

By the late twenties and early thirties, Ray Bradbury was fully immersed in the worlds of L. Frank Baum's *Wizard of Oz*. Today, in our semi-literate society, we remember the classic MGM Studios'

1939 motion picture, but the stories of Oz were chronicled in book form for 40 years before that movie, and Bradbury would speak fondly and often about this series for the remainder of his life. Those big oversized volumes with color covers, a plethora of interior black and white illustrations, elegant print font and page decorations, and the occasional color frontispiece were just short of the Holy Grail for Bradbury and children of all ages in the 1920s and '30s. Thick pulpwood pages carried tales of fictional and not-so-fictional worlds. There were adventure, romance, treasure, happiness, and newly-found friends in the Oz books. There were also perils, monsters, and outright evil. And, unashamedly, there was escape.

The world of *Fahrenheit 451* does not offer any real escape to Montag or his not-so-fictional counterparts…until the end. Montag is stuck until his epiphany of escape through books and people who embrace and even *are* books. Wicked witches and Gnome Kings and their ilk are not vanquished in Guy Montag's reality—at least not for a long time—as they are in the Oz tales.

A little more than ten years before Ray Bradbury's birth, Edgar Rice Burroughs (1875-1950) introduced two archetypal adventure heroes. History would make the second of these heroes more famous—Tarzan of the Apes—but it was the first that had an even bigger impact on Bradbury: interplanetary explorer John Carter, who debuted in 1911 in the pulp magazine serial novel, *A Princess of Mars*. Burroughs' John Carter appeared in novels and novellas for the rest of Burroughs' life. Best described as Space Opera—Westerns in the sprawling frontier of the great cosmos, forerunners of *Star Trek* and *Star Wars*—these adventures framed the imagination of young Bradbury. John Carter, in a not-so-distant future, fights totalitarian governments, despots, classicism and racism of various forms, and evil empires and entrepreneurs.

Some of the same historical and cultural realities of the early twentieth century define the near-future world of Guy Montag as well. Oppressive government and a class structure straight out the political theories of Karl Marx are central themes, and warnings, of *Fahrenheit 451*.

Ray Bradbury was a devotee of silent movies from his childhood on. While Edison and other international scientists had produced silent movies since the turn of the century, the height of the era of nitrate-based silent film arrived just about the time that Bradbury arrived on Earth. Adaptations of Victor Hugo's *The Hunchback of Notre Dame* (1923), Gaston Leroux's *The Phantom of the Opera* (1925), and Arthur Conan Doyle's *The Lost World* (1925) defined Bradbury's early life. Then in the early days of sound motion pictures came *King Kong* (1933), with stop-motion animation by Willis O'Brien, who also had done the stop-motion animation for *The Lost World*, and then there came installments of Universal Studios' monster movie series based on Frankenstein's monster, Dracula, the Mummy, the Invisible Man, and others. Bradbury loved these movies; more importantly, he loved the literature of these movies.

Many of these movies featured monsters. Each was an abomination of nature, or of humanity's own meddling with nature. Later in the 1950s, Ray Bradbury would create stories and screenplays for movies. Each of Ray Bradbury's big-screen movies featured monsters, be they from outer space, from under the sea, and even the great white whale himself, Moby Dick. In its own way, *Fahrenheit 451* is very much a Ray Bradbury monster story. In this story, however, the monster takes a variety of forms and even some intangible forms. The monsters of *Fahrenheit 451* include the government, the book-burning firemen, the fire trucks with their mythic salamander iconography, the clamoring full-wall televisions, the Mechanical Hound, and the people themselves.

Also in the 1920s and '30s, Ray Bradbury was a card-carrying member of the public library. His Aunt Neva and extended family introduced him to newspaper comic strips, including *Buck Rogers* and *Flash Gordon*. He lovingly cut the *Buck Rogers* strips out of discarded newspapers and pasted them in scrapbooks. In their way, members of the Bradbury family were pioneers of Popular Culture Studies. They embraced comic strips as closely as they held classic world literature. Young Bradbury was well read. He read international authors and playwrights (including Hugo, Dumas,

Scott, and Dostoyevsky), many American authors and local, regional authors as well. He figuratively devoured the works of Edgar Allan Poe, Jules Verne and H.G. Wells. He read and wrote poetry; in his own hand, he illustrated stories he had read; and he wrote sequels to some of his favorites. Jack Williamson, Henry Kuttner, Edmond Hamilton, and Leigh Brackett (champions and headliners of *Amazing Stories* and other pulp magazines) personally mentored Ray in his later teens and made him a writer. Bradbury often boasted that no other author, he thought, paid as much tribute in their work to other authors as he did. From the start, if one wanted to attack Ray Bradbury, that person attacked the books, and the people behind the books, that Bradbury loved. The enemy never won—and the enemy does not win in *Fahrenheit 451*.

As early as 1933, the Nazi party began burning books in Germany. The motivation was primarily anti-Semitism, but any books that were deemed "un-German" were targeted. Indeed, the list of some of our most revered authors singled out for literary execution is staggering—Helen Keller?! This very destructive period of Nazi Germany history is, sadly, although perhaps a little mercifully, not so well remembered today. Perhaps the most popular image of more recent times is the Nazi book burning scene in the motion picture *Indiana Jones and the Last Crusade* (1989), where a fictitious Hitler signs the Grail diary of Professor Jones, Sr. In real life, the level of purely destructive censorship involved in the Nazi book burning shook Ray Bradbury to the core. He was not alone. This tragic cultural history touched a very sensitive nerve in the readers of *Fahrenheit 451* in 1953 and years that followed. Bradbury's classic novel brought back the horror of not only the book burning, not only the censorship, but the perversions and atrocities of Nazi Germany. Ray Bradbury's audience, then as now, was and is emotionally tethered to the story line. We need to be; it should be no other way.

While books are the main mark for censorship in *Fahrenheit 451*, throughout his life Bradbury was quick to note that other forms of censorship are equally damning. He pointed out that victims of censorship could be not only those who employ print, but also those who use non-print media such as painting, motion pictures, radio, television, and more to convey their messages. Politics, discourse, and education can be severely compromised, and even people killed as well. In his essays and articles, Bradbury often provided specific examples of these atrocities.

Like the later storm troopers of the *Star Wars* franchise, the firemen of *Fahrenheit 451* are goose-stepping reminders of a Hell not so long ago. Thankfully, Montag is introspective and evolves from his government-assigned occupation and life. But our hero's transition does not come easily. His struggles are not only central to the book—they are our struggles as individuals and members of society, too.

When World War II was officially over, the Cold War began. Suspicions and dissentions marked this multigenerational era of international politics. Axis powers were being humanely rebuilt and guided by some of the victorious Allies, but the Allies themselves were turning on each other. Impending apocalypse was averted for the moment, but the possibility was far from gone.

In fact, it was beginning again to gain momentum. Joseph McCarthy's "witch hunts" for Communists and communist sympathizers reached fever pitch. Ultimately, and thankfully, his own Republican Party eventually deflated him, though he had already disgraced himself long before.

The popular medium of comic books were the target of some well-meaning, if not often misguided do-gooders. Critics of the medium, who gained some traction with the "intellectual" and "moral" communities, included Dr. Frederic Wertham. Wertham, a famous expert on and defender of early twentieth-century serial killers, was the author of the infamous book, *Seduction of the Innocent* (1954). This volume, presented from a psychological/sociological perspective, purported to analyze panels and images from selected comic books actually taken out of context, and claimed that the relatively new popular medium was the scourge of our youths' mental, emotional and intellectual health. (Ironically, toward the end of his life in the 1970s, Dr. Wertham spent considerable time in print recanting what he said and what he believed he had been misrepresented saying.) Wertham's advocacy of wholesale censorship, which reached the halls of the United States Congress, is well remembered today.

In larger, urban markets, the late 1940s and early 1950s saw the advent of network television. This new audio-visual medium brought news, comedies, sporting events, and genre dramas—such as Westerns, detective fiction, suspense, and science fiction— to the living rooms of families that could afford what was then most assuredly a luxury. Television captivated people, much like computers and cellular telephones do today. Then, like now, the results were not all positive. Viewers considered television as the purveyor of unassailable truth—there was little critical assessment of the content and machinations of the new medium. And, like computers and cell phones today, television introduced a degree of unattractive antisocial behavior among its consumers.

The multi-walled television in the Montags' home is the most powerful and destructive narcotic in Mildred's life—and this, even considering the array of drugs the government of the novel allows and provides its citizens in an effort to stratify emotions, thinking, and behavior. The cartoon White Clown, master and monster of ceremonies of the television broadcasts, commands a cult status enviable to any radical evangelist or talk show host alive today. Mildred and her friends are transfixed by their interactive television family, and "reality" is prescribed by that same television family. Viewers descend to a level of non-social interaction that makes them no more than the "zombies" we fear in today's culture.

Throughout *Fahrenheit 451*, jet bombers fly overhead. These warplanes bring death and destruction, and they are the catalysts for the conflict at the story's end. When Guy Montag flees from the intellectually, emotionally, and technologically compromised city and escapes to the peace of the river and the countryside, he is pursued by the Mechanical Hound. When he catches up with Granger and the "human books," he sees and hears the jets destroy the city. The real-life Cold War has arrived and become part of the inferno that is the world of *Fahrenheit 451*.

Two criticisms of Bradbury's work, including *Fahrenheit 451*, are that these stories use and misuse rather formulaic, even unimaginative, genres of "popular literature" and are flawed by illogically plotted story lines. Both assessments are inaccurate. *Fahrenheit 451* fits neatly into no generic category. It is neither wholly dystopian fiction nor utopian fare; the world does "go to Hell in a handbasket" around Montag, but he himself evolves and achieves self-worth and purpose, which previously he never had. Neither is this novel, strictly speaking, "science fiction," a popular genre whose definition varies greatly between practitioners, fans, and scholars of the form. Furthermore, *Fahrenheit 451* does not really even need to be genrefied. If we insist on labeling it, then terms and categories like "fantasy" and "speculative fiction" and "cultural critique" are most accurate because of their wide scope of parameters. Remember, too, that stories deemed "fantasy" and "fiction" should not be condemned as wholly unrealistic or fallacious. The fictions of any given social-historical-cultural period can tell us a great deal about peoples and societies and intellectual thought— sometimes as much as or more than so-called "nonfictions." Fiction, unlike nonfiction, does not have the pretext of being entirely real and accurate. Further, in the strictest sense of the term, there is no such thing as nonfiction, since all narratives are bound by biases, perceptions, perspectives, subjectivity, and human error.

Fahrenheit 451 is a good story that entertains and, in doing so, makes us think. The novel evokes personal experience and cultural inheritance. It is fair to say that Ray Bradbury never intended a purely logical, neatly packaged intellectual tract that was to be force-fed his readers. Rather, Bradbury produced a most disturbing and beautiful tale, which is full of errors in logic, that is sometimes unclear in its meaning, and which because of this, as much as any other novels of our times, reflects twentieth and early twenty-first century social and cultural history. Hence, it is replete with chaos, and only partial answers and explanations regarding our purposes as individuals and as members of larger national and world societies. *Fahrenheit 451* is the result of the keen observations and personal experiences of its author; it is also a cultural artifact, which reflects who we were, who we are, and who we might become.

For 60 years, *Fahrenheit 451* has served as an entertaining yet serious warning—not of what has to be, but of what unfortunately increasingly is—and to an extent, we have listened. But we have heeded only some of the author's words of prevention. Bradbury has forced us, at least at some level, to examine ourselves and our culture, and to analyze who we are and where we are going. This is the source of true power for the written narrative. But there is, too, an element of deadly accuracy in regard to Ray Bradbury's vision. The video image and the sound bites, the texts and tweets of today are as skewed a reality, as much a pseudo-event of epic proportions, as any detailed and forewarned in *Fahrenheit 451*. Yet, as the novel continues to warn new generations of readers and thinkers, the echoes of Bradbury's personal experiences of a now-vanished century, along with the cultural inheritance and the historical milieu that informed his art, continue to become part of *our* personal experience, *our* cultural inheritance, *our* historical milieu; in this, we are most fortunate indeed.

Genre, Censorship, and Cultural Changes: Critical Reception of Ray Bradbury's *Fahrenheit 451* from the 1950s to 2000s

Robin Anne Reid

After Ray Bradbury's death, the *New York Times* quoted a special Pulitzer citation he received in 2007 that praised his "deeply influential career as an unmatched author of science fiction and fantasy" (Jonas). In September 2013, seventy versions of *Fahrenheit 451* are available, in multiple formats, including study guides (Bowker's). The novel, published in 1953, is considered important enough that the National Endowment for the Arts (NEA) chose it as one of thirty-four "Reading Choices" for their "Big Read" program, which offers grants to support community events focused on a single book. Bradbury's novel is the only science fiction novel on the list. The NEA's webpage on *Fahrenheit 451* identifies it as the beginning of science fiction's movement from the category of genre fiction to that of "mainstream of American literature" and as being "both a literary classic and a perennial bestseller," and this reflects the scholarly and popular consensus. That consensus is that Bradbury's poetic style of writing and the themes of the novel transcend the limitations of science fiction as a popular genre sufficiently to be considered a literary classic—in other words, a work important enough to be widely taught, and which thus is the focus of academic scholarship.

While a broad consensus exists on the importance of Bradbury's novel in terms of its stylistic qualities and its critical commentary on censorship, book-burning, and American culture, critical scholarship shows a range of interpretations. A growing and complex body of scholarship explores political questions and the novel's historical context as well as Bradbury's use of figurative language, such as metaphors. There are six main topics of scholarship. The first is the question of the novel's genre categorization, specifically the question of whether the positive ending situates the work in dystopian, utopian, or related genres. Second is disagreement over the question of which specific cultural events of the 1950s the narrative warns as being most likely to bring about a dystopian future. Third is scholarship focusing on analyzing the aesthetics of the novel, primarily Bradbury's use of figurative language, such as metaphors and symbols, a topic strongly connected to the critical argument that Bradbury's work can be considered as literary, rather than as genre science fiction. Fourth are articles and resources for teachers and students that address some of the first three topics, but in the context of teaching the novel. Fifth, scholarship on the 1966 film adaptation of the novel by François Truffaut focuses on questions of the quality of the adaptation and the issue of what elements of the novel were retained, or discarded. Finally, the sixth and most recent area is biographical work, situating Bradbury's fiction within the context of his life and providing new and vital information on Bradbury's life and writing process. A notable aspect of the scholarly reception and coverage of the novel and film that is outside the scope of this project is the existence of scholarship in languages other than English. Essays on *Fahrenheit 451* (both the novel and the film adaptation) have been published, for example, in French (Grigore-Muresan, Mangeot, Païni), German (Drescher, Heurmann), Italian (Laino), Korean (Hwang), and Spanish (Fernández U., Millán de Benavides).

Is the Postapocalyptic Ending Dystopian or Utopian?
The majority of scholarship on the novel considers the questions of how it fits—or does not fit—into genre categories. The question driving this scholarship is whether the novel should be read as a dystopia (the worst possible future), or whether the utopian ending places it in that category, or whether it exists in a category that exists on the blurred boundaries between the two genres. A number of critical essays dealing with this topic discuss the novel in relationship to major dystopian works of the 20th century.

Kevin Hoskinson considers *Fahrenheit 451* a "Cold War Novel," but his 1995 evaluation of the ending of the novel is that it is optimistic, promising hope for a utopian future: "Bradbury's optimism for a recivilized world is also evidence in the conclusion of *Fahrenheit 451*. The seed for the optimistic ending to this dystopian work is actually planted just before the bombs strike" (354). Susan Spencer's 1991 essay, "The Post-Apocalyptic Library: Oral and Literate Culture in *Fahrenheit 451* and *A Canticle for Leibowitz*", also focuses on the positive nature of the ending of the novel in the context of Walter Ong's work on the differences between oral and print cultures, especially those periods of change from orality to increasing print literacy, which requires technology. Spencer argues that *Fahrenheit 451* is more positive than *A Canticle for Leibowitz* in Bradbury's focus on the importance of literature.

Other articles present more ambiguous interpretations of the ways in which the novel can be read. One of the earliest articles on genre categorization is Mary Weinkauf's 1975 essay, "Five Spokesmen for Dystopia." Rather than focusing on the ending, however, she analyzes the role of Captain Beatty, arguing that he is one of the dystopian characters who failed to create better worlds, i.e. utopias. That desire, she argues, is why the boundaries between the genres are blurred. In a 1982 essay, John Huntington argues that Bradbury's novel falls into the dystopian category because of the novel's construction of good and evil: books and nature are symbolic of utopias, while technology (including the Mechanical Hound and the Bomb) are evil.

Yet, as Huntingdon points out, books are produced by technology. The production of books during the centuries since the invention of the printing press has made books increasingly a part of mass culture, rather than being available only to an elite class. In his 1983 essay "Mass Degradation of Humanity and Massive Contradictions in Bradbury's Vision of America in *Fahrenheit 451*", Jack Zipes makes a similar argument when he argues the novel's handling of the conflict between book-loving intellectuals (such as Montag learns to become) and the masses of people in the novel is elitist in nature. Zipes concludes that whether the ending of the novel is utopian is debatable, since the hope for the future is a group of intellectuals who have memorized books, the same books that existed during the past events, which led to an authoritarian state and book-burning. Jacqueline Foertsch in "The Bomb Next Door" (1997) argues for Bradbury's novel being an example of an "alterapocalyptic" novel rather than a postapocalyptic novel: If a postapocalyptic work is one that focuses on a world after a nuclear conflict, then "alterapocalyptic" is a term for those novels in which "the bomb is copresent in a still-recognizable universe but curtained menacingly offstage, enabling totalitarian powers to maintain an oppressive society" (174).

An early essay that was not originally published in an academic journal considers the importance of the novel as a "Putropia," a term coined by the author meaning the "20th century corruption of the Utopian romances" (Williams 357). This 1956 essay by Raymond Williams, a British academic considered one of the originators of cultural criticism, which is the method of studying scholarship by situating a work of literature in its historical context, deals with the same issues that Zipes considers some decades later. However, Williams' language and judgment are even more direct and negative. The essay was originally published in *The Highway*, the journal of the Workers' Educational Association, and reprinted in *Science Fiction Studies* in 1988 as an early example of criticism about science fiction. The Workers Educational Association was founded in 1903 and still exists in Britain as a charitable, non-profit organization founded to provide adult education (WEA website). Williams covers *Fahrenheit 451* in some detail, arguing that Bradbury's novel centers on the conflict between the "isolated intellectual, and…the 'masses' who are at best brutish, at worst brutal," noting "that to think, feel, or even speak of people in terms of 'masses' is to make the burning of the books and the destroying of the cities that much more possible" (358), a conclusion directly connecting the possibility of cultural revolution to the kind of elitism portrayed in the novel.

Minority or Majority Culture as a Cause of Censorship
A major feature of dystopian novels is their didactic tone; they are written to warn readers against the contemporary cultural elements

that the author is criticizing. The critical work on *Fahrenheit 451* often disagrees on what specific events of the 1950s are presented by the novel as the cause of the future, whether it is the elite who hold political power, the majority culture, or minority groups who are singled out by Captain Beatty as causing the start of the censoring of materials. Scholarship discussed in the previous section tends to focus primarily on political events as the most important cause (Hoskinson). However, the 1950s also saw the rise of a consumer culture supported by the growth of communication technology, such as television and mass marketing (Seed, Zipes, Williams, McGiveron). Situating a work of literature in its historical context requires discussion of a complex range of historical events, which themselves constantly are being reevaluated in terms of relative importance by scholars in the academic discipline of history.

Hoskinson situates the novel firmly in the historical context of the Cold War, specifically such political events as the rise of Joseph Stalin, the Soviet Union's development of atomic weapons, and the actions of Joseph McCarthy and J. Edgar Hoover, which created a widespread fear of Communist agents. This reading of the novel identifies the major events and causes of the future as being the conflicts between national powers, both armed with nuclear weapons. Other critics, however, argue that mass culture, including advertising, is far more likely to be the primary cause of the future. Focusing on dystopian novels published after World War II, David Seed in "The Flight from the Good Life: *Fahrenheit 451* in the Context of Postwar American Dystopias" (1994) argues that the common conflict is between the protagonists' desire to maintain their individuality and the power of social and political structures that were growing in power during the 1950s. Seed points to the "consumer culture completely divorced from political awareness....[and] total separation of political action from everyday social life" (228). Jonathan R. Eller and William Touponce argue in *Ray Bradbury: The Life of Fiction* (2004) that "The main target of *Fahrenheit 451* is not censorship, as is often supposed, but rather mass culture" (186), especially the power and presence of marketing.

Other critics have made similar arguments, including Jack Zipes, who criticizes the tendency of academics to spend time debating genre terms and definitions rather than focusing on the context and political aspects of narratives. His 1983 essay is one of the earliest arguments concerning the influence of the Cold War, the growth of television, the spread of advertising, and the military industrial complex on the novel. Zipes also argues that despite the powerful elements driving the novel, the narrative has a fundamental contradiction built into it because it identifies the basic cause of the destruction in the novel as an aspect of human nature, rather than the impact of operations of social institutions and power structures. The contradiction, or gap, in the text has also been analyzed by Rafeeq O. McGiveron in "What 'Carried the Trick'? Mass Exploitation and the Decline of Thought in Ray Bradbury's *Fahrenheit 451*" (1996): there is "a noticeable gap between the message that the author and we the readers receive from the novel and the message that the text actually seems to support" (245). McGiveron, while noting that Bradbury's own "Coda" to the novel emphasizes Captain Beatty's speech blaming minorities as the cause, provides a close reading of Beatty's speech, along with information Clarisse provides Montag, as evidence that the majority population's demand for conformity and easy entertainment is the primary cause of the anti-intellectualism and active censorship by the firemen. McGiveron notes that "we are more likely to see the dangers of minority pressure in the novel because of the widespread decision that such dangers exist in our own society," because "the current debate about political correctness also helps shape how we read Bradbury" (248).

Aesthetics: Science Fiction or Literature?

The extent to which popular genres such as science fiction, mysteries, romances, and westerns are inherently inferior to mainstream literature has been debated at length by academics of English, often centering on the question of aesthetics, or quality of the style of writing. Bradbury's novel, as noted by the National Endowment for the Arts, was one of the earliest works published as science fiction to cross from the category of popular (mass) or genre work into the category of literature. Eller and Touponce cover the revision and publication history of the novel, which was published by Ballantine Books. The press was founded in 1952 with a "specialty in science fiction, fantasy, westerns, and mystery novels," and a focus on paperback originals (rather than reprints), thus being part of a change in publishing aimed at developing more mass production of books after World War II.

Much of the discussion of whether Bradbury's work is "literary" or not depends on the quality of his writing style, an aesthetic issue (aesthetics being the branch of philosophy that deals with question of what beauty is). While most of the scholarship in this section discusses the Bradbury's writing style, one scholar argues that the novel is best understood as existing in another literary genre that originated in the nineteenth century, specifically the nineteenth-century prose romance (Kagle).

George E. Connor argues that "the significance of metaphor is probably the single most analyzed aspect of Bradbury's fiction," identifying eight articles on figurative use of language (Spelunking 409). "Spelunking with Ray Bradbury: The Allegory of the Cave in *Fahrenheit 451*" (2004) is a detailed examination of the use of Plato's allegory of the Cave as a central metaphor, analyzing how the major characters all fit the categories of humans identified in the allegory. Donald Watt, in "Burning Bright: *Fahrenheit 451* as Symbolic Dystopia," analyzes how fire, the central symbol of the novel, both symbolizes destructive forces and also is the central image of home (1980). Rafeeq O. McGiveron has written two essays on imagery and metaphors in the novel. In the 1997 essay, "'Do You Know the Legend of Hercules and Antaeus?' The Wilderness in Ray Bradbury's *Fahrenheit 451*," McGiveron analyzes the images associated with nature and technology in the novel, both those that are symbolic and those that are descriptive of settings, including the wilderness at the end. In his 1998 essay "'To Build a Mirror Factory': The Mirror and Self-Examination in Ray Bradbury's *Fahrenheit 451*," McGiveron explores the metaphor of mirrors in the novel and their thematic importance, arguing that:

"With Montag's failures and successes, Bradbury shows that all of us, as individuals and as a society, must struggle to take a long, hard look in the mirror. Whether we look at ourselves from another's perspective or from the perspective of a good work of art, we need this self-examination to help avoid self-destruction" (287).

In a unique move, Steven E. Kagle analyzes how Bradbury's fascination with Herman Melville's *Moby Dick* influenced Bradbury's work. In the 1992 essay, "Homage to Melville: Ray Bradbury and the Nineteenth-Century American Romance," Kagle argues that "Bradbury's place in literary history is closer to that of Melville and other nineteenth-century writers of the prose romance than it is to twentieth-century writers of science fiction" (19). Kagle considers not only structural elements of *Fahrenheit 451* but also Bradbury's authoring of the screenplay for the 1956 adaptation of *Moby Dick* by John Huston, and of a radio play adaptation for the BBC in 1968.

Teaching *Fahrenheit 451*

Some of the earliest scholarship on Bradbury's work was related to teaching. A 1968 essay in *The English Journal*, Charles F. Hamblen's "Bradbury's *Fahrenheit 451* in the Classroom," establishes major points with which other pedagogical scholarship tends to agree. Hamblen argues that, while science fiction is not often considered important to teach, certain dystopias are included in the curriculum, those by authors such as H. G. Wells, Aldous Huxley, and George Orwell. Hamblen relates his successful experiences teaching *Fahrenheit 451*, noting that his students were able to deal with the commentary on mass entertainment's effect on people, exemplified by Montag's wife, and the satiric presentation of Captain Beatty's defense of the censorship and anti-intellectualism of the future American society. Peter Sisario, in the same journal, follows Hamblen's essay with a 1970 article on the literary and Biblical allusions in the novel. Wade E. Reynolds, in "*Fahrenheit 451*: Three Reasons Why It's Worth Teaching" (1986), identifies the following reasons for bringing the novel into the classroom: the style, specifically usage of simile and metaphor; the relevance of the themes of the work to students' lives; and its usefulness as an introduction to the genre of science fiction.

Besides the pedagogical articles, a number of resources for teachers and students also exist, some by authors of the academic articles discussed above, including McGiveron and Watt. The resources range from short, narrowly focused explications of structural elements to books meant to be read alongside the novel or as models of how to do critical analysis (Baker, Brown, de Koster, Reid), as well as collections of reprinted scholarship (Gerall and Hobby, Watt). The existence of the film adaptation of the novel also allows for a comparative approach to teaching the film alongside the novel, as John Katz discusses in his essay on "An Integrated Approach to the Teaching of Film and Literature."

Film as Interpretation

Film studies, as one subset of literary studies, has been growing during the past decades. The most developed analysis of Truffaut's film adaptation of the novel is a 1985 essay by George Bluestone, which covers disappointments noted by some critics, relating to changes made in the film. These changes include the deletion of retired literature professor Faber, and the reduction of Clarisse's role. The other problem analyzed by Bluestone is the problem of how to represent the "living books" in the scene at the end of the film, which visually gives the impression of flat characters repeating their memorized books in ways that seemed machine-like.

Biographical and Bibliographical Scholarship

William F. Nolan's *The Ray Bradbury Companion*, published in 1975, is a reference work containing bibliographic information and numerous photographs and images. In 2004, Jonathan R. Eller and William F. Touponce published *Ray Bradbury: The Life of Fiction*, which discusses Bradbury's major works in the historical context of their composition, their publication history, and their connections to his shorter or unpublished works. Sam Weller based his 2006 biography of Bradbury on extensive interviews with Bradbury himself, as well as with others who knew the writer personally and professionally. Additionally, Bradbury gave Weller access to his private papers and documents, and the resulting work, *The Bradbury Chronicles: The Life of Ray Bradbury*, has been widely praised for the ways in which Weller was able to connect the details of Bradbury's life to his work, published and unpublished.

The most recent biographical work on Bradbury is Jonathan Eller's 2011 *Becoming Ray Bradbury*, which focuses on the author's first thirty years and also draws on interviews with Bradbury. Eller utilizes his extensive bibliographic work as well as his access to Bradbury's papers, with a focus on the creators in fiction, art, and film who were inspirations to Bradbury. This biography covers Bradbury's life up to the point when *Fahrenheit 451* was finished, and Bradbury scholars are no doubt looking forward to publication of material that covers the later years of Bradbury's work.

Works Cited

Baker, Brian. "Ray Bradbury: *Fahrenheit 451*." *A Companion to Science Fiction*. Ed. David Seed. Malden, MA: Blackwell, 2005. 489-99. Blackwell Companions to Literature and Culture 34.

Ballantine Books. "About Ballantine Books." Web. <http://ballantine.atrandom. com> 29 Sept. 2013.

Bluestone, George. "Three Seasons with *Fahrenheit 451*." *Sacred Heart University Review* 6.1-2 (1985): 3-19.

Bowker. *Books in Print*. R. R. Bowker LLC. Web. <http://www.booksinprint. com> 29 Sept. 2013.

Brown, Joseph F. "'As the Constitution Says': Distinguishing Documents in Ray Bradbury's *Fahrenheit 451*." *The Explicator* 67 (2008): 55-58.

Connor, George E. "Spelunking with Ray Bradbury: The Allegory of the Cave in *Fahrenheit 451*." *Extrapolation: A Journal of Science Fiction and Fantasy* 45 (2004): 408-18.

De Koster, Katie. *Readings on Fahrenheit 451*. San Diego: Greenhaven, 2000. Greenhaven Press Literary Companion to American Literature.

Drescher, Horst W. "Der Aussenseiter Im Utopischen Roman Der Moderne: George Orwell, Nineteen Eighty-Four, und Ray Bradbury, *Fahrenheit 451*." *Anglia: Zeitschrift fur Englische Philologie* 96 (1978): 430-46.

Eller, Jonathan R. *Becoming Ray Bradbury*. Urbana, IL: U of Illinois P, 2011.

Eller, Jonathan R. and William F. Touponce. *Ray Bradbury: The Life of Fiction.* Kent, OH: Kent State UP, 2004.

"Fahrenheit 451 by Ray Bradbury." *The Big Read.* National Endowment for the Arts. Web. <http://www.neabigread.org> 10 Sept. 2013.

Fernández U, Ana Francisca. "Simbología Del Fuego En *Fahrenheit 451* De Ray Bradbury." *Káñina: Revista de Artes y Letras de la Universidad de Costa Rica* 6.1-2 (1982): 73-76.

Foertsch, Jacqueline. "The Bomb Next Door: Four Postwar Alterapocalyptics." *Genre: Forms of Discourse and Culture* 30.4 (1997): 333-58.

Gerall, Alina and Blake Hobby. *"Fahrenheit 451* (Ray Bradbury): 'And the Leaves of the Tree Were for the Healing of the Nations': Reading and Civil Disobedience in Ray Bradbury's *Fahrenheit 451." Civil Disobedience.* Ed. Harold Bloom and Blake Hobby. New York: Bloom's Literary Criticism, 2010. 141-49. Bloom's Literary Themes Ser.

Grigore-Muresan, Madalina. "La Défense De L'imaginaire Dans *Fahrenheit 451* De Ray Bradbury." *Cahiers du Gerf* 22 (2001): 79-94.

Guijarro González, Juan. "'Back to the Future' or Out of the Past? The Sociopolitical Subtext of Ray Bradbury's *Fahrenheit 451." Actas Iii Congreso De La Sociedad Española Para El Estudio Dos Estados Unidos/ Spanish Association for American Studies (Saas): Fin De Siglo: Crisis Y Nuevos Principios/Century Ends, Crises and New Beginnings.* Ed. María José Alvarez Maurín et al. León, Spain: Universidad de León, 1999. 191-97.

Hamblen, Charles F. "Bradbury's *Fahrenheit 451* in the Classroom." *English Journal* 57 (1968): 818+.

Heuermann, Hartmut. "Ray Bradbury: *Fahrenheit 451* (1953)." *Die Utopie in Der Angloamerikanischen Literatur: Interpretationen.* Ed. Hartmut Heuermann and Bernd-Peter Lange. Düsseldorf: Bagel, 1984. 259-82.

Hoskinson, Kevin. *"The Martian Chronicles* and *Fahrenheit 451:* Ray Bradbury's Cold War Novels." *Extrapolation: A Journal of Science Fiction and Fantasy* 36 (1995): 345-59.

Huntington, John. "Utopian and Anti-Utopian Logic: H. G. Wells and His Successors." *Science Fiction Studies* 9 [27] (1982): 122-46.

Hwang, Eunju. "Ray Bradbury's *Fahrenheit 451* and Society of Controlled Knowledge." *Journal of English Language and Literature/Yŏngŏ Yŏngmunhak* 58.4 (2012): 589-609.

Jonas, Gerald. "Ray Bradbury, Who Brought Mars to Earth With a Lyrical Mastery, Dies at 91." NYTimes.com. *New York Times* Books. 6 June 2012. Web. 25 Sept. 2013.

Kagle, Steven E. "Homage to Melville: Ray Bradbury and the Nineteenth-Century American Romance." *The Celebration of the Fantastic: Selected Papers from the Tenth Anniversary International Conference on the Fantastic in the Arts*. Ed. Donald E. Morse, Marshall B. Tymn, and Csilla Bertha. Westport, CT: Greenwood, 1992. 279-89. Contributions to the Study of Science Fiction and Fantasy 49.

Katz, John. "An Integrated Approach to the Teaching of Film and Literature." *Screen* 11.4/5 (1970): 56.

Laino, Guido. "Destinazione 'Good Old Days': Il Viaggio Nel Tempo in *Fahrenheit 451*." *Cuadernos de Literatura Inglesa y Norteamericana* 9.1-2 (2006): 25-36.

_____. "Nature as an Alternative Space for Rebellion in Ray Bradbury's *Fahrenheit 451*." *Literary Landscapes, Landscape in Literature*. Ed. Michele Bottalico, Maria Teresa Chialant, and Eleonora Rao. Rome, Italy: Carocci, 2007. 152-64. Lingue E Letterature Carocci 47.

Mangeot, Philippe. "Zone Franche: *Fahrenheit 451* (1966)." *Cahiers du Cinéma* 592 (2004): 27-28.

McGiveron, Rafeeq O. "Bradbury's *Fahrenheit 451*." *The Explicator* 54 (1996): 177-80.

_____. "'Do You Know the Legend of Hercules and Antaeus?' The Wilderness in Ray Bradbury's *Fahrenheit 451*." *Extrapolation: A Journal of Science Fiction and Fantasy* 38 (1997): 102-09.

_____. " 'To Build a Mirror Factory': The Mirror and Self-Examination in Ray Bradbury's *Fahrenheit 451*." *Critique: Studies in Contemporary Fiction* 39 (1998): 282-87.

_____. "What 'Carried the Trick'? Mass Exploitation and the Decline of Thought in Ray Bradbury's *Fahrenheit 451*." *Extrapolation: A Journal of Science Fiction and Fantasy* 37 (1996): 245-56.

Millán de Benavides, Carmen. "Ekpyrosis." *Aleph (Manizales, Colombia)* 137 (2006): 31-36.

Nolan, William F. *The Ray Bradbury Companion: A Life and Career History, Photolog, and Comprehensive Checklist of Writings with Facsimiles from Ray Bradbury's Unpublished and Uncollected Work in All Media*. Detroit: Gale, 1975.

"Our Books." *The Big Read*. National Endowment for the Arts. Web. <http://www.neabigread.org> 10 Sept. 2013

Païni, Dominique. "Cocteau, Hitchcock, Truffaut…Et Retour." *Cinéma* 4 (2002): 83-90.

Reid, Robin Anne. *Ray Bradbury: A Critical Companion*. Westport, CT: Greenwood, 2000. Critical Companions to Popular Contemporary Writers Ser.

Reynolds, Wade E. "*Fahrenheit 451*: Three Reasons Why It's Worth Teaching." *Virginia English Bulletin* 36.2 (1986): 117-21.

Seed, David. "The Flight from the Good Life: *Fahrenheit 451* in the Context of Postwar American Dystopias." *Journal of American Studies* 28 (1994): 225-40.

Spencer, Susan. "The Post-Apocalyptic Library: Oral and Literate Culture in *Fahrenheit 451* and *A Canticle for Leibowitz*." *Extrapolation: A Journal of Science Fiction and Fantasy* 32 (1991): 331-42.

Watt, Donald. "Burning Bright: *Fahrenheit 451* as Symbolic Dystopia." *Alienation*. Ed. Harold Bloom and Blake Hobby. New York: Bloom's Literary Criticism, 2009. 71-83. Bloom's Literary Themes.

————. "Burning Bright: *Fahrenheit 451* as Symbolic Dystopia." *Ray Bradbury*. Ed. Martin Harry Greenberg and Joseph D. Olander. New York: Taplinger, 1980. 195-213. Writers of the 21st Century Ser.

Watt, Donald J. "Hearth or Salamander: Uses of Fire in Bradbury's *Fahrenheit 451*." *Notes on Contemporary Literature* 1.2 (1971): 13-14.

Weinkauf, Mary S. "Five Spokesmen for Dystopia." *Midwest Quarterly: A Journal of Contemporary Thought* 16 (1975): 175-86.

Weller, Sam. *The Bradbury Chronicles: The Life of Ray Bradbury*. New York: HarperCollins, 2005.

Williams, Raymond. "Science Fiction." *Science Fiction Studies* 15.3 [46] (1988): 356-60.

Workers Educational Association. Web. <http://www.wea.org.uk> 1 Sept. 2013.

Zipes, Jack. "Mass Degradation of Humanity and Massive Contradictions in Bradbury's Vision of America in *Fahrenheit 451*." *No Place Else: Explorations in Utopian and Dystopian Fiction*. Eds. Eric S. Rabkin, Martin H. Greenberg, and Joseph D. Olander. Carbondale: Southern Illinois UP, 1983. 182-98. Alternatives Ser.

The Phoenix and the Fireman: Dialogistic Inversion in Ray Brabury's *Fahrenheit 451*

Joseph Michael Sommers

"Language lives only in the dialogic interaction of those who make use of it."

—M. M. Bakhtin, *Problems of Dostoyevsky's Poetics*, 183

"There was a silly damn bird called a phoenix back before Christ, every few hundred years he built a pyre and burnt himself up. He must have been first cousin to Man. But every time he burnt himself up he sprang out of the ashes, he got himself born all over again. And it looks like we're doing the same thing, over and over, but we've got one damn thing the phoenix never had. We know the damn silly thing we just did."

—Ray Bradbury, *Fahrenheit 451*, 163

A critic, or any writer really, uses the epigraph for a variety of means and concerns, most often, I think, to provide a frame for the body of the narrative it is set before. As a Bakhtinian critic, someone who uses the works of M. M. Bakhtin to frame and try to better comprehend texts, I frequently employ two epigraphs so as to construct not a hermeneutic, or necessarily explanatory, frame but, rather, what I think to be a set of brackets: one that opens a conversation and one that rejoins that conversation in progress. For critics such as myself, such approaches to literature lie at the heart of what is called Dialogism. This is a difficult term to define, with a meaning that shifted for Bakhtin over time and space—easy enough, as the term was never actually used by him but instead was given to his concept Bakhtinian scholars. The term, however, comes down to a basic principle that:

> everything means, is understood, as a part of a greater whole—there is a constant interaction between meanings, all of which have the potential of conditioning others. Which will affect the other, how it

will do so and in what degree is what is actually settled at the moment of utterance. (*Diologic* 426)

Or, to look at the epigraphs above, two quotations from two separate works by two separate authors that came from two separate time periods have been juxtaposed with each other in an effort to begin the conversation of: 1) introducing what is contained in this essay, 2) what Bakhtin, at the time of writing, meant by the idea of dialog, 3) how the reader of this essay could see these concepts working in Bradbury's *Fahrenheit 451* or, rather, 4) how *Fahrenheit 451* is a dialogical text. And so on. By way of my intentions, the epigraphs above are meant to demonstrate what Granger tries to teach Guy Montag in the third section of *451*: Bradbury in his dystopic novel has his character Granger, a former academic, explain to Montag, a former fireman, the lost meaning behind the symbol of the phoenix that Montag had worn proudly upon his chest during his service as a fireman (163). It is a moment filled with irony and Bakhtinian dialog as Montag, who has literally burnt his former life to ashes by way of daring to read outlawed books, and was likely scheduled to die for doing so, has come about face and risen from those ashes through the interlocution and dialog with Granger. In Bradbury's dystopia, people literally cannot remember even the most basic things moment to moment because they have stopped reading. What Granger does with Montag, where Montag both becomes a phoenix and breaks the cycle of being the phoenix, is by enacting that which has become taboo; as Granger states, "We're remembering" (164). None of which goes into the kind of depth that explains the dialogism of Christ and the Phoenix, or fire as a principle of both life and destruction, or even the concept of "the fireman" who have moved from putting out fires to setting them in a book whose concept is set in a far-flung future from when it was originally written to when it is being discussed today. But that's a different conversation for a different essay.

At present, what concerns this study is the peculiarity of *Fahrenheit 451* as an operating dialog and dialogic novel. Specifically, the character of Guy Montag, as constructed by Bradbury, seems to be an inherently dialogical set of monads, or units of philosophical thought, through which Bradbury explores the multiplicity of many big ideas relevant to his time period, such as American McCarthyism and its chilling parallels, in his mind, to things such as book-burning in Nazi-occupied Europe during World War II. However, interestingly enough, Bradbury's voice as author seems to slip into other characters, which Montag encounters, such as Clarisse McClellan, Professor Faber, and Granger. Using dystopia, in which the author oft makes chilling indictments of the past and present with the nightmarish future to come, Bradbury becomes inherently monologic, not unlike like Chief Beatty. Both included in the conversation and yet excluded by being told how to read the novel, the reader thus is turned into Guy Montag, left to wonder whose version of the truth might be the take-away from the book.

A Bit More on Dialogism and How It Works

While dialog is a relatively simple enough concept, dialogism is not. Bakhtinian dialog, as the name implies, concerns language in its systemization, in its vessel, which, in this case, is the novel, and in those persons using language. That is to say, dialog necessarily implies voices, usually many voices (a term called 'polyglossia') and, ideally, different kinds of voices (a term called 'heteroglossia') that are uttered into the site of the discourse (which is, again, the novel). The easiest way to understand the concept would be to think about the novel as a busy train station where many voices are heard and overheard, while a few primary people are having a conversation with one another. As a result of all the noise and interaction occurring around these few primary people, little bits of all the other voices in the station creep into their conversation.

Additionally, whatever else is on these few primary people's minds—personal concerns, political concerns, observations about the passers-by and -thru outside of the small group (or even about the people within it), whether or not they left the toaster on when they left the house, etc.—also factor into the voices that are internal and external to the site of the novel. This is just like in real life, where someone might be listening outwardly to one person telling her about the latest comic book movie, while thinking about something completely different inside her head. Yet this person nods in agreement only as a method to buy time to formulate a smart response about comic book movies while someone else in her group approaches from behind to tell her about the terribly overpriced churro he just purchased from a vendor, and so on. This is a rather dynamic way of looking at language and language usage, as something always alive and always picking up the valences of all the prior usages of that language set forth into the exchange of information, which, if one thinks about it, is an impossible and insurmountable amount of information for anyone to try to process. The difference with a novel is that readers can see all of these interacting and interchanging voices as they read what has been presented to them by the author.

The author of the novel, as such, is the great funnel of dialog to the reader. If dialogism is, as *The Dialogic Imagination* states, a sort of "epistemological mode of a world dominated by heteroglossia" (426), then the novel forms the brackets by which one particular conversation exists and is offered up to the reader, who then can engage, intertextualize, and continue the conversation to whatever extent desired. Importantly, this also means that the reader can engage with the conversation even with a lack of knowledge about the elements in the conversation, outwardly changing the meaning either through ignorance or by deliberately imposing or shifting values based upon such markers as time and space. An example of the latter would be what has been termed "political correctness"; whereas in a certain time and place, it was deemed permissible in common parlance for a man to call a young woman "foxy" or a "hot mama," such talk in a generalized, social setting would most likely be seen as derogatory or sexist in the current American moment. In Bakhtinian dialog, though, such contributions to the discourse within the novel hold that the reader, to engage effectively with the reading, would be aware not only of the semantic and connotative discourses, but also the culture surrounding the writing. This is not to say that Bakhtin would argue for a forced interpretation. In fact, he would likely argue against such things, since such forced or entrenched readings from a dominant discourse would be what is termed *monologia*, an authoritative discourse that does not permit the freedoms that interpretive dialog does. Bakhtinian theory, stemming from revolutionary ideals and theories, generally does not work towards the ends of closing down thought as much as it works towards expanding it.

As Bakhtin notes in the essay "From Notes Made in 1970-71," "The speaking subjects of high, proclamatory genres—of priests, prophets, preachers, judges, leaders, patriarchal fathers, and so forth—have departed this life. They have been replaced by the writer, simply the writer" (*Speech Genres* 132). These authoritarian figures represent a threat to Bakhtin's view of the novel as the novel is a place where the "sacred" word is beset with "rejoinder among equally privileged rejoinders" (133). For Bakhtin, the word and its language is life, and those who would seek to commandeer life have little business in the novel where the life of the common person is allowed to breathe free of authoritarian controls and constraints. Admittedly, this presents what might be considered a somewhat naïve view of the author as one who, in presentation of many and different voices, would seek to expand the concept of language through the presentation of dialog within the novel. In fact, as Gary Saul Morson and Caryl Emerson observe:

> Bakhtin always treats the novel as the form best satisfying his favorite values and expressing global concepts.... The novel is sure to be the genre that is most dialogic. More than any competitor, it treats character, society, and knowledge as unfinalizable; it is closest to prosaic values, an appreciation of centrifugal forces, and a sense of the world's essential messiness. (303)

However, what happens when a novel, like *Fahrenheit 451*, is a piece of inherently dystopian fiction, wherein the author seeks to make a readily monological point to an audience of readers, even if the author does so by way of presenting the folly and madness that is part of the authoritarian society presented in the novel? Can subject matter negate dialog when an author presents himself to be authoritarian[1] in a work didactically preaching an anti-authoritarian

---

agenda? *Fahrenheit 451* offers itself up as a resplendent litmus test for Bakhtinian dialog as Bakhtin does not make much comment upon dystopia or anti-utopia novels. The critic thus must infer and apply Bakhtin's existing theories upon a genre of the novel, about which he himself made little remark. As such, when an author utilizes a form, the novel, seemingly in a manner for which Bakhtin did not suppose it would be used (arguable monologia), the opportunity makes an advantageous site to tax the boundaries of both the text and the critical lens being applied to the text.

Dialogic Inversions in *Fahrenheit 451*

Perhaps it might be best to examine first some of the underpinnings of *Fahrenheit 451*. This will be all the more difficult because 451 is a text that, arguably, came into being from a variety of pretexts. Nevertheless, that argument does come directly from Ray Bradbury himself. In *Match to Flame: The Fictional Paths to Fahrenheit 451*, Bradbury chronicles the events that precipitated the writing of 451, from his concerns regarding censorship during the period known as American McCarthyism in the 1950s and 1960s, paralleling previous Nazi and Stalinist trends, to notable short works of fiction he authored, such as "Bright Phoenix," "Chief Sensor," and "The Pedestrian" (9, 68). All of these early thoughts, ideas, and short writings became the foundation for what would become the 1953 first printing of *Fahrenheit 451* published by Ballantine Books. This sort of contextualization of the author's mindset is the sort of work easily accomplished in the digital era by way of little more than using an internet search engine or a good encyclopedia, but for the Bakhtinian critic, in Bakhtin's day, this sort of contextualization would have had to be tracked down by way of searching voluminous amounts of material that might not have had quite such a simply acquired digital footprint. Yet, this information does not even begin the task of engaging 451 dialogically; it simply allows us insight into the variety of the streams of voices in the author's head. What matters is always on the page.

And one can begin as simply as examining our protagonist, Guy Montag, a fireman, who in Bradbury's alternative reality, is charged not with putting out fires but with burning: burning not only the books and homes of those who violate the law against having books, but also sometimes even the malefactors. The first thoughts the reader is given in the text are Montag's; while he is not the narrator of *Fahrenheit 451*, the omniscient voice of the text tells the reader, first, that "It was a pleasure to burn" (3). Further, it attributes the following to Montag's thoughts:

> It was a special pleasure to see things eaten, to see things blackened and *changed*. With the brass nozzle in his fists, with his great python spitting its venomous kerosene upon the world, the blood pounded in his head, and his hands were the hands of some amazing conductor playing all the symphonies of blazing and burning to bring down the tatters and charcoal ruins of history.
> ...Montag grinned the fierce grin of all men singed and driven back by flame.
> He knew that when he returned to the firehouse, he might wink at himself, a minstrel man, burnt-corked in the mirror. (3-4)

Simple analysis of this passage informs the reader that the narrator attributes to Montag a sort of hyperbolic sexual pleasure for burning, metaphorically charging "his great python" with the "brass nozzle in his fists" spitting forth kerosene to the extent that "blood pounded in his head." As the reader would not normally attribute that to the notion of what a fireman in the reader's universe does, is obvious from the novel's title and the inversion of the fireman's vocation that this novel is some kind of alternative history or future concern.[2]

Yet dialog becomes increasingly interesting with the analysis of the operating discourses attributed to Montag's thought: the narrator paints Montag as a man proud in his vocation, observing himself covered in soot and soaked through to the pores of kerosene to the extent that he cannot wash the smell away (6). And, as a good fireman is and should be, Montag is not one to think lofty thoughts or have brazen idylls—no such work, meaning books, exists to inform his imagination as such and spur it to loftier heights. Yet "his hands were the hands of some amazing conductor playing all the symphonies of blazing and burning to bring down the tatters and charcoal ruins of history" (3)—this is not the vapid thought of man engaging in little more than sports and the parlor walls; this is an authoritative man whom the narrator describes from the first page of *451* as a catalyst of *change* in a period where complacency and the status quo are privileged. This is the way, as the reader comes to learn in the novel's second section, that a scholar thinks.

Granted, these thoughts are the narrator's and not Montag's. Narrators are, of course, not always trustworthy. This narrator seems to undercut the authority of Montag from outset. This narrator offers the reader scant glances into Montag's mind, where he divines Whitmanesque notes of precision and concern with "the air [that] seemed charged with a special calm as if someone has waited there" (5). These are not merely the thoughts of the observant man, as a fireman must be observant and vigilant; the word choices given to Montag's thoughts articulate a man conflicted between his job of burning books and the fancy that might be contained within them. Of course, if the narrator was merely hinting by describing Montag's thoughts earlier, he did not necessarily cement them by offering a direct moment to validate such concerns. Until, he does:

> The girl's face was there, really quite beautiful in memory: astonishing, in fact. She had a very thin face like a dial of a small clock seen faintly in a dark room in the middle of a night when you waken to see the time and see the clock telling you the hour and the minute and the second, with a white silence and a glowing, all certainty and knowing what it had to tell of the night passing swiftly on toward further darknesses, but moving also toward a new sun.
> "*What?*" asked Montag of that other self, the subconscious idiot that ran babbling at times, quite independent of will, habit, and conscience. (10-11)

Here the narrator deliberately outs Montag as a man of poetry using simile, metaphor, and enjambed lines, among of other literary devices. Worse, Montag *admits it*. He outright says that he is not being misrepresented by the narrator here; he really does think poetically. In the next paragraph "he searched for a simile [and] found it in his work—torches" (11). Montag cannot control this "idiot" voice in his own head, all the more ironic as it is a remarkably well thought-out idiot, as opposed to the reduced mental state of most all other people in this world, like his wife, Millie, who nearly kills herself accidentally because she has lost the capacity to remember how many sleeping pills she has taken at one time (14). The narrator actually tells us that Montag remembers things. He does not live in a perpetual present. He is a man who against all of his offices and virtues exemplifies everything he should not be.

Why would the narrator do such a thing? It clearly could get Montag killed, and it is not information that necessarily need be betrayed. And when the narrator does do this to others in the novel, the consequences are high. Clarisse, the young girl who inspired the aforementioned thought from Montag and who can also see the poet within him, dies as a result of her irregularity within this system (47); Professor Faber, who aids Montag in his attempts at cultivating his intellect, has his home set upon by firemen and has a homicidal mechanical hound loosed after him before going into exile (136); Granger already has been forced into exile, becoming a living volume of Plato's *Republic* (151). In fact, as Granger shows Montag, the authoritative regime controlling this world has faked Montag's death, since they can no longer find him and perform the public execution themselves. As a result, Montag finds home with the living volumes; he possesses knowledge of the Book of Ecclesiastes, and some of Revelation, and he has come back from the dead as a living, breathing Book of Ecclesiastes (149-51). In essence, he becomes the change he originally felt was a fireman's purpose and, not unlike the sigil of the phoenix upon his chest in that life, returns from the ashes. However, his purpose has changed, too.

All of which brings this reading back to the interlocution of the narrator into the text. Regardless of how Bakhtin sees the novel, dystopic fiction functions differently than novelistic discourse: dystopic fiction is inherently pedantic. It hopes to teach the reader by way of frightening the reader. This could not be seen any clearer than Bradbury's voice occupying *451*'s primary antagonist, Chief Beatty. As shown, Bradbury's optimistic insertion of his voice into characters are all part of the counter-culture to the dominant discourse of the novel's dystopic setting, save Montag, who acts as the novel's fulcrum towards change. Beatty is Bradbury's voice, showing readers his world's past and present, inspiring them to rethink their future:

> I've had to read a few [books] in my time, to know what I was about, and the books say *nothing*! Nothing you can teach or believe. They're about nonexistent people, figments of imagination, if they're fiction. And if they're nonfiction, it's worse, one professor calling another an idiot, one philosopher screaming down another's gullet. All of them running about, putting out the stars and extinguishing the sun. You come away lost. (62)

The dialogism here is as thick and acrid as the oily smoke coming from a kerosene fire. Beatty tells Montag, and the reader, of the evils of reading books—that they cannot teach. Yet, he instructs Montag and the reader in these matters by virtue of the voluminous amounts of reading and scholarship he has done to arrive at this thesis. Further complicating the matter is that what Beatty argues *is true*! Scholarship has long been fostered upon the idea of appreciable argument and advancement from argument— argument, in other words, that answers fewer questions but creates further and better questions. From Plato forward, humankind has been charged with the idea of one of its greatest social merits: being inherently inquisitive. Beatty vilifies himself here by articulating, and waving in the reader's face, nothing more than the reality of our history, something which might be best forgot if we are to be "happy" living in the fictionalized "happy world"[3] Bradbury creates for us here (62).

Of course, with the novel being a dystopia, the reader knows that this abandonment of argument and questioning is not the desired outcome of the author, an understanding reinforced by watching Bradbury punish this world with nuclear destruction at the novel's end. This, however, is not bracketed information; by being so totalitarian in his punishment of this world of memory loss and un-thought, Bradbury acts as might a monologic despot. He uses the fear of death and complete erasure of humanity to reinforce his point and package his argument, for who would allow that the universe he presents, one of nuclear death for being inherently stupid, is superior to the one he advocates through pain and strife? "Read, children!"—Bradbury's narrative voice seems to scream—"Read! Read this book and others like it so that the America that you live within, one threatened by the Red Scare and McCarthyism, does not turn into the failed empires of the Nazis and the Stalinists! As that is the trajectory I foresee." And yet, while that may appear inherently dialogical—resistance to authoritative and totalitarian discourses is good, yes, language should still be freeing and dialogic—the entirety of *Fahrenheit 451* has been couched in a religious discourse, that of the parable. As Bakhtin notes earlier, this is a voice that closes down conversation instead of opening it up and letting it expand, not unlike removing the lid from Pandora's Jar.

What we are left with is something akin to a paradox: Bradbury's novel seems to demand freedom. It is a novel that chooses to close the hermeneutic loop as opposed to letting it spiral off into the cosmos. Then again, to close off the discussion of what is and can be seen as dialogical would, by Bakhtin's construction of dialogism, be monological. So, perhaps, the only way to leave this particular reading of this particular text would be to not close, but leave the discussion and allow it to continue.

Notes

1. Note that the root word of authoritarian is actually author.
2. Remember, although the book was published in 1953, the setting seems to be sometime towards the end of the twentieth century.
3. Part of the dark humor of this section is that this "happy world" Beatty describes is literally on the brink of nuclear annihilation by book's end (160).

Works Cited

Bakhtin, Mikhail Mikhaïlovich. Trans. Caryn Emerson and Michael Holquist. Ed. Michael Holquist. *The Dialogic Imagination: Four Essays*. Austin: U of Texas P, 1981.

Bakhtin, Mikhail Mikhaïlovich. Trans. and ed. Caryl Emerson. *Problems of Dostoyesvsky's Poetics.* Minneapolis: U of Minnesota P, 1984.

Bakhtin, Mikhail Mikhaïlovich. Trans. Vern W. McGee. *Speech Genres and Other Late Essays*. Austin: U of Texas P, 1986. Theory and History of Literature Ser 8.

Bradbury, Ray. *Fahrenheit 451*. 1953. New York: Del Rey, 1991.

Bradbury, Ray. *Match to Flame: The Fictional Paths to Fahrenheit 451*. Colorado Springs: Gauntlet, 2007.

Morson, Gary Saul and Caryl Emerson. *Mikhail Bakhtin: Creation of a Prosaics*. Stanford, CA: Stanford UP, 1990.

From "Government Control of This and That" to "The Whole Culture's Shot Through": Behavior, Blame, and the Bomb in *The Martian Chronicles* and *Fahrenheit 451* ___

Rafeeq O. McGiveron

Ray Bradbury's *Fahrenheit 451* is a work both grim and yet hopeful, the portrayal of a frenetically hedonistic society so deeply troubled that the author can present a nuclear war as positive, as much an opportunity for change and the rediscovery of human values as for destruction. It is interesting, though, to examine Bradbury's 1953 novel in light of his earlier book that ends with atomic fire and the hope for rebirth, *The Martian Chronicles*. Only three years separate the publication of these two works, but although both exemplify the major fears of the time of their writing—not just the external threat of nuclear war but also the internal threat of postwar consumerism and conformity, and the resulting loss of true humanness—their foci of pessimism are intriguingly different.

In *The Martian Chronicles*, despite the great destruction caused by the settlers from Earth, humanity as a whole is presented in a more positive light than it is in *Fahrenheit 451*. Indeed, while certain particularly hateful characters are shown here and there, many other very ordinary people are portrayed as inoffensive, even well-intentioned, and as much evil appears to be caused by the seemingly far-removed "government" as by the actions of individuals; by *Fahrenheit 451*, of course, Bradbury presents the pleasure-seeking—or at least discomfort- and thought-avoiding—populace as being the driving force behind anti-intellectualism and interpersonal disconnection, with laws for the banning of books and the dumbing-down of school being established by the government almost as an afterthought. Curiously, however, whether from the author's real estimation or whether from plot necessity, the horror of the atom bomb has receded somewhat in the later novel. Still, although Bradbury's retreat between 1950 and 1953 from the notion of near-complete human extinction from nuclear holocaust to a brief, easily contained atomic blitzkrieg may be a step back from reality, his sociological and psychological shifts in *Fahrenheit 451* probably better reflect the evolution of the modern world since the Second World War.

Fire Captain Beatty in *Fahrenheit 451* contrasts the supposedly sedate nineteenth century's "horses, dogs, carts, slow motion" with the accelerating pace of the modern world (58), but in many respects, *The Martian Chronicles* harks back to a culture, which has not yet completely anesthetized itself with high-speed mass entertainment "leveled down to a sort of pastepudding norm" (*Fahrenheit* 58). Yes, the rape of a world and the destruction of its ancient and magnificent culture by the diseases of uncaring newcomers is a savage thing. Yet even this treatment of the American frontier myth upon a fantastic ochre Mars is, in a way, less brutal and soul-destroying than everyday life in Bradbury's later novel. Written on the cusp of the television age, when minds still might turn outward to intellectual or experiential curiosity and to relationships rather than wallow in the pleasures of the full-color mass-market drug flickering in the parlor's crystal screen, *The Martian Chronicles*, for the most part, portrays the "average" person less as a force for evil or even for mere ignorance than as basically decent, and caught up in the flow of self-destructive historical trends beyond human control.

Certainly reprehensible characters exist in *The Martian Chronicles*, although they do not necessarily seem representative of the whole society. Sam Parkhill of the fourth expedition to Mars in "—And the Moon be Still as Bright," for example, is the crewman most cruelly eager for a literally bloody vengeance when Captain Wilder must order his men to hunt down archaeologist Jeff Spender, who has begun killing off his fellow crewmembers, whom he considers vanguards of Earth's destructive culture. For fun, Parkhill shoots apart one of the dead Martian "chess men" cities (72), a habit he has not lost when he returns four years later in the plot as the unimaginative, crassly grasping owner of a hot dog stand in "The Off Season." His credo is "[T]he old got to give way to the new. That's the law of give and take. I got a gun here" (134). Although one of the last Martians, showing up unexpectedly, assures him, "We mean you no harm," Parkhill's rejoinder is "But I mean you harm!" (134), and soon he shoots his way out of the encounter with a brutal and vandalistic relish. White Southern racist Samuel Teece of "Way in the Middle of the Air" is even more distasteful, condescending and mean-spirited as he gloats at the thought of impeding any of the oppressed blacks who might escape to Mars. And, of course, he is a murderer far worse than the panicky Parkhill, one who, "laughing to himself, his heart racing like a ten-year-old's," has reveled in "[h]ow many nights over the years, how many nights" of lynchings (100).

In addition, while Parkhill and Teece may represent some of the worst that the culture of the modern materialistic West has produced, Bradbury, with his imagery, reminds us that despite the perhaps benign motives of some, the colonization of Mars also ultimately must be a thoughtless and destructive process, an "invasion" (78) even when almost none of the planet's native inhabitants remain alive to see the offense. The language of the narrative, after all, is that of violence and force, comparing the arriving rockets to drums of war "beating in the night" or to "locusts"; the newcomers do not just arrive but run, "with hammers in their hands to beat the strange world into a shape that [is] familiar to the eye, to bludgeon away all the strangeness…" (78). Even the naming of the supposedly "new" land is shown as destruction, for just as the "fiery cauldrons" of the rockets "burn the land," "breaking" and "shattering" the past, the new Terran names forcibly obliterate the old Martian "names of water and air and hills," and great pylons then are "plunged" down, violating phallic markers that show "the mechanical names and the metal names from Earth" (102).

Of course, it is Jeff Spender of "—And the Moon be Still as Bright," which Edward J. Gallagher correctly terms the book's "thematic center" (63-64), who enunciates Bradbury's most unified and coherent critique of "the whole crooked grinding greedy setup on Earth" (*Martian* 64). According to the sensitive and imaginative archaeologist, whereas the Martians "blended religion and art and science because, at base, science is no more than an investigation of a miracle we can never explain, and art is an interpretation of that miracle" (67), the culture of Earth "lost [its] faith and went around wondering what life was for" (66). His fellow crewmen, he has discovered in asking about their possible sympathies toward a hypothetical remaining Martian, live by very simple and bleakly self-centered rules: "Catch as catch can, finder's keepers, if the other fellow turns his cheek slap it hard, etc...." (59; ellipsis Bradbury's). These oafs, he tells Captain Wilder, are "professional cynics", interested only in a "keep[ing] up with the Joneses" (67). Such an evaluation is echoed by the father of "The Million-Year Picnic" at the end of the book, when he tells his family, "Science ran too far ahead of us too quickly, and people got lost in a mechanical wilderness, like children making over pretty things, gadgets, helicopters, rockets; emphasizing the wrong items, emphasizing machines instead of how to run the machines" (179-80).

Yet despite the often-correct evaluations of these justifiably embittered characters, and despite the author's haunting and evocative imagery, we should not forget that Bradbury still portrays humanity in general in a significantly more charitable light in *The Martian Chronicles* than he does in *Fahrenheit 451*. Spender is "ashamed" of the others' noise and disrespect on the grave of a dead civilization (53), but Wilder points out that, until egged on by Biggs, who is the worst of them, the rest "looked pretty humble and frightened" (54-55). Indeed, Wilder soon afterward takes an exploring party into the nearby empty Martian city of "moon-silvered towers" and intricately worked tile, and the men are somber again, "whispering now, for it [is] like entering a vast open library or a mausoleum" (56). As Spender recites Byron's "So We'll Go no More a Roving," these military rocket crewmen actually listen, and as they regard the ancient mosaics beneath their feet in silence, "[t]here [is] not a sound but the wind"...until the drunken Biggs vomits (57).

Thus despite Biggs and other members of the "if the other fellow turns his cheek slap it hard, etc." school of thought, there actually exist a surprising number of well-intentioned characters in *The Martian Chronicles*. Some are intellectuals trained in university graduate schools like Spender or like Dr. Hathaway, who a quarter-century later reports making a yearly pilgrimage to the tomb of his ex-shipmate, the idealist turned killer[1] (159). Some, however, are fairly ordinary, like those who are moved by Spender's recitation of Byron, or like Cheroke, whose technical specialty we never learn but who, despite his unwillingness to join Spender in his killing spree, knows the history of the Native Americans in Oklahoma and hence would be "all for" any remaining Martians (59). While a commissioned officer such as the sympathetic Captain Wilder must hold a bachelor's degree of some kind, most likely it is in engineering or physics or somesuch rather than in any "slippery stuff like philosophy or sociology" (*Fahrenheit* 65), yet despite his very practical training, Wilder understands the basic truths of Spender's arguments against greed and materialism, so much that he thinks to himself, "I'm Spender all over again" (71).

Later, back on Earth in "Way in the Middle of the Air", once the colonization of the fourth planet has begun, when the venomous Samuel Teece attempts to keep a teenaged employee from joining his family in the black exodus to Mars, the tolerant Grandpa Quartermain offers to take the youth's place polishing the brass. Even more surprisingly, Teece's other cronies on the hardware store's drowsy midday porch—most likely some of the same Klansmen, with whom Teece has taken many a midnight murderous ride—somehow balk at Teece's vindictiveness as well. At an earlier crack from Grandpa, Teece has commented, "I'm not bad at shootin' white folks neither" (93), but at the look in the others' suddenly unsympathetic faces, he realizes he now is outnumbered. Those loungers with their eyes "almost puffed shut" (95) may not be marching in any civil rights parades, but they at least have come to soften their hateful stances enough to help a fellow human for once rather than hurt. I am not sure their shift makes sense, but it certainly is heart-warming.

Moreover, those who come to Mars include not only the exploiters who burn, break, and bludgeon but also the immigrants who are content, essentially, to leave the red world as it is, those whose only imprint is "the hard clatter" of a novelist's typewriter, the "scratch" of a poet's pen, or the contented silence of the amiable loafing of an ex-beachcomber (88). Whereas archaeologist Spender from the fourth expedition to Mars expounded a philosophy of savoring and "relish[ing] life" (66) informed by history, visual aesthetics, even literature, in "Night Meeting" a simple gas station attendant explains to a young customer a stance no less worthy for being homespun and experiential rather than erudite. The old man, whom the younger calls "Pop," enjoys the pleasant loneliness of the Martian countryside beneath the foothills beyond because "all you got to do is open your eyes and you're entertained":

> "I'm just looking. I'm just experiencing. …. Keeps me alert and keeps me happy. You know what Mars is? It's like a thing I got for Christmas seventy years ago—don't know if you've ever had one— they called them kaleidoscopes, bits of crystal and cloth and beads and pretty junk. You held it up to the sunlight and looked in through at it, and it took your breath away. All the patterns! Well, that's Mars. Enjoy it. Don't ask it to be nothing else but what it is." (79)

In some respects it is hard to argue with; one might even replace the word *Mars* with *life*.

Edward J. Gallagher is correct, of course, in contrasting the undemanding outlook of Pop with the grasping of Sam Parkhill, but I believe he errs in lumping "The Musicians" and "The Martian" into the same group as Parkhill's chapter (69). Yes, each of these other stories shows destruction of a kind, but in neither is there ill will, or true greed. While "The Musicians" shows Terran boys in the old native towns "playing the white xylophone bones beneath [an] outer covering of black flakes" (89)—in other words, desecrating Martian corpses, whose flesh rather conveniently dries into something akin to autumn leaves—I nevertheless am reminded of Captain Wilder's supposition that the spirits of the superior Martian dead would be tolerant of the brash Earthlings rather than critical: "They probably don't mind us being here any more than they'd mind children on the lawn, knowing and understanding children for what they are" (54). In "The Martian", one of the few remaining natives is drawn to an elderly human couple and, using his powers of telepathic projection to appear as their young son who died of pneumonia, lives with them, "accepted and happy at last" (124). Although he can be "trapped" by competing longings, and although such a conflict of emotions kills him in the end, the relationship, which he himself seeks out with the kindly LaFarges is one of mutual companionship rather than exploitation, for the Martian actually is "in need of love as much as" the lonely couple (124). If there is a selfishness in wishing to have one's dead children returned, it is a very understandable and forgivable one, something far removed from love of money or possessions and much more akin to the Martian notion of "relish[ing] life" (66).

Therefore, despite the evaluation of the father in "The Million-Year Picnic" that "[l]ife on Earth never settled down to doing anything very good" (179), many perfectly ordinary characters in the book—the kind who in *Fahrenheit 451*, of course, would be compulsive watchers of television or users of drugs or purposeful hit-and-run drivers—are quite decent folk indeed, and settle down to things like living, laughing, and loving. In fact, certain philippics notwithstanding, Bradbury actually puts much of the blame for the self-destruction of humankind upon depersonalized forces such as "government" and "war" rather than upon people themselves. Railing against these abstractions may not help us understand how the world really works, or how choices made or not made go into constructing our political landscape, but it certainly riles up righteous indignation and keeps the plot moving.

On the day of the launch of the third expedition to Mars, for example, Pritchard in "The Taxpayer" clamors to be let aboard, "[t] o get away from wars and censorship and statism and conscription and government control of this and that, of art and science!" (31). In this list of threats to freedom, sanity, and even life, we can see, naturally, the echoes of the time of Bradbury's writing: the profound psychic shock of the beginning of the atomic age, exacerbated by increasingly powerful weapons tests in the Pacific; the deteriorating international situation, including the tense Berlin Blockade, the Soviet development of the atom bomb, and the Communist victory in the Chinese Civil War; and increasing Red scares in the United

States. With Bradbury extrapolating such international tensions and with the growth of big government and the Cold War national security state fifty years in the future, Pritchard's plea is a sweeping condemnation, and a powerful one. Yet it is, of course, a rather simplistic one as well. People vote in *The Martian Chronicles*, do they not? Presumably, they write their congressional representatives, hold town hall meetings, perhaps stage protest marches. We see none of this, however, not even the superficial televised debates of the candidates of the Ins versus Outs later shown in *Fahrenheit 451* (105-6). Instead, control seems to come from some unreachable, inescapable, and hence easily condemnable "above," a faceless bureaucracy eager to extend nuclear hegemony to Mars (*Martian* 64), censor thought and expression with what Gary K. Wolfe correctly terms "encroaching governmental restrictions" (42), and force the well-intentioned Captain Wilder on a twenty-year expedition out to the gas giants, so that he cannot "interfere" with the destructive colonial policy (*Martian* 159).

Some colonists in *The Martian Chronicles* have come to Mars to tear up a new world or to build hot dog stands, but the overarching "government"—either as a thing to be followed or a thing to be avoided—plays a great part as well. Many, after all, have come simply for work, often heeding "a government finger pointed from four-color posters" (72). Others have left Earth "to get away from things—politics, the atom bomb, war, pressure groups, laws" (132)—but of course "red tape" naturally follows (102-3), including that of the anti-fantasy killjoys of the Bureau of Moral Climates, precursors to the book-burning "firemen" of *Fahrenheit 451*. Yet although this government agency exists because "[t]hey passed a law" (105), and the conversation of the impassioned Stendahl and his completely perplexed architect in "Usher II" suggests that the public either accepts or at least is ambivalent about such laws, Bradbury still has not yet laid the majority of the blame upon the public itself, as he will do in *Fahrenheit 451*.

Finally, when the nuclear war anticipated in "The Taxpayer" finally occurs, it is shown not as the result of any particular issues—

or, despite the reference of the father in "The Million-Year Picnic" to "those evil men" back on Earth (179), of the decisions of policy-makers—but instead simply as a catastrophe both inexplicable and inescapable. One moment, the nighttime sky over the dead Martian sea bottom shimmers serene and lovely, and then the next moment, the green star of Earth seems to catch fire, "coming apart in a million pieces, as if a gigantic jigsaw puzzle ha[s] exploded. It burn[s] with an unholy dripping glare for a minute, three times normal size, then dwindle[s]" (143). No one knows exactly how it happens, no one knows why, and yet arrive the war does, with an apocalyptic intensity, which can destroy the entire continent of Australia in a single stroke (145). How a conflict of such power could continue across more than twenty years is hard to imagine, but somehow, in another example of what Christopher Isherwood tolerantly calls Bradbury's "characteristically casual implausibility" (57), it does. Still, when one family at last escapes to Mars—with, it is to be hoped, a neighbor family following soon after—as finally the last radio on Earth goes silent, it is clear that a culture of materialism and conformity has been "burned clean" from humanity's scorched and poisoned home world (179). Yet the death of irradiated billions notwithstanding, Bradbury's ending is optimistic, for it suggests that these two families will be able to "strike out on a new line" (180) and, as Marvin Mengeling puts it, "return us to the ideals and concepts that once were stabilizing elements in life" (99).

In *The Martian Chronicles*, therefore, we see many notions later explored in *Fahrenheit 451*. Kevin Hoskinson suggests that Bradbury's "fear at a future that must accommodate atomic weapons had intensified" in the three years between these novels (353), but I would argue that Bradbury's hesitance to reduce the world to glowing radioactive glass in the war that concludes the later tale belies this. Had Bradbury wished, after all, that he could have incorporated space travel into *Fahrenheit 451* such that Earth might be destroyed, while certain survivors escape. Instead, however, eschewing a true doomsday scenario that grew ever more possible as the 1950s went on, especially after the development of the hydrogen bomb, the author keeps his nuclear war here apparently "small" enough to allow for what Hoskinson more correctly calls "Bradbury's optimism for a recivilized world" (354). In fact, Granger, leader of the book-memorizing intellectuals, whom former book-burner Guy Montag conveniently stumbles upon during his escape from his former colleagues, asserts that a nuclear blast seen from the camera in the nose of a V-2 rocket "two hundred miles up" is "a pinprick" or "nothing" (170). This evaluation may have had some truth in the fission age—significantly less in the fusion age—but when Montag is not sure whether in America alone a hundred cities have been destroyed or a thousand (176), Bradbury seems to be fudging his science a bit more than usual.

Where he seems more true to life and more pointed in his criticism than in *The Martian Chronicles*, though, is in his treatment of human behavior and its causes. Only three years separate the publication of *Fahrenheit 451* from that of the tales of the Mars[2], but the pessimism of Bradbury's portrayal of humanity has deepened significantly. In *The Martian Chronicles*, it is not only intellectuals and free spirits who end up with profound and life-affirming thoughts and emotions but also very average people indeed: military rocket crewmen who give poetry a chance, Grandpa Quartermain with his touching sympathy for a black youth's desire for freedom, the longing LaFarges with their desperate love for their lost child, the old gas station attendant who is satisfied to take the grand kaleidoscope of the world—any world—simply for what it is. Yet aside from the professors and the atavistic oddballs, where are such characters in *Fahrenheit 451*? They simply do not exist. No, for as Beatty says, people live for one thing: "For pleasure, for titillation" (63). The average people thus watch four-wall television "that [says] nothing, nothing, nothing and [says] it loud, loud, loud" (47), race jet cars or try to run down animals or even people with their glittering "beetle cars," and take drugs from sleeping pills to heroin.

Although government does indeed play a role in the dumbing-down of society and its increasing focus on the superficial rather than the meaningful, Bradbury in *Fahrenheit 451* has abandoned the bogeyman of "government control of this and that" (*Martian* 31) and sharpened his focus to critique instead the individual's desire for mind-numbing pleasure. Montag's sensitive and imaginative young neighbor Clarisse details an educational system based on the rote memorization of basic facts and the suppression of questioning (31), and Chief Beatty sagely explains the agenda of reprogramming the "odd ducks" by "lower[ing] the kindergarten age year after year until we're almost snatching them from the cradle" (64). The government, of course, controls the military that has "started and won two atomic wars since 1990" (80), and it controls the "firemen" who burn any houses found to contain books and use their deadly eight-legged Mechanical Hound to hunt down any dissidents.

Bradbury will not let us forget, however, that it is the populace at large that actually supports, and that itself even has begun, the slide into mindless hedonism. *The Martian Chronicles* scarcely admits the possibility of such widespread guilt, but *Fahrenheit 451* actually insists upon it. Beatty, discussing the speeding-up of modern life and the homogenizing effect of the mass market upon books and magazine, explains to Montag that "[t]echnology, mass exploitation, and minority pressure carried the trick"[3] of removing challenging thought from art and entertainment:

> Magazines became a nice blend of vanilla tapioca. Books, so the damned snobbish critics said, were dishwater. No *wonder* books stopped selling, the critics said. But the public, knowing what it wanted, spinning happily, let the comic books survive. And the three-dimensional sex magazines, of course. There you have it, Montag. It didn't come from the Government down. There was no dictum, no declaration, no censorship, to start with, no! (61)

Lest we imagine that Bradbury sets the all-knowing Captain Beatty up as some government apologist to be disbelieved, he has Professor Faber, the moral and intellectual guide for the wavering Montag, make essentially the same point: "The public itself stopped reading of its own accord." When pleasure and conformity are so much easier than uncertainty and individuality, the firemen now are "hardly necessary to keep things in line. So few want to be rebels any more." Indeed, "[t]he whole culture's shot through" (94).

By *Fahrenheit 451*, therefore, Bradbury has shifted from the easier tropes of *The Martian Chronicles*, which portrayed a basically decent humankind powerless beneath the overarching control of government and the completely inexplicable threat of looming war to a more complex, more pessimistic outlook. In *Fahrenheit 451*, he shows a self-destructive society created, in large part, by people's own desire for simplicity, comfort, and pleasure. Yes, in real life, government can grow intrusive and oppressive, market forces can indeed close out options, and international affairs can explode without warning. However, to blame the intellectual and moral decay of society on the "crimes against humanity" and "the state and private industry" as Jack Zipes does, while sniffing dismissively at the notion that great masses of people "allegedly" enjoy consumerism and intellectual ease (191) seems to miss a component of individual responsibility that should not be ignored. Pleasure is pleasurable, after all; one may enslave oneself to it with disturbing ease and with the worst of consequences. Bradbury's estimation of "man's 'nature'" (Zipes 191) might not be perfect, but I do believe he is onto something, and with its increasing complexity over that of *The Martian Chronicles*, *Fahrenheit 451* serves as an even more apropos reminder of the importance of striving toward true humanity.

Notes

1. I cannot help finding Kent Forrester's evaluation of Spender as a "mass murderer" (51) just a little harsh; yes, the body count in Spender's undeclared war is high, but he is at worst a terrorist rather than an ordinary killer.

2. The time of the novel's setting most likely is not far removed from that of *The Martian Chronicles* either. Although Peter Sisario has written that *Fahrenheit 451* takes place "five centuries" in the future (201), perhaps because of Beatty's assertion that the "intellectual pattern for the past five centuries or more" is "[o]ut of the nursery into the college and back to the nursery" (*Fahrenheit* 58), it seems better to read those five centuries as beginning with end of the Middle Ages; Bradbury in 1953 therefore looks only a century or less into the future.

3. For a fuller discussion of the primacy of individual choice in these trends, see McGiveron.

Works Cited

Bradbury, Ray. *Fahrenheit 451*. 1953. New York: Del Rey, 1980.

_____. *The Martian Chronicles*. 1950. New York: Bantam, 1979.

Forrester, Kent. "The Dangers of Being Earnest: Ray Bradbury and *The Martian Chronicles*." *The Journal of General Education* 28 (1976): 50-54.

Gallagher, Edward J. "The Thematic Structure of *The Martian Chronicles*." *Ray Bradbury*. Ed. Martin Harry Greenberg and Joseph D. Olander. New York: Taplinger, 1980. 55-82. Writers of the 21st Century Ser.

Hoskinson, Kevin. "*The Martian Chronicles* and *Fahrenheit 451*: Ray Bradbury's Cold War Novels." *Extrapolation* 36 (1995): 345-59.

Isherwood, Christopher. Rev. of *The Martian Chronicles*, by Ray Bradbury. *Tomorrow* Oct. 1950: 56-58.

McGiveron, Rafeeq O. "What 'Carried the Trick'? Mass Exploitation and the Decline of Thought in Ray Bradbury's *Fahrenheit 451*." *Extrapolation* 37 (1996): 245-56.

Mengeling, Marvin E. "The Machineries of Joy and Despair: Bradbury's Attitudes toward Science and Technology." *Ray Bradbury*. Eds. Martin Harry Greenberg and Joseph D. Olander. New York: Taplinger, 1980. 83-109. Writers of the 21st Century Ser.

Sisario, Peter. "A Study of the Allusions in Bradbury's *Fahrenheit 451*." *English Journal* Feb. 1970: 201+.

Wolfe, Gary K. "The Frontier Myth in Ray Bradbury." *Ray Bradbury*. Eds. Martin Harry Greenberg and Joseph D. Olander. New York: Taplinger, 1980. 33-54. Writers of the 12st Century Ser.

Zipes, Jack. "Mass Degradation of Humanity and Massive Contradictions in Bradbury's Vision of Humanity in *Fahrenheit 451*." *No Place Else: Explorations in Utopian and Dystopian Fiction*. Eds. Eric S. Rabkin, Martin H. Greenberg, and Joseph D. Olander. Carbondale: Southern IL UP, 1983. 182-98. Alternatives Ser.

CRITICAL
READINGS

Speaking Futures: The Road to *Fahrenheit 451* _____

Jonathan R. Eller

> "A man cannot possibly speak futures, unless he has a strong sense of the past."
>
> —*Ray Bradbury*

When his Muse spoke, Ray Bradbury could turn out a richly poetic and emotionally charged story draft within a single day, often within a few hours. But his ability to start longer works of fiction came much more slowly, sometimes stretching out into months or even years of rewriting and revising. He often told of the powerful nine-day burst of creativity that resulted in the main text of *Fahrenheit 451*, composed during long stints on the pay typewriters of UCLA's Powell Library in 1953. But the opening pages of *Fahrenheit 451* shifted many times as he slowly developed his novel out of false starts and several drafts of his "Fireman" novella between 1946 and 1953. A closer look at these openings offers a great deal of insight into the way that Bradbury first crafted an enduring literary classic, and how he tried several very different ways to bring readers into the near future of *Fahrenheit 451*.

His own creative ignition point was sparked by his highly emotional identification with the great authors of all cultures, preserved in countless libraries, great and small, public and private. He never attended college, but he knew libraries and their magic from childhood, and from the very beginning of his reading life, he identified his favorite writers with the physical artifacts of their books; to burn the book was to burn the author, and in his mind, the great tragedies of history included the multiple burnings of the great classical library at Alexandria, Savonarola's Bonfire of the Vanities in Renaissance Florence, and, in his own lifetime, the public book burnings of Fascist Germany during the 1930s (Bradbury interview).

Bradbury was most concerned about the future, however, and the complex behaviors that start civilizations down the path toward obscuring and eventually destroying the literature that instills human values and makes an examined life possible. He read Huxley's *Brave New World* around 1940, which reinforced his own evolving appreciation of Juvenal's timeless rhetorical question: Who watches the Watchers? In 1949, he also read Orwell's *1984*, which presented the dual nightmare of history constantly re-written in a language purged of modifiers. But his 1944 reading of Arthur Koestler's *Darkness at Noon* fueled the emotional core of his creativity on this issue. He quickly realized that Koestler fully understood the behaviors that culminated in Stalin's purges and show trials of the late 1930s; his few unpublished speaking notes from the 1950s provide more than a hint of the emotions that Bradbury drew out of his reading: "...only a few perceived the intellectual holocaust and the revolution by burial that Stalin achieved... Only Koestler got the full range of desecration, execution, and forgetfulness on a mass and nameless graveyard scale" (Eller 89).

Bradbury also had a sense of how such cultural tragedies began. For these insights, he could draw more readily on his own experiences as a boy, crossing America during the darkest years of the Great Depression. His father's search for work led the family west from their hometown of Waukegan, Illinois, first to Tucson and back (1932–33) and finally, in the late spring of 1934, all the way out to Los Angeles. Each small town along the way offered the magic of a public library, but the young boy found that many of his beloved mysteries, fantasies, and science fiction books were not on the library shelves at all. He found that L. Frank Baum, Edgar Rice Burroughs, and sometimes even Edgar Allan Poe or Ambrose Bierce were not welcome in public or school libraries (Bradbury interview).

By the end of World War II, as his own story sales began to transition out of the genre pulps and into the mainstream magazine world, he saw a more pervasive and subtle discrimination against these genres opening out across America as the world began to polarize around the ideologies of two postwar superpowers. He was beginning to write cautionary tales about the death of the imagination, and by the summer of 1946, he had hit upon a forceful

---

inversion of cultural norms: what if firemen were trained to set fires, rather than to extinguish them? This conceit became his slow-burning match to flame.

But where to enter the time stream of this inverted world? A few precious opening pages from his first germ of the novel, later dated in Bradbury's hand as June 1946, were discovered by his close friend and bibliographer Donn Albright just a few years before Bradbury's death. These pages reveal that he initially chose to enter this nightmare world through the aperture of a futuristic fire station and its bizarre fire-producing apparatus. It was a natural progression from the world he actually lived in, for his father and brother worked in a similar world. His father, an experienced lineman, was what Bradbury would describe as a troubleshooter for the Venice Beach power and light company, and his older brother Skip was a lineman as well. Ray, nearly 26, and Skip still lived in their father's home, a utility company rental on the lot of a local power substation (Eller 53, 132–34). As he typed the opening words to "The Fire Men," Bradbury was writing at his small desk in the garage, gazing at the reflected lights of the power station just a few feet away. It was natural that these words would center on similar machineries that exposed the dark heart of the future fireman's trade:

> The tools lay in the aluminum shed while the four men, facing each other, laid out their cards and talked lazily about their work. The tools gleamed with brass and copper, they glinted fiercely in the fluorescent light. Some of them were round and long and contained silent flame. Some of them were claws that held and made torches of whatever they touched. Some of them were chemicals that frosted and dissolved items like snails properly salted. (Bradbury, "The Fire Men" 1)

At this point, Bradbury was far more interested in the instruments of destruction than in the firehouse itself. The images and metaphors are unpolished, but nonetheless powerful and charged with Bradbury's emerging gift for suggesting rather than fully describing the dark terrors within. The firemen are playing cards in the station; we learn from their desultory conversation that most books had been destroyed in something called "the first Big Fire," and that there has not been an alarm sounded locally in the last three years. "I hear they got a Poe over in Cincinnati yesterday," one fireman observes; "Lucky bastards," says another (Bradbury, "The Fire Men" 1).

In this world, as Bradbury first imagined it, the dark fantasies of witchcraft, magic, and the traditional weird tale must be destroyed. The broader mainstream literatures are not in the picture at all. When an alarm suddenly sounds, the fire crew responds to an antiquated house where an old woman hides with her forbidden treasures: "Poe and Hawthorne and Bierce and Dunsany and Machen. Witches and vampires, warlocks and familiars, ghosts and goblins, trolls and elves. All the forbidden fruits of an ancient and superstitious world, all the rotten variety of sick minds that must be found and burned. This new clean world had no place in it for myth, legend, or superstition. Burn it!" (Bradbury, "The Fire Men" 3)

This "new clean world" seems to echo Huxley's brave new one, yet it still lacks the scope of literary destruction found in the final pages of *Fahrenheit 451*. But Bradbury was already asking the more universal questions, and here, nearly four years before his spring 1950 first full draft of "The Fireman," he imagines one fireman, Scoles, who stops and wonders: "What *were* the books? What was in them? What was it all about. He had never questioned himself or others. There must have been something in them. Millions had read them and been frightened by them. Frightened? How could a book frighten you? He had never been frightened by much of anything in his life, much less a book. What was it, then?" (Bradbury, "The Fire Men" 3)

Scoles is forerunner to Guy Montag, and like Montag he grasps at the forbidden fruit; his hand closes on a small volume by Edgar Allan Poe, and here, the 1946 fragment pages end.

* * * *

At this point, however, Bradbury put his firemen away and concentrated on the incredibly rich mixture of short story ideas

Critical Insights

that constantly and unpredictably welled up from his subconscious mind. He published eighteen tales in 1946, another eighteen in 1947, twenty-one in 1948, and sixteen in 1949. In all, he published one hundred twenty professional stories during the 1940s, and he was not yet thirty years old. Many more remained unfinished in his files, along with an occasional title page or brief outline for a novel concept. None of these long fiction ideas ripened, and so his reputation continued to grow as a gifted writer in the short story form. Some of his detective pulp fictions contained a few chapter divisions and were billed as novellas; these few were, nonetheless, short stories, rarely exceeding eight thousand words in length (Eller and Touponce 439–503).

He would, like Mark Twain before him, have to feel his way along the path to longer fictions. By the end of the 1940s, he had managed to sustain and publish two novella-length tales that would eventually rank among his better-known works of this period, "The Creatures That Time Forgot" (1946, revised as "Frost and Fire") and "Pillar of Fire" (1948). The latter presented his first sustained warning about the impending death of the imagination, offered through the lens of a future world that has never known the fear and wonderment of magic, superstition, or the great works of literature that had once sprung from these sources.

For the most part, classic tales of the grotesque and arabesque defined the subject range of his fictional probes into such themes. As Bradbury worked on through the late 1940s to craft stories about the growing climate of fear and its threat to creativity, he remained focused on the classics of mystery and horror fiction that were increasingly targeted by school districts and library boards. "Pillar of Fire," "Carnival of Madness" (transformed into "Usher II" for *The Martian Chronicles*), and "The Mad Wizards of Mars" (collected in *The Illustrated Man* as "The Exiles") all focus on the specific threat to genre forms in postwar America.

Ironically, it would be one of his failed novel concepts of this period that would release his imagination to investigate the consequences of a future world where all literature and art is condemned to flame. *Where Ignorant Armies Clash by Night* (1947–

48) portrays a post-apocalyptic world where entertainment centers on ritual assassinations and the ceremonial burning of cultural artifacts from the past—artifacts such as books and paintings, symbolizing the civilization that had created this ravaged world through nuclear war. The surviving fragments of this unfinished novel contain a climactic moment when the celebrated Assassin must burn a volume of Matthew Arnold's poetry as prelude to the main event: the destruction of perhaps the last copy of the works of William Shakespeare (*Ignorant Armies* 318–30).

The Assassin is conflicted, however, and reads to the massed crowd from Arnold's "Dover Beach," then publically burns the volume of Arnold's poetry before escaping with the precious volume of Shakespeare. There is no redemption in any of these half-finished fragments; the Assassin is killed against the backdrop of a hopeless world, where it is judged better to have never been born. This novel proved to be a nihilistic dead-end for Bradbury—he had to have hope, he had to find a life-affirming mythos for the times, if he was to develop sustained works of novel-length fiction. To simply "conform or die" did not represent a way to deal with Modernity; he was still looking for a third way, and a protagonist who could find that way out of the darkness. *Ignorant Armies* only survives in a few fragment episodes, but the Assassin's crisis of conscience— and his reading from "Dover Beach"—shows Bradbury moving unmistakably toward some of the pivotal scenes he would reprise in a different future world for *Fahrenheit 451*.

Although the real postwar world seemed to be on the brink of a third world war where two superpowers now held the secret of the atom, he nevertheless was writing from the near side of this looming nightmare. With such thoughts in mind, he picked up his firemen once again in the late winter or early spring of 1950. They seemed to offer a more compelling symbol of cultural inversion than his Assassins had offered: everyone depends on the Fireman, but what if the New Normal requires the Fireman to set fires, rather than to put them out? This became his settled intention for a timely cautionary tale, one he felt he could sustain and project into the form of his third and longest novella.

In August 1950, Bradbury left Venice Beach and settled his young family into a new home off Westwood Boulevard in Los Angeles; from here, it was a short commute by bus to the UCLA library, where he soon settled into what he later described as nine days of uninterrupted creativity in the library's basement typing room. Occasional breaks browsing the vast library shelves provided inspiration, and he soon had a one hundred-page typescript titled *Long After Midnight*.[1] Initially, he experimented with a nightmare opening: his principal fireman, now named Montag, dreams he is an old man hidden away among a vast treasure of books in his small apartment. A young neighbor boy spies through the keyhole, sees the aged Montag handling his precious books, and raises the alarm:

> A crowd rushed up the street. Health officials burst in, followed by police, fierce with silver badges. And then himself! Himself as a young man, in a Fire uniform, with a torch. The room swarmed as the old man pleaded with himself as a young man. Books crashed down. Books were stripped and torn. Windows crashed inward, drapes fell in sooty clouds.
> Flame crackled. They were charring out the room, with controlled, scientific fire. A vast wind of flame devoured the walls. Books exploded in a million live kernels.
> "For the love of God!"
> The ancient lawn of the room sizzled.
> The books became black ravens, fluttering.
> Mr. Montag fell shrieking to the far end of the dream.
> He opened his eyes.
> "Blackjack," said Mr. Leahy. (*A Pleasure* 174)

Montag's nightmare is really a deep reverie; the words of his fire captain jolt him back to reality, where he sits in a card game at the fire station. By this time, reveries were not an uncommon element of Bradbury's fiction, and the events of this dream may also reflect his recent reading of George Orwell's *1984*; it seems to echo the incident where Orwell's Winston Smith sees the boy in the next apartment turn in his own father for disloyalty to Big Brother.

During August 1950, Bradbury evolved this new dream-reverie to frame a variation on his original 1946 fire station opening. Within a month, however, he had discarded the dream, re-titled the novella "The Fireman," and opened the narrative directly into the world of the fire station, just as he had done with the initial pages in 1946. This time, however, the focus was on the men rather than their machines:

> The four men sat silently playing blackjack under a green drop-light in the dark morning. Only a voice whispered from the ceiling:
> "One thirty-five a.m. Thursday morning, October 4th, 2052, A.D. ..." ("The Fireman" 4)

"The Fireman" would reach print, with relatively few structural variations from the earlier "Long After Midnight" draft, in the February 1951 issue of *Galaxy Science Fiction*. But the novella, now around 25,000 words in length, had also picked up a very significant counterpoint to the harsh realities of the late-night firehouse—the solitary midnight walker, Clarisse McClellan.

In a sense, Clarisse owed her fictional existence to the imaginative spark behind a Bradbury story titled "The Pedestrian"; in fact, this story stood closer to the origins of *Fahrenheit 451* than any of his other cautionary tales. "The Pedestrian" had emerged from a late-night walk along Wilshire Boulevard, where he was stopped and questioned by a police officer. The exchange was uneventful, but it rekindled Bradbury's long-standing sense that the image of the solitary urban walker was quickly becoming a relic of the past. For Bradbury's city-dwellers, locked away from the buckling sidewalks and abandoned plazas, reality is merely an illusion, simulated on large-screen televisions or narrated through tiny Seashell earphones. The pedestrian of the future would be both rare and dangerous—a threat to the new behavioral norm.

Although "The Pedestrian" was published in August 1951—six months after "The Fireman" reached print—Bradbury had actually finished and submitted the story to his New York agent, Don Congdon, in March 1950. As he turned to work on "The Fireman" narrative, the doomed pedestrian of his earlier short story, who is accosted and swallowed up by an automated police car, began to transform into other possibilities. He soon envisioned his solitary fireman, walking late at night, encountering a young girl, a neighbor, who knows his name, and knows his occupation. She will ask the unanswerable question: "Why do you do what you *do*?" ("The Fireman" 14)

Clarisse is vital to Montag's awakening, but in "The Fireman" her entry is buried under a series of opening events designed to establish the particulars of Montag's world: the men play cards at the station, reflecting with casual humor on the house and books they had most recently burned; they respond to a call, an unusual one, where the homeowner—a solitary woman—beats Captain Leahy to the mark and strikes the match herself, so that she may die among her kerosene-soaked treasures; Montag, shaken, returns home late that night, realizing that he has never really known or loved his sleeping wife, a woman totally absorbed by the technological marvels and entertainments of the day.

Here, finally, Clarisse enters the narrative, but her arrival is late and limited to a single scene; her stay is far too short before she is "disappeared"—by a reckless driver perhaps, as Montag's wife maintains, or by the authorities who watch her every move. Montag cannot be sure. She has shown him simple but long forgotten ways to apprehend the natural world, but neither Montag nor the reader can fully appreciate her significance. At this stage of narrative development, Bradbury had not given her the significant presence required to fully release Montag's quest for answers in a world where all questions are suspect.

* * * *

By the end of 1952, Bradbury and his agent had secured a contract with Ballantine Books for a new story collection built around an expanded version of "The Fireman." Cold War anxieties were growing ever stronger in American politics, and the resulting Climate of Fear periodically manifested in McCarthyesque tirades against publishers and writers of anti-authoritarian or counterculture literature.

Books were not often burned, but comics were occasionally put to the match, with varying degrees of media news coverage. In January 1953, Bradbury found the master metaphor he was looking for—the temperature at which book paper combusts—and began, among many distractions, to expand "The Fireman." In June, he returned to the typing room of the UCLA library and channeled another intense blaze of concentration through the pay-as-you-go keyboards.

This time the uninterrupted creativity inspired by the library interlude was tempered by his conscious desire to expand the incidents of the original work without deviating very far from the established sequence of events. By late July, *Fahrenheit 451* had doubled in size from the underlying "Fireman" bedrock and went to proofs at just under fifty thousand words—by far the longest work of fiction he had ever come close to completing. Bradbury managed to expand Montag's interactions with Clarisse and the reclusive professor Faber, as well as his confrontations with the dangerous Fire Chief Leahy, now renamed Beatty (Eller 275–80).

But Montag's awakening still needed to be foregrounded in a way that would open out with great emotional impact into the dystopic world of the new novel, a world full of wonders and entertainments that masked a slow progression toward atomic disaster and an unexpected redemption in the hidden retreats of the Book People. "The Fireman" had introduced Clarisse into the narrative thread, yet that intermediate version also obscured her crucial role in the process of revelations. Now, however, as he transformed a promising but unevenly-paced novella into his first novel-length fiction, he realized what was needed. In February 1953, months before his final breakthrough in the UCLA library, he described his emerging insights in a letter to his British publisher, Rupert Hart-Davis: "[T]he young girl who lives next door is really the pivotal character; without her and her influence … our Fire Man may not have changed when he did."

He went on to tell Hart-Davis that Clarisse represented the only way to inject significant character growth into the story. As the months passed, Bradbury also came to realize that timing meant everything to the emerging characterizations. Gradually, as he worked on into the summer of 1953, he brought Montag's fateful first encounter with Clarisse into the opening pages of the novel, taking care to develop a masterful physical presence for her in words and images that centered on sensation and contact.

In these revisions, Montag now senses her before he sees her, and through the greatly expanded descriptions, Bradbury provides a fascinating depth to what the fireman sees. In the novella, she had been little more than a manifestation of Montag's own conscience, and perhaps a bit of his subconscious; she had answered his unremarkable questions and asked a few insightful ones that left him thinking. But in revision there is a tangible presence that emerges through Bradbury's new descriptions of Clarisse: "Her face was slender and milk-white, and in it was a kind of gentle hunger that touched over everything with tireless curiosity. It was a look, almost, of pale surprise; the dark eyes were so fixed to the world that no move escaped them" (*Fahrenheit* 3).

In another revision, we find out *how* she knows what he does for a living—she smells the kerosene that he can never quite wash away in the fire station showers. Other revisions open out into an intoxicating array of poetic sensations. Montag hears the motion of her dress and the movements of her hands, and he smells fresh apricots and strawberries as they walk, a seasonal impossibility among the falling leaves of the autumn night. Through these heightened senses, he comes to see himself, with startling clarity, reflected in her presence:

> He saw himself in her eyes, suspended in two shining drops of bright water, himself dark and tiny, in fine detail, the lines about his mouth, everything there, as if her eyes were two miraculous bits of violet amber that might capture and hold him intact. Her face, turned to him now, was fragile milk crystal with a soft and constant light in it. It was not the hysterical light of electricity but—what? But the strangely comfortable and rare and gently flattering light of the candle. (5)

In this way Bradbury developed a far more subtle and poetic doubling of Montag than he had initially planted in the discarded opening dream of the *Long After Midnight* version, where an elderly Montag encounters and is destroyed by his younger self. After he has seen his double in her reflective eyes, Clarisse will ask the questions he has never dared to ask himself—at least not consciously: "How long have you worked at being a fireman?" "Do you ever *read* any of the books you burn?" "Is it true that long ago firemen put fires *out* instead of going to start them?" Montag offers the official responses, and laughs nervously at her continuing cascade of questions. But when she asks why he laughs, Montag has no answer. Her conclusion is proverbial in its brevity and impact: "You laugh when I haven't been funny, and you answer right off. You never stop to think what I've asked you" (5–6).

As they talk, they are walking through the same cityscape found in both "The Pedestrian" and the "Fireman," an urban sprawl with broken and neglected sidewalk pavement, empty as a tomb yard, reflecting the solitude and desolation of a desert landscape. These descriptions are not new, but her final question is a complete departure from the novella form: "Are you happy?" (7). This simple question will begin to crack the walls of denial and repression he has used for many months to hide the secret actions of his hands. As he enters his own house, he glances up at the vent where he has hidden the precious books he has taken from various burnings—books he has never tried to read (8). This revealing glance at the vent was written by Bradbury at the last minute, a paste-in addition to the final typescript of *Fahrenheit 451* (Typescript 9).

Bradbury's new and expanded opening—evolved from the brief encounter with Clarisse that Bradbury had originally buried far deeper in the "Fireman" novella—provides a vital psychological frame for Montag as he enters his house and sees his sleeping wife. He is now fully equipped for the subjective thoughts that cross his mind. He can really see what is missing in their lives, and catches an imaginary glimpse of the closeness that he and Mildred will never know. Bradbury then fashioned a subsequent week of late night walks with Clarisse, using the remaining dialog from the original novella scene as a basis for expanded conversations that sharpen Montag's ability to sense the natural world in all its subtle grandeur. And when

Clarisse is lost, the grief he feels is genuine and believable, setting the stage for all that follows.

Bradbury had now laid out a compelling path into the novel, one that could fully engage a universal audience in the choices that Montag must make if he is to find meaning in a broken and valueless world. But at this late stage in Bradbury's revisions, readers could only catch intimations of that world through the new dream-like opening dialog between Montag and Clarisse. The earlier firehouse openings had set a broader, discrete context for this future world and Montag's perverse role in it, but these scenes were now merged into the new novel's deeper structure. Bradbury needed a short framing passage to provide the necessary glimpse of Montag's world and his state of mind just before he encounters Clarisse.

He decided to build this frame around the kind of reverie he could write so well. Through the long process of revisions, Bradbury now knew his principal character thoroughly, and he eventually found a way to present Montag's fiery world through a concise montage-like progression of vivid opening metaphors: the hose and nozzle forming "this great python spitting its venomous kerosene upon the world," handled by Montag like "some amazing conductor playing all the symphonies of blazing and burning to bring down the tatters and charcoal ruins of history," followed by flashing highlights of a typical book-burning that quickly establish the time-honored routine of destruction in the reader's mind (1–2).

But what about *Montag's* mind? The new opening frame concludes with an unforgettable image of the mask that Montag uses to both hide and repress his innermost thoughts: "Montag grinned the fierce grin of all men singed and driven back by flame. …. Later, going to sleep, he would feel the fiery smile still gripped by his face muscles, in the dark. It never went away, that smile, it never ever went away, as long as he remembered" (2). This was the face he projected to the world; this was also the face he used to repress any rational or sequential thoughts about the books that his hands were hiding within his fireman's tunic under the blazing 451 badge, books that he would place, unexamined, in the ceiling vent of his home. All the background of Montag's profession—and his secret repressions—were now compressed into 250 opening words that radiated out from a single sentence that would, in hundreds of editions and many languages across time and place, become one of the most famous opening lines of modern literature:

"It was a pleasure to burn."

* * * *

The long evolution of Bradbury's dystopian masterpiece was not limited to the opening pages, but these rarely seen variations clearly show Bradbury on his way to learning how to write long fiction. Like Mark Twain, who needed the anecdotal and episodic structures of *Roughing It, The Innocents Abroad,* and *Life on the Mississippi* to work up to *Huckleberry Finn*, Bradbury preferred to gather and bridge related stand-alone tales into such novelized story cycles as *The Martian Chronicles* and *Dandelion Wine*. *Fahrenheit 451* also emerged from his mastery of shorter forms of fiction, but his newfound ability to sustain the transition of a single narrative idea into a compelling and enduring novel would provide the template for the culminating work of his early career, *Something Wicked This Way Comes*.

The road to *Fahrenheit 451* is also the story of a writer navigating treacherous literary paths through the early Cold War and the cultural Climate of Fear that often transcended the political theaters of the House Un-American Activities Committee and the McCarthy era's Senate hearings. Bradbury knew the tenuous place of great ideas and great art in the history of the Western world, and he had an abiding sensitivity to the early signs of intolerance and authoritarianism. The evolving world of *Fahrenheit 451* is best studied through successive stages of fragile typescript pages, carefully preserved to this day—pages that show how a strong sense of past and present is essential for any writer who dares to envision the future.

Note

1. The quotations from *Long After Midnight* are taken from *A Pleasure to Burn*, which is the only easily accessible edition of the preliminary versions of *Fahrenheit 451*. This text was first edited by Albright with Eller as textual editor and published in a limited press edition as *Match to Flame* (Colorado Springs, CO: Gauntlet Publications, 2006). This published text is itself based on Donn Albright's archival photocopy, the only complete form of the now untraceable original typescript; the original was sold, in two segments to two different private purchasers, by Bradbury's long-time friend Forrest J. Ackerman.

Works Cited

Bradbury, Ray. *Fahrenheit 451*. 1953. Author's carbon of the submitted typescript, photocopy in the Albright Collection, Center for Ray Bradbury Studies, Indiana University School of Liberal Arts, Indianapolis.

———. *Fahrenheit 451*. 1953. 60th anniversary ed. New York: Simon & Schuster, 2013.

———. "The Fire Men." 1946. Typescript fragment (title page and pp. [1]–[3]), photocopy in the Albright Collection, Center for Ray Bradbury Studies, Indiana University School of Liberal Arts, Indianapolis.

———. "The Fireman." *Galaxy Science Fiction* Feb. 1951.

———. Letter to Rupert Hart-Davis, 26 Feb. 1953. Bradbury's reference copy (Bradbury Center), from the Hart-Davis Collection, University of Tulsa.

———. Personal interview with the author. 11–14 Mar. 2002.

———. *A Pleasure To Burn*. Ed. Donn Albright (Jonathan Eller, Textual Editor). New York: Harper Perennial, 2011. Based on the limited press hardbound edition (Burton, MI: Subterranean, 2010).

———. *Where Ignorant Armies Clash by Night*. 1947-48. Novel fragment in Ray Bradbury. *Match to Flame: The Fictional Paths to Fahrenheit 451*. Colorado Springs, CO: Gauntlet, 2006. [274]–345.

Eller, Jonathan R. *Becoming Ray Bradbury*. Urbana, IL: U of Illinois P, 2011.

Eller, Jonathan R. and William F. Touponce. *Ray Bradbury: The Life of Fiction*. Kent, OH: Kent State UP, 2004.

"Classics Cut To Fit"? *Fahrenheit 451* and Its Appeal in Other Media

Phil Nichols

In explaining how the book-burning world of *Fahrenheit 451* came to exist in the first place, Ray Bradbury's Fire Chief Beatty apportions some of the blame to media adaptations, with their tendency to over-simplify or dumb down the books from which they are derived: "Classics cut to fit fifteen-minute radio shows, then cut again to fill a two-minute book column, winding up at last as a ten- or twelve-line dictionary resumé" (52).

Curiously, when Bradbury wrote these lines, he was himself on the brink of becoming a script writer for film and television, and his work in the visual media would involve adapting existing stories to suit the screen, such as Herman Melville's *Moby Dick* (Weller 210). As a writer who would cross boundaries between media, Bradbury was drawn to the spectacle of film, but also argued that his own writing translated directly from one form to another without difficulty. Later in his career, though, he would somewhat gleefully recall the indignity he had suffered when asked to cut one of his own full-length radio plays into three-minute episodes to better suit the scheduling requirements of NBC radio (Bradbury, *Now and Forever* 118).

The continuing attraction of *Fahrenheit 451* to adapters in various media suggests that Bradbury's story lends itself to translation into other forms, but in addition to the tremendous variation in the approaches of the playwrights, comic-book artists, and filmmakers who have produced such adaptations, we can see that they each pick up on different potentialities located within Bradbury's novel. To date, there have been one film adaptation (with a second version stuck in "development hell" for over a decade), two radio dramatizations, an unauthorized television version, a graphic novel, and Bradbury's own perennially popular stage play.

While Beatty's view on "classics cut to fit" appears to echo some of Bradbury's own negative feelings about adaptation, the reality is that media adaptation is often about exploring alternative interpretations of a text. This chapter will use current theory from the field of "adaptation studies," particularly Linda Hutcheon's *A Theory of Adaptation*, to understand the ways various artists have derived inspiration from *Fahrenheit 451* and, sometimes surprisingly, produced works which shine a new light on Bradbury's novel.

Radio Drama

In *Fahrenheit 451*, the book-burning fireman Guy Montag steals one of the books he is supposed to destroy. He takes it home and forces his wife to listen to him read a text, which bears a remarkable parallel to his own life experience:

> "...I dreamed, and behold, I saw a man clothed with rags, standing in a certain place, with his face from his own house, a book in his hand, and a great burden upon his back. I looked, and saw him open the book, and read therein; and, as he read, he wept, and trembled; and, not being able longer to contain, he brake out with a lamentable cry, saying, What shall I do?" (Bunyan 13)

The text is a passage from John Bunyan's *The Pilgrim's Progress*, the seventeenth-century allegory about a sin-burdened man who must leave the "City of Destruction" and make his way to the "Celestial City." The parallel to Montag's own story is remarkable, not only relating to his state of discomfort with his world at that point in the story, but indicating a likely future direction for his actions—he does, of course, eventually escape from his city, observe its destruction in an atomic war, and find a more idyllic place of harmony that gives hope for the future rebirth of civilization.

At this point, an attentive reader of *Fahrenheit 451* might be somewhat puzzled. Where exactly in Bradbury's novel does this reference to *The Pilgrim's Progress* occur? The answer is: It does not. Bradbury uses all manner of literary allusions in his novel, but there is no reference to Bunyan, despite its appropriateness.

The allusion is actually to be found in a radio play, a dramatization of *Fahrenheit 451* written by David Calcutt and produced by BBC

Radio in 2003. Calcutt does not just use *The Pilgrim's Progress* for a throwaway quotation, but instead uses it to establish some of the mystery of Guy Montag and his role in life. The play begins with the passage being read over a dreamlike sound collage, and the quotation returns as if in a haunting dream, just as Bunyan's entire book is framed as being "delivered under the similitude of a dream."[1] Later, *The Pilgrim's Progress* turns out to be the book that Montag steals, and at the play's end, it also becomes the text which Montag chooses to commit to memory.

Calcutt's play clearly has strong connections to Bradbury's novel. Linda Hutcheon defines an adaptation as "an extended, deliberate, announced revisitation of a particular work of art" (170), a definition, which accurately encompasses Calcutt's play. Clearly, though, the play is not identical to Bradbury's novel. In fact, the first reaction of a naïve listener might be to object that Calcutt has changed *Fahrenheit 451*, that he has not followed the "true" story, in which Montag actually steals many books and first reads from *Gulliver's Travels* and *The Life of Samuel Johnson* rather than from *The Pilgrim's Progress*—Calcutt has not faithfully adapted the Bradbury novel.

There is no doubt that such a position, which adopts an argument for "fidelity," is quite common and still informs some published reviews whenever, say, a book is adapted into a film, or a film is adapted into a computer game (Hutcheon 7). However, in the community of critics of literature, film, and popular culture, the fidelity argument has long been dismissed on the grounds that fidelity is impossible to achieve—the differences between one medium and another are legion, and the adjustments required when taking a work into a new medium are unavoidable.

In recent decades the critical discourse has moved beyond fidelity and instead explores more interesting ideas, such as how one work of art can inform another, or how one work can comment on another. Thinking of adaptations as translations or re-mediations—literally being transformed from one medium to another—enables us to think of an adaptation as being inevitably multi-layered

---

(Hutcheon uses the word "multilaminated"), and often leading the reader's or viewer's thoughts to oscillate actively between the original work and the adaptation even as they read or watch (6). Hutcheon suggests we even avoid referring to an "original work," so that we do not inadvertently presume that the "source" work is somehow more important than an adaptation.

Part of the pleasure of experiencing an adaptation is in the combination of repetition and variation: re-experiencing what we remember of the adapted work, and newly experiencing the novelty of the adaptation (Hutcheon 4). Bradbury's *Fahrenheit 451* already uses an eclectic mix of literary allusions, but with careful parallels between the events of the novel and the texts he is quoting (Sisario 201). This aspect of the novel seems to challenge adapters to seek out allusions of their own. Calcutt responds to this challenge, as do the other adapters mentioned later in this chapter.

Calcutt is a British playwright, and although his play is non-specific about the setting of *Fahrenheit 451*, all the performers in the BBC broadcast are English. In choosing *The Pilgrim's Progress* as a recurring motif in his version of Bradbury's work, Calcutt anchors the otherwise American story in a firmly British milieu. What is more, Bunyan's Christian allegory illuminates the quest of Guy Montag as a personal journey, and elevates Montag's actions into something of a religious quest. Through the selection of this one allusion, then, Calcutt answers Bradbury's challenge, succeeds in making *Fahrenheit 451* his own, and prompts the listener to re-examine the role(s) which Bradbury originally assigned to his protagonist.

Calcutt uses one other narrative tactic which introduces a debate over *Fahrenheit 451*'s book people and their likely effectiveness in bringing about the renaissance they so firmly believe in. Picking up on the word play in Bradbury's novel, Calcutt has characters reciting nonsense rhymes, such as "Hey Diddle Diddle" and "The man in the moon came down too soon and asked his way to Norwich." Such rhymes have come down to us through centuries of oral culture, perpetuated through childhood playground games, and in the process, they have lost any literal meaning they may once have had—perhaps through corruption over time, or perhaps through the loss from our culture of the things to which the rhymes once referred. Inspired by the equally nonsensical advertising jingles in Bradbury's novel, in Calcutt's play the nonsense rhymes anticipate our later discovery that the book people are trying to memorize entire books, and prompts us to consider a key question: will they succeed in transmitting the memorized works down through the ages without corruption or loss of meaning? This is a question that is considered only briefly by Bradbury's novel, but is certainly rich for discussion. Indeed, when Bradbury was originally developing *Fahrenheit 451*, he debated these issues with science fiction magazine editor Horace Gold and the Italian art critic Bernard Berenson (Eller, "Story" 175, 187). The same questions inform, in part, Walter M. Miller's post-apocalypse novel *A Canticle for Leibowitz* (1959).

The French film critic André Bazin wrote of adaptations being a "refraction" of the texts on which they are based (20). Just as a lens focuses a selective view of an image, or just as a prism splits out a rainbow of colors from a white light source, so an adaptation can reveal a new view of an existing work. Far from being a disrespectful tampering with Bradbury's story, Calcutt's radio play provides a new outlook on Bradbury, as does a more famous adaptation of *Fahrenheit 451*, the 1966 film directed by François Truffaut.

Film

François Truffaut was a French filmmaker who had begun his career as a film critic. Mentored from an early age by André Bazin, Truffaut was passionate about film, but also immensely passionate about books and literature (Toubiana and De Baecque 29-69). Growing up in Nazi-occupied Paris in the Second World War, Truffaut was all too aware of the dangers of dictatorship and censorship and found in Bradbury's *Fahrenheit 451* an elegant portrayal of a single literate man's breaking free from cultural repression. Like other adaptations of *Fahrenheit 451*, Truffaut's film is selective in the details it responds to in the novel. Truffaut "refracts" the novel for us, partly based on his own experiences. The contexts in which he developed his adaptation provide an exciting dialogue with the novel.

From a political viewpoint, Bradbury was writing his novel in the 1950s, at the height of the Cold War when the United States and Soviet Russia were on the verge of a world-destroying atomic war. Bradbury was influenced by what he knew of Stalin's regime, partly informed by books, such as Arthur Koestler's *Darkness at Noon* (1941). Koestler's novel provided a devastating account of the revisionism of Stalinist history, in which a man might be a hero one day and an enemy of the state the next (Eller, *Becoming* 88-90). Bradbury was also influenced by the censorship of opinion that he saw at home, as the House Un-American Activities Committee (HUAC) expanded its reach to take in, among other suspected "subversives," Hollywood scriptwriters (Weller 193-97). Guy Montag's world is a hybrid of an imagined science-fictional city of the future and of Bradbury's conception of the intrusive, confrontational interrogations of the Stalin regime and the equally intrusive, confrontational HUAC.

Truffaut's film, on the other hand, was made in the 1960s entirely in Europe and undoubtedly informed by European experience. The locations, in reality mostly in England, are more suggestive of Northern Europe. The visual appearance of the Firemen in their black uniforms has distinct echoes of the Second World War Nazi SS. Whether deliberately or accidentally, the casting of heavily-accented German actor Oskar Werner in the lead role subtly reinforces the feeling that we are dealing with an analogue of the Nazi regime, and this is further strengthened by a recurring character played by another German actor, Anton Diffring, who for viewers at the time would be recognisable almost entirely from his roles as a Nazi officer in various war films such as *The Colditz Story* (1955), *Reach for the Sky* (1956) and *Operation Crossbow* (1965). The "Nazi" reading of Montag's world even appears to be self-consciously referenced in the film, as we see the Fire Chief make a point of insisting that even Hitler's *Mein Kampf* be burned.

Another element of the film, which is striking from a visual point of view, is undoubtedly confusing to many viewers: the casting of Julie Christie in the dual roles of Mrs. Montag *and* Clarisse McClellan. The film itself makes no attempt to explain the facial similarity of the two characters, and no other characters even appear to be conscious of the resemblance of the two. The most obvious reading of this odd circumstance is that Montag somehow sees the two women as complementary, that the occasionally sensuous Linda lacks the intellect of the creative-minded Clarisse. Compared with Truffaut's other films, such as the earlier *Jules et Jim* and *Le Peau Douce*, *Fahrenheit 451* shows a pointed absence of physical affection between characters. While *Fahrenheit 451* on its own might appear an emotionally cold film, the context provided by Truffaut's other films suggests that this is a deliberate strategy for *Fahrenheit 451*, Truffaut's extension of the logic of Montag's world: the *incidentally* limited human relationships of Bradbury's novel become refracted into a *consequentially* limited set of relationships, preparing the viewer for an ending which comes across as considerably more bleak than in Bradbury's novel.

Bradbury's novel is full of science-fictional technology, much of which firmly establishes the intrusion of mass media and mass communications. At the time he wrote the novel, television was on the rise and would soon take over from radio as the most popular form of mass entertainment. Bradbury's short story "The Murderer," published in the same year as *Fahrenheit 451*, takes a similarly hostile view of the intrusion of the telephone and other personal communications. While the novel and short story still speak to us on these issues today because of the rise in our modern lives of large flat TV screens, smartphones, and people isolated by their ubiquitous personal headphones, it is important to remember that Bradbury was, in the 1950s, being anticipatory and providing a warning. In a 1975 interview he put it this way: "I am not so much a science-fiction writer as a fantasist, moralist, visionary. I am a *preventor* of futures, not a *predictor* of them. I wrote *Fahrenheit 451* to prevent book-burnings, not to induce that future into happening, or even to say that it was inevitable" (Aggelis 99).

Hutcheon points out that when a work in a "telling" medium (such as a book) is transformed to a "showing" medium (such as a film), the audience's awareness of the transformation is heightened, as passive or tacit elements of the fictional world must be made visible and concrete (22-27). Most visible in Truffaut's film is his choice of technology. Eschewing modern technology, he instead shows us antiquated objects from the fire truck, which looks like something from the 1940s, to the telephone, which could be from the earliest days of the twentieth-century. In isolation, these items appear strange, but Tom Whalen points out that there are, throughout the film, constant reminders of a past that has become somehow detached from the present: a rocking chair, an eye-test chart, a pastoral landscape glimpsed on a matchbox (184). Taken together, these all serve not only to emphasise the poor memories of the characters in the film and to indicate what has been lost, but also to suggest that there is a different world in the past to which books can make a connection. The science-fictional aspects of Bradbury's novel tend to create a timelessness. Truffaut's film questions the origins of this, using the antiquities as an answer to that question.

At the same time, though, Truffaut's film reflects *his* times as much as the novel reflects Bradbury's times. The film begins with images of TV antennas, and so like Bradbury's novel continues the reflection on the rise of television. A central feature of the Montag house in the film is the interactive TV screen, and Truffaut takes delight in making fun of the triviality of the medium just as Bradbury does. But Truffaut was working in the era of Marshall McLuhan, the futurist who spoke of television—and other pervasive media— giving rise to a "global village" (McLuhan 6), and so his depiction of television takes on a doubly mocking tone: Montag's only good use for the TV is to use it as a reading lamp and another book-hoarder uses a TV as a convenient place to hide books.

Truffaut's choices of technology evolved as he developed the screenplay for *Fahrenheit 451*, partly in response to other films of the time. Whereas his original intention was to make a science fiction film "set in the future and backed up by inventions and gadgetry" (Truffaut 125), the first gadget-laden James Bond film came out during the long gestation period for *Fahrenheit 451* and prompted revulsion from Truffaut, who would later reflect that "that film marks the beginning of the period of decadence in the cinema... Until then the role of the cinema had been by and large to tell a story in the hope that the audience would believe" (qtd. in Peary 130). In the journal he kept during the making of the film, Truffaut described his strategy like this:

> Obviously it would be going too far to make *Fahrenheit 451* a period film yet I am heading in that general direction... I am trying for anti-gadgetry – at one point Linda gives Montag a superb cut-throat razor and throws the old battery-model Philips in the waste basket. In short, I am working contrariwise, a little as if I were doing a "James Bond in the Middle Ages." (130)

As a result of Truffaut's dislike of James Bond, we now have a film version of *Fahrenheit 451* that makes a striking visual impact, and whose production design immediately prompts questions: What kind of world is this? How did it come to be?

Just as David Calcutt's radio play poses questions about the idea of memorizing books, so does Truffaut's film question the degree to which texts would need to be eliminated in Montag's world. In Bradbury's novel, certain types of books and texts are allowed to exist—instruction manuals, for instance, and written records that would help the government function. But Truffaut stretches the loss of text further, eliminating written words entirely from Montag's world. Buildings just have numbers, not names. People read comics that have no captions or speech balloons. The files in the fire department contain images and numbers, not names or text. This is a bold decision and must, in part, have come from the requirement to concretize Montag's world; while a novel can be vague about some details of how things look, a film cannot help but *show* things. A logical extension of this choice is that almost nobody in Montag's world will be able to read, the possible exceptions being any people who were alive before the current regime came about, and anyone who has been surreptitiously taught to read.

The absence of text in the film makes the book-burning scenes all the more tantalizing, as we catch occasional glimpses of title pages succumbing to the flames, and our eye is drawn hungrily to the text. This is one instance where an argument of "medium-specificity" (Hutcheon 33-38) might be valid, in that the visual showing of the burning books can have a stronger, almost visceral impact than the verbal "telling" of the same scene in a novel. Moreover, when Truffaut has Montag read a book for the first time, we see Montag savor every letter on the page, including the name of the publisher and the copyright details. This Montag is radically different from Bradbury's Montag, who could already read and desires books for the wisdom they contain. Truffaut's Montag is like a child learning to read for the first time, and to reinforce this notion Truffaut, like David Calcutt, chooses a new literary allusion for Montag's first reading. In the film, Montag reads from Charles Dickens' *David Copperfield*:

> Whether I shall turn out to be the hero of my own life, or whether that station will be held by anybody else, these pages must show. To begin my life with the beginning of my life, I record that I was born (as I have been informed and believe) on a Friday, at twelve o'clock at night. It was remarked that the clock began to strike, and I began to cry, simultaneously. (Dickens 3)

Just as Bradbury's novel challenges adapters to choose their own literary allusions, so it prompts us to engage in another game: which book would we choose to save for posterity? (Bradbury explicitly uses this very challenge in his introduction to Tim Hamilton's 2009 graphic novel adaptation of *Fahrenheit 451*.) Truffaut rises to this challenge through those extensive shots of books going up in flames, showing loving detail of the texts and the paper slowly yielding to the heat. Truffaut also takes delight in making his own selection of books to rescue from oblivion, even allowing Bradbury's *The Martian Chronicles* to be memorized by one of the book-people.

Truffaut's film, like Calcutt's play, responds to the games and challenges of Bradbury's novel. His reflection on Bradbury's presentation of Montag's world brings the film to a different interpretation of how elements of that world interrelate. His refraction of *Fahrenheit 451* invites the viewer or reader to look again at Guy Montag and his intellectual re-birth.

And not just the reader is inspired to look again at Montag by Truffaut's film: Bradbury himself was inspired by the film to re-consider some elements of his own creation when he adapted *Fahrenheit 451* for the theatre.

On Stage

Ray Bradbury's working methods typically included many attempts to re-write, adapt, and further develop all of his major works for other media. *Fahrenheit 451* is one of the earliest examples of this, with Bradbury writing and publishing it first as a novella in a magazine, later expanding it into a short novel for book publication, and shortly afterwards attempting to re-write it as a stage play for the actor-director Charles Laughton (Eller, "Story" 167-86). It is likely that Bradbury took some inspiration for this latter venture when he saw Sidney Kingsley's Broadway stage transformation of Arthur Koestler's *Darkness at Noon,* a novel which had influenced Bradbury's development of *Fahrenheit 451* in the first place (Eller, *Becoming* 90).

Unfortunately for Bradbury, it appears that his initial approach to staging *Fahrenheit 451* was too much tied to the structure of the novel; he was trying to be "faithful" to the original work. In personal correspondence with the art critic Bernard Berenson, Bradbury wrote in 1956, "much to my sorrow, I discover that I have not as yet learned all the essentials of the theatre and that what I produced was more gimcrackery and surface-static than idea and interplay of character" (Eller, "Bradbury-Berenson" 41). At this point, Bradbury was working to a three-act structure—unusual, but not unheard-of—in the commercial theatre), mirroring the three sections of the novel.

Disappointed by his experiences, Bradbury would put off further work on *Fahrenheit 451* for many years, eventually returning to it in the 1970s, by which time he proved to be less tied to his original conception. He also took inspiration from some of François Truffaut's creative choices and decided that, like Truffaut, he would keep the character of Clarisse alive, bringing her back at the close of the play to welcome Montag into the book-people's world. This is an unusual situation and shows the Bradbury novel, Truffaut film, and Bradbury play to be in dialogue with each other. It also supports Hutcheon's point that it is unwise to think of one work as "an original" and another work as a derivation.

The final, published version of Bradbury's play, which came out in 1986 but actually was developed from 1979 onward (Eller, "Story" 206-7), has a two-act structure, and this condenses the narrative. The play advances the story at a faster pace than the novel, but retains nearly all of its key plot points. Montag's journey remains similar to the novel, and Bradbury keeps elements like the Mechanical Hound from which other adaptors, including Calcutt and Truffaut, have shied away. Where the play shows most difference from the novel is in the characterization.

In the interests of dramatization, the play's version of Montag is much more self-motivated. No longer is he full of pro-system swagger and only able to conceive the world differently at Clarisse's prompting. Instead, this Montag has already questioned the status quo before even meeting Clarisse. Indeed, his slightly rebellious behavior is part of what attracts Clarisse to him. Mrs. Montag does not fare so well in her transformation to the stage: Mildred is a bit less intelligent in the play. For example, she is unable to understand how the interactive TV play really works, whereas in the novel, it is Mildred who explains it to Guy.

The greatest achievement of the stage play is the enhancement of Fire Chief Beatty. Although obviously a powerful figure in the novel, it isn't entirely clear how he came to be like he is. In the stage play, Bradbury takes the opportunity to re-examine this pivotal antagonist, and his refraction of the character provides a fascinating new insight into him. In his essay "Investing Dimes," Bradbury explains the creative process behind this revision of *Fahrenheit 451*, and he tells how he imagined Beatty explaining himself: "It's not owning books that's a crime, Montag, it's reading them! Yes, that's right. I own books, but don't read them!" (72). From this utterance, Bradbury works through the logic of Beatty's background: a long time ago Beatty had been a rabid consumer of books, until a succession of bad life experiences wore him down. At his lowest point, he would turn to books for consolation, and yet:

> I looked in the mirror and found an old man lost behind the frightened face of a young man, saw a hatred there for everything and anything, you name it, I'd damn it, and opened the pages of my fine library books and found what, what, what!? …Blank! Oh, the words were there, alright, but they ran over my eyes like hot oil, signifying nothing. Offering no help, no solace, no peace, no harbor, no true love, no bed, no light." (74)

From the point of view of adaptation theory, Bradbury's play also offers direct evidence that an adaptation can be something other than a one-way process. Two important character-related elements of the play take inspiration from Truffaut's film: the reappearance of Clarisse and the educating of Montag.

On the question of Clarisse and her re-appearance after her reported death, Bradbury writes that, like Truffaut, "I felt the…need to save her, for after all, she, verging on silly star-struck chatter, was in many ways responsible for Montag's beginning to wonder about books and what was in them. In my play, therefore, Clarisse emerges to welcome Montag, and give a somewhat happier ending to what was, in essence, pretty grim stuff" ("Investing Dimes" 75).

When Montag first picks up a book and reads, Bradbury follows Truffaut's lead by having Montag slowly read his way through the text. The stage directions could almost be a description of Truffaut's staging of the corresponding scene in the film:

> ([...] *The illumination from the TV will be his lamp. He sits down and at last opens one book, turning the pages with fascination. He traces his finger under the title.*) A…Tale of…Two Cities…by…Charles… Dickens. (*More clearly.*) Charles Dickens. (*He turns a page, squints, and starts to read, painfully.*) Chapter One. It was the Best of Times… it was… the… worst of… times… (*Fahrenheit 451* [play] 51)

Notice also that Bradbury has followed Calcutt and Truffaut in playing his own allusion game: he has replaced Montag's first reading text with an alternative selection, Dickens' *A Tale of Two Cities*!

It is somewhat unusual for a novelist to dramatize his own novel, but it is highly unusual for it to happen so long after the novel was written, and yet more unusual for an author to acknowledge influence from another adaptor of his work. Bradbury's stage play, then, is a remarkable instance of an adaptation which refracts both its source and other attempts at adaptation.

Examining the various ways that *Fahrenheit 451* has been "cut to fit" into different media need not be reduced to a series of tick-box comparisons. While it can be fun to discuss whether one version of a story is faithful to another, or by extension, whether one telling is "better than" another, there is more reward in a critical reading that considers how each new adaptation throws new light on previous incarnations of a text. It is precisely because of what Bazin called "refraction" that *Fahrenheit 451* is a fascinating case study, with successive adaptations never failing to encourage a new view of Bradbury's story and Guy Montag's world. While each adaptation inevitably reflects the viewpoint of the artist responsible for the adaptation, there is a clear sense of the potentials of Bradbury's novel providing a series of challenges to the creative interpreter of the book, and it is undoubtedly this aspect of the book which has maintained its popularity in a range of popular media.

Note

1.   The complete title of Bunyan's work is The Pilgrim's Progress from This World to That Which Is to Come; Delivered under the Similitude of a Dream.

Works Cited

Aggelis, Steven L. *Conversations with Ray Bradbury*. Jackson: UP of Mississippi, 2004.

Bazin, André. "Adaptation, or the Cinema as Digest." *Film Adaptation*. Ed. James Naremore. New Brunswick: Rutgers UP, 2000. 19-27.

Bradbury, Ray. *Fahrenheit 451*. 60th anniversary edition. New York: Simon & Schuster, 2013.

_____. *Fahrenheit 451* [play]. Woodstock, IL: Dramatic, 1986.

_____. "Investing Dimes: *Fahrenheit 451.*" *Zen in the Art of Writing.* Santa Barbara, CA: Odell, 1994. 69-78.

_____. *Now and Forever.* New York: Morrow, 2007.

Bunyan, John. *The Pilgrim's Progress.* 1678. Mineola, NY: Dover, 2003.

Calcutt, David. *Fahrenheit 451.* BBC Radio 4, London. 5 July 2003. Radio.

Dickens, Charles. *David Copperfield.* 1850. Mineola, NY: Dover, 2004.

Eller, Jonathan R. *Becoming Ray Bradbury.* Champaign, IL: Illinois UP, 2011.

_____. "The Bradbury-Berenson Correspondence." *The New Ray Bradbury Review* 2 (2010): 28-66.

_____. "The Story of Fahrenheit 451." *Fahrenheit 451.* Ray Bradbury. 60th anniversary ed. New York: Simon & Schuster, 2013. 167-87.

Fahrenheit 451. Dir. François Truffaut. Perf. Oskar Werner, Julie Christie, Cyril Cusack. Universal, 1966.

Hamilton, Tim. *Ray Bradbury's* Fahrenheit 451*: The Authorized Adaptation* [graphic novel]. New York: Hill and Wang, 2009.

Hutcheon, Linda. *A Theory of Adaptation.* New York: Routledge, 2006.

McLuhan, Marshall. *Understanding Media.* 1964. New York: Routledge, 2005.

Miller, Walter M., Jr. *A Canticle for Leibowitz.* 1959. New York: EOS, 2006.

Peary, Gerald. "*Fahrenheit 451*: From Novel to Film." *Omni's Screen Flights/ Screen Fantasies.* Ed. Danny Peary. Garden City, NY: Columbus, 1984. 127-32.

Sisario, Peter. "A Study of the Allusions in Bradbury's *Fahrenheit 451.*" *The English Journal* 59 (1970): 201+.

Toubiana, Serge and Antoine De Baecque. *Truffaut: A Biography.* New York: Knopf, 1999.

Truffaut, François. "Journal of *Fahrenheit 451.*" *Bradbury: An Illustrated Life.* Jerry Weist. New York: Morrow, 1966. 124-39.

Weller, Sam. *The Bradbury Chronicles.* New York: Morrow, 2005.

Whalen, Tom. "The Consequences of Passivity: Re-Evaluating Truffaut's *Fahrenheit 451.*" *Literature/Film Quarterly* 35 (2007): 181-89.

Fahrenheit 451 and the Utopic Dystopia: Bradbury's Vision Compared to Those of More, Orwell, Huxley, Wells, and Dick

Wolf Forrest

Ever since humans first banded together for the common good, and primitive clans developed, a better world has been the goal, although the powerful and avaricious among those have taken the opportunity to create one only for the select few. After thousands of years, democracies like Athenian Greece were an experiment designed to replace aristocentric societies like Pharaonic Egypt, as learned men and women saw the value of spreading hope to those willing to elevate their economic and social standing. Always, however, forces outside human control, like disease and natural disasters, and the continuance of oppressors who spread their stain of "might makes right," flexed out in wars, eat away at the struggle for equality and betterment.

When Ray Bradbury wrote *The Fireman*, he might not have anticipated that it would evolve into one of the most influential novels of the 20th century and join a host of literary tomes dedicated to the exploration of worlds both optimistic and nihilistic. It began with a simple premise: what if firemen started fires instead of putting them out? A simple inversion, really, that evolved into an examination of how men control others by various means.

There have been many attempts to document perfect societies in literature through the ages—Plato's *Republic* is probably the earliest surviving piece and certainly the Book of Revelation in the New Testament describes the ultimate human paradise—but Thomas More, a Latin and Greek scholar as well as a religious figure, was the first to give it a name. In his 1516 book *Utopia*, he created a mythical island kingdom whose name is based on the homophonic pun *ou* (no) or *eu* (good) plus *topos* (place). The debate continues as to whether this dense work, whose meaning still eludes, is political treatise or satire. Ultimately a martyr, More opposed the Protestant Reformation and, ironically, burned some of Martin Luther's books.

As a result of his friendship with the philosopher Erasmus and his reaction to the loneliness of Antwerp More conceived *Utopia* as a response to Erasmus' *The Praise of Folly*. Its precept that private property was a vice that entered the world with the fall of Adam and Eve (Marius 165) suggests the origin of Communism as a political entity. Yet this perfect world is not often perfect. The reformist idealism wrought by the Utopians is undermined by the sinfulness of human nature (Fox 58). And, despite their lives of relative ease, they are restricted in their travels, wear uniformly drab clothing, and are limited to essentials in their consumer goods. Offbeat science fiction writer R.A. Lafferty wrote a satire of More's *Utopia* called *Past Master*, in which More was summoned to the future to preside over a paradise named Astrobe, with unintended consequences.

Samuel Johnson's *Rasselas,* about a prince searching for the ideal place to live, is in part a response to the philosopher Leibniz's assertion that, despite the ills that plague mankind, this is the best of all possible worlds. Samuel Butler's *Erewhon* deserves mention, for it satirizes Victorian society by creating a Luddite utopia where machinery is banned. Even adventure writer Jack London toyed with the concept of dystopia, penning *The Iron* Heel, which involves the discovery of a manuscript centuries after it was written (much like the plot of Walter M. Miller's later post-apocalyptic *A Canticle for Leibowitz*).

The first major film to depict a dystopia was Fritz Lang's *Metropolis*[1] (1927), based on a script he wrote with his wife, Thea von Harbou. Taking many themes from the writings of H.G. Wells, it mirrors the German social, engineering, and artistic fabric emerging from the rubble of World War I, and it also anticipates the rise of Fascism. As a dystopia with a happy ending, it is comparable to *Fahrenheit 451* in that out of oppression comes opportunity. When Maria, the laborers' rabble-rouser, speaks of motivation she exhorts, "The mediator between head and hands must be the heart." (The motto of the concentration camp at Buchenwald was, "Break the body, break the spirit, break the heart" [Shandler 75].) As a robotic false Maria is created by the overlords to undermine her efforts, a pattern of doppelgängers begins to emerge in the growing body of dystopic art.

Dystopic works of literature that need or desire a happy ending usually have some clandestine or underground force opposed to the ruling state. In history, we see the French Resistance fighting the Nazi regime in World War II, or the leftists battling Franco's forces during the Spanish Civil War, or Joan of Arc sacrificing herself for a cause. Bradbury's citizens do what they can—by committing a book to memory for the purposes of verbally passing its precious contents down through the generations, they preserve what would have been the province of the printed word.

Bradbury opens his novel with the incendiary "[i]t was a pleasure to burn." Are we reading the words of an outlaw arsonist? Sadly, the duty of those whom the novel's citizens have entrusted with their safety is to start fires rather than put them out. The firemen wear salamander pins on their lapels, the salamander being an ancient symbol of a fireproof organism, one also supposedly able to extinguish fire with the exceptional coolness of its body (Ashton 323-26). Of course, in real life, salamanders need constant moisture to survive, and aside from evoking the near-mythical abilities attributed to the animal by ancient folklore, the term *salamander* also can refer to a portable stove or heater. Bradbury was keenly aware of such dualities, and his emotional construct is rooted in his love of reading, for the historical record he uncovered about the burning of the library at Alexandria, along with his subsequent exposure to the book burnings in Nazi Germany, left him shaken.

In ancient times, the Cynics of Diogenes were obligated to search for truth, stripped from its veneer of social posturing as a form of self-protection. In this regard, Bradbury is a cynic with a capital C. His characters are noble—not in the form of heroic fantasy figures like Burroughs' John Carter of Mars (which he adored) or Howard's Conan the Barbarian, but in their simplicity and utter humanness and their search for truth, even when they are violating some civil code.

A third generation fireman, Montag has a job not subject to analysis, particularly as he enjoys his work. Is he the proletariat destroying the tools of the privileged? Of course, a book can be seen as an elitist tool: to take advantage of it, one must be able to read. Is the printed word more dangerous than visual aids? Would Bradbury's world have censored paintings like *The Torment of St. Anthony*, Bosch's triptych, or even the depiction in Wyeth's *Christina's World* of a crippled girl trying to reach a farmhouse? Most likely, for Bradbury specifically points out that museums show only abstract art, nothing that might portray people or inspire thought or questioning.

Fahrenheit 451 does not address the concept, or role, of religion in the world in which Montag lives, beyond its exploitation by advertisers, perhaps damning by omission its unimportance. Other writers of dystopic or utopic worlds, however, deal with the issue of religion by mocking it, or finding a substitute. H.G. Wells was a hopeful optimist, a Fabian socialist, who stressed gradual rather than revolutionary reform and supported the implementation of eugenics in its purest form. He believed technology could solve any problem. His prescience in predicting the outbreak of World War II almost to the year in *The Shape of Things to Come* is noteworthy, but, like Orwell's *1984,* suppression of religion as an impediment to education is the State's directive—and in particular here the dismantling of Islam, a view that in today's culture seems inflammatory at best.

Wells' greatest novels—*War of the Worlds, The Time Machine, The Invisible Man, The Island of Dr. Moreau, The Shape of Things to Come,* and particularly in *A Modern Utopia* and his non-fiction omnibus *The Outline of History*—evince a utilitarian humanism. *Moreau* is the ultimate eugenics experiment, raising animals to the "evolved" level of humans through surgery, while in *The Invisible Man*, a scientist experimenting with a drug is driven insane by its side effects. Griffin, in the latter novel, becomes the victim of his environment in an effort to control it, his own utopia spoiled by the most basic of human failings. Wells does not capitulate to a character like Griffin; he does not expect human reason to be a source of truth and goodness. Griffin is presented as the symbol of pure—

and purely selfish—intelligence (Williamson 83). He may not seem like the central character in a dystopic novel, but his rationale is comparable to many despots in history, whose singular vision caused much agony before their fall. Certainly *any* form of government is anathema to those at the bottom of the socio-economic well—then the whole world seems dystopic.

Aldous Huxley's writing is a reaction to the humanistic universes postulated by Wells. *Brave New World,* which takes place in the year 632 A.F.—*After Ford,* a nod to Henry Ford's implementation of the assembly line, which figures importantly in the novel, and also to the displacement of religion—relies on a seemingly glowing overview of the future to drive home the irony. (It is interesting how many of the non-utopian, or dystopic, characteristics in novels are actually desirable by people who are not automatons.) As a palliative to Yevgeny Zamyatin's *We,* a harsh dystopia condemning the citizenry to isolation from the green earth while granting State-authorized sexual license, Huxley's world gives its citizens pleasure, in large part from the drug S*oma* and also from having the State minister to their every need.

George Orwell's two most famous works, *1984* and *Animal Farm*, are a study in contrasts birthed from the same egg. In the former, the ultimate totalitarian state works its magic through propaganda. The latter uses satire against a socialistic world that has run amok and a children's approach to envision the perfect society through the machinations of barnyard denizens who view the human players as the true enemy. Unfortunately, in an attempt to improve their world, using homilies like "Two legs bad, four legs good" and "All animals are equal, but some are more equal than others," they fall victim to the same shortcomings as their former overlords. Bradbury's intellectual, yet surprisingly humble, book-memorizing citizens do not seem to have such flaws, but the Thought Police of *1984* would have rounded them up in no time. The agents of the sinister Ministry of Love, after all, know that the mask that every thinking person carries is a danger to those who cannot perceive it, and Oceana's military scientists have spared no effort to pierce that mask to the 'thoughtcrime' beneath. Huxley wrote to Orwell after the publication of *1984*, citing its importance but criticizing his treatment of "the ultimate revolution" and stressing that the transformation of society would only be accomplished through the "total subversion of the individual's psychology and physiology" (Baker 22). After constant propaganda and surveillance, brainwashing in *1984* comes about through drug manipulation and threat of torture and death. By *Fahrenheit 451*, of course, the "brainwashing" is subtler and less violent, but no less insidious.

In *Brave New World*, whose title is taken from a line in Shakespeare's *The Tempest*, the science of the State has replaced the magic of Prospero. Reproduction is a focal point in *Brave New World*, where "standardized humans are thereby produced in 'uniform batches'" (Matter 95). In Bradbury's universe, despite Fire Chief Beatty's casual references to three-dimensional pornographic magazines and heroin-fueled orgies, there still is an aseptic quality to any notion of sex, as if the books were the children, the fruits of perpetuity, which must be guarded against the State. When sexual impulses that would have been forbidden in *1984*—or would have been government-directed or monitored in *We* or *Brave New World*—are left to the discretion of individuals, pleasure control must come in other forms. Where science has outstripped ethics (Baker 23) in *Brave New World*, the universe of *Fahrenheit 451* has produced a conundrum for both the lawmaker and philosopher.

A return to Eden is a common theme for novels based in the future. In More's *Utopia*, his paradise turns England's model of reform upside down. It may be that More placed his ideal society on an island to reduce the chance of plague, which would certainly negate a feeling of well-being, but England was an island nation, too, and certainly not immune to such ills. Wells' time traveler encounters a paradise where no one has to work, and the human race is divided into two camps: the passive Eloi and the cannibalistic Morlocks, neither of which depends on intellectual stimulation or fulfillment. Further, the Morlocks have a complex symbolic function, representing an exaggerated fear of the nineteenth-century proletariat as well as traditional mythical images of a demonic (or dystopian) world (Bergonzi 53). Religious components in a future society, or the lack of same, also are central to conflict and resolution of many literary works. Karl Marx's assessment that religion was the opiate of the masses suggests a connection between drug use in these future novels and fervent religious belief as an analgesic to oppression. Does one turn inward or outward when one's consciousness is altered through pharmaceuticals or meditation/prayer? Or through reading a book? Is self-discovery self-contained, or is information sought from others for confirmation? And, once infused with power, does the individual share or intimidate?

Dystopias work best when paranoia is at its extreme, and Philip K. Dick is the dystopic writer whose art perhaps most reflects the sensibility of someone who has actually lived in one of these terrible worlds and is merely writing reports on the conditions found there. Certainly, police states, such as those of Zamyatin's *We* and Orwell's *1984*, foster anxiety and suspicion, but the often fractured worlds of Dick reflect the paranoia that seeped from the author himself. Dick wrote, "The ultimate in paranoia is not when everyone is against you, but when *everything* is against you" (Umland 7), and on at least one occasion, an interviewer who had set up a tape recorder realized *he* was being recorded by Dick (Platt 146). Or was it just curiosity?

One component of Dick's writing is the fluidity of perception—like the Heisenberg principle, where a particle's speed, but not its location, can be known, and vice versa, and the observer effect, where observing or measuring a phenomenon changes the phenomenon. His novels—including *The Man in the High Castle*, an alternate universe in which the Axis Powers win World War II; *The Three Stigmata of Palmer Eldritch*, depicting commonplace mass drug use; *A Scanner Darkly*, about drug informants who themselves are addicted; and, of course, *Do Androids Dream of Electric Sheep?*, filmed as *Blade Runner*—often highlight the problem of determining exactly what, or who, is real. He shares with Huxley the trait of using drugs to control the populace, and his extreme dystopias, like "We Can Remember it for you Wholesale," wherein the State implants false memories in an individual to achieve its own objectives, and "Minority Report," in which people arrested merely for thinking about committing crimes, show echoes of the Thought Police of *1984*, and a recurrence of *doppelgänger* themes.

A signature topic in much of Dick's work, however, what is perceived as an objective reality is a shared experience. The shared experiences via the drug Can-D in *The Three Stigmata of Palmer Eldritch*, for example, blur the character distinctions more than they serve to reinforce the individuals' beliefs, as do the Empathy Boxes of *Do Androids Dream of Electric Sheep?* In *Eldritch*, the ultimate nature of reality is put to a test. Can humans ever know reality, or forever be trapped in their own subjective world? The question, of course, is based on the assumption that the universe has form and meaning, and the problem for humans is to discover what that form and meaning is (Warrick 109). Dick's writing is also influenced by Gnosticism, the notion that the universe we experience is the product of a flawed creator whose intent may or may not be benevolent, while behind it lies a benevolent God intent on repairing the flawed empirical world (Link 75). In *Fahrenheit 451*, the passing on of books through oral recitation is a recapitulation of the way the shared experiences of tales and myths originally were spread, and Bradbury's insistence on saving the *essence* of books, rather than books themselves, can be seen as the manifest of God, for by recycling the essence, his characters are maintaining the spirituality.

"The Fireman" first appeared as a 25,000 word novelette in the February 1951 issue of *Galaxy* magazine. Bradbury's story "The Pedestrian" was its genesis, part of the "five ladyfinger firecracker tales" that formed the basis of *Fahrenheit 451*, along with "The Bonfire," "Bright Phoenix," "The Exiles," and Usher II" (Weller 200). The novel was expanded to 50,000 words, double the novelette's length, and serialized in the second, third, and fourth issues of *Playboy*, then sold to Ballantine Books, where it was published in 1953. That same year McCarthyism and Red-baiting were at their peak and the junior senator from Wisconsin was orchestrating his own-book burning mission to rid the country of subversive literature. Another stalwart of censorship and book-burning, Joseph Stalin, died that year in Soviet Russia. "The Fireman" takes place in a specific year, 2052, as the firemen play cards under a talking clock as war is imminent. This scene occurs later in the expanded novel, after the reader is introduced to Clarisse, to Montag's wife and her first bout with drug overdose, and to the Mechanical Hound.

It is impossible to discuss Bradbury's book without also including the 1966 film version by Francois Truffaut. In the movie, Truffaut illustrates the shunning of the printed word by having a narrator speak the opening credits. An early scene shows Montag in bed next to his wife, reading the comics section of a newspaper with no captions or dialogue balloons. We see images of the Ku Klux Klan, a group that has also used burning to intimidate. Bradbury may have been critical of Truffaut for using the same actress, Julie Christie, albeit with different hairstyles, to play the roles of Montag's wife Linda (Mildred in the novel) and confidant Clarisse McClellan, but the *doppelgänger* use does serve a purpose. As with Dick's assertion that perception is everything, the two similarly appearing women represent the passive citizen and the rebel, and Montag is not moved by this visual anomaly. Early in their relationship, Clarisse's question to Montag—"Do you ever read the books you burn?"—haunts him as might a similar question to a bomber pilot: "Do you ever see the faces of those you kill?" When Montag dreams, it is of a school, where books used to be kept, and Truffaut utilizes a dizzying tracking shot seen in *Vertigo* to accentuate his newfound ambivalence.

Bradbury has stated that *Fahrenheit 451* is his only science fiction work, and that books like *The Martian Chronicles* are really myths[3] that rely on the essence of Greek or Egyptian storytelling (Bouzereau). But *Fahrenheit* is also beholden to the myth of Orpheus and Eurydice. Montag not only seeks the secrets of Hades (why men/books must burn) but also is on a quest to save his *imago*—though he does not realize it. He wonders about Clarisse when she disappears and is told she was hit by a car. His further enlightenment is motivated by her *joie de vivre* and seeming unconcern about the banning of books. The characters of the novel exist to either support Montag, as Clarisse and Faber do, or to oppose him, as Mildred and Captain Beatty do (Reid 57), whereas in the film Montag's process of discovery is self-contained. Clarisse's comments to Montag about her peers are also noteworthy, when she states that young people are given destructive outlets for their boredom, including car- and window-smashing in a controlled environment. Mildred talks about going out driving and killing animals with the car when she feels stressed, as if they were props or avatars in a video game.

Faber's role in the novel, particularly as someone whom Montag recalls from an earlier meeting, is also absent in the film, the professor being replaced instead by another doppelgänger, Fabian, a fireman who has a similar-sounding name but none of the former's functions in the plot. Faber[4] is a former English professor who lost his position as the humanities were eliminated from the State's educational system. Montag wants Faber to understand how he has come to a point of awareness, and Faber teaches the unsettled fireman to see for himself that people's idle time is filled with mindless entertainment, for true leisure might lead to conversation, to reading, to thought. When Mildred requests a fourth wall for her interactive telescreens, it may be referencing the fourth wall in theater, the invisible barrier between the audience and the players on stage. When a character breaks the fourth wall, he or she communicates directly with the audience, acknowledging the artifact of the play and thereby stressing the "unreality" of this type of interface; the electronic fourth wall, however, would not be "broken" so easily.

In *The Time Machine*, the passive Eloi from the year 802,701 have libraries but have forgotten their purpose, and the books have decayed with time. Other than the withered flowers Weena gave him, the time traveler in the novel leaves nothing of his intent behind, while at the end of the 1960 film *The Time Machine,* the character takes three books back to the future, a cornerstone to build a new civilization. Montag and Faber likewise wish to start society anew with the wisdom of books, and they at first decide to print new copies of their own for distribution through an underground network.

Despite Bradbury's repeated reference to books as feathers or moths or birds, or as having pores, however, he also stresses that books themselves are not living, only vehicles with no innate worth other than to carry the message; indeed, Montag and Faber soon realize that memorizing books will have a far greater effect than merely printing new ones. In our own time, with the digital shorthand of texting, and the decreasing emphasis on cursive writing, the printed word, and the flow of words, becomes even more precious. As Jack Zipes writes, "The dystopian constellation of conflict in *Fahrenheit 451* is not really constituted by the individual versus the state, but the intellectual versus the masses" (191).

Guy Montag's epiphany is different from that of Winston Smith, who in *1984* has a conflicted relationship with Julia, who herself can be compared to Clarisse. A spin doctor for the Ministry of Truth and a promulgator of Newspeak, Smith nevertheless keeps a secret diary of his thoughts and feelings; he "has a legitimate love of the traditions of the past, and that love is combined with a genuine concern for the language and literature of Oldspeak, and for the right to independent thought" (Stansky 113). With Montag, however, the death of the woman who chooses to burn with her house full of books is a galvanizing moment. When Beatty learns of Montag's defection, Montag, in a supposed dream of Beatty's, reiterates Newton's assertion about the reasons behind his scientific success, telling Beatty that he is a dwarf on a giant's shoulders and sees the further of the two. Beatty here and elsewhere shows himself to be quite literate, apparently having read a great number of the books he burned. Montag's hands have developed a life of their own, and after his theft of a Bible from the woman's house and, ultimately, a climactic late-night raid upon the disillusioned fireman's own home, he kills Beatty. Montag escapes, and war is declared.

Wars are a major force in many dystopias. They may become the impetus to tighten government control or restructure society, as in *Things to Come* or *1984* or some of the works of Philip K. Dick. Alternately, they may serve instead as a cleansing, as in *Fahrenheit 451*. In *Fahrenheit 451,* Montag mentions that two nuclear wars have been fought since 1960, and during his flight from the authorities after killing Beatty, another brief war breaks out. Apparently for the first time, however, America either has lost or at least has taken a major blow. The future is extraordinarily hazy, but it is to be hoped that now society can be reshaped anew. Montag commits to memory the Book of Ecclesiastes[5], a perfect choice for someone who is conflicted about his life and his life's work, for although its meaning has been a subject for debate, its message of living in the present certainly pushes Montag onto an appropriate path.

The brief war has cleansed the city of evil men and, certainly, any books that remained, while Montag and the others, who have committed books to memory, can start again, giving civilization a chance to right its wrong. The film version, which minimizes the threat of the atom bomb, save for one small reference, explores that transfer of knowledge in an intimate setting, as the fall changes to winter, as oral tradition manifests itself in the repetition of books to the next generation. So how did Bradbury regard this adaptation? "I was happy with *Fahrenheit 451*. I think it's a beautiful film, with a gorgeous ending. A great ending by Truffaut" (Platt 179). Thankfully, Bradbury's future had yet to find a way to read minds, then de-program them.

Censorship still exists in the real world. *Brave New World*, along with *Tom Sawyer*, *Lady Chatterley's Lover*, *The Last Temptation of Christ*, *Naked Lunch*, *Uncle Tom's Cabin*, *Our Lady of the Flowers*, and a multitude of others repeatedly turn up on a list of banned books in classrooms because of racial insensitivity, historical inaccuracy, sexual or religious matters, or widespread drug use. Ironically, *Fahrenheit 451* was subjected to censorship in the form of minor revisions by its publisher Ballantine, which prompted Bradbury to write an afterword to a new printing of the novel in 1980, when the revisions and edits were reversed. And there is criticism, albeit tongue-in-cheek, because these books do not accurately reflect the future—our present—that the authors predicted; Alandra Petri, for example, in criticizing efforts to remove *Brave New World* from school reading lists in today's schools, wryly notes the novel's "error" in blaming Ford, not Zuckerberg, for the future's problems. *Fahrenheit 451* and films like *Privilege* influenced novels like *Bug Jack Barron* and other films like *Rollerball, Network, and Brazil. Brave New World* mentored *A Clockwork Orange*. The line between the medium and the message becomes increasingly blurred, and instead of the media manipulating the user, the user manipulates the media. Such forms of entertainment seem prophetic when real incidents erupt. Pastor Terry Jones' threatened burning of the Koran got enormous publicity for him and his church; conversely, a *fatwā* was issued against Salman Rushdie for publishing *The Satanic Verses*, a book that fundamentalist Muslims thought *should* be burned.

What books such as *Fahrenheit 451* do is to spotlight the extremes of human behavior regarding the governance of humanity as a whole. Science influences religion, while religion influences science less so, but examples of the latter are there nonetheless, the work of Gregor Mendel and Teilhard de Chardin bearing witness. Politics influences science and religion, and ethics serve to cart around these scattered disciplines. Utopias and dystopias are two sides of the same coin, and for every gleaming technocracy, there are those who fear the hidden costs of maintenance. Newton's second law of thermodynamics certainly applies here: "For every action there is an equal and opposite reaction." The cynic (with a small c) sees a utopic/dystopic world, where only the basest and vilest of human characteristics would predominate.

The near future, at least, seems more Warholian than Orwellian. The self-indulgent behavior seen on social media is a perfect foil to outside control, and bombardment by so many various forms of advertising, sound bites, and celebrity misdeeds, along with the personal sharing of data, pictures, and thoughts seemingly on a whim would suggest that any governments or corporations with an ax to grind would find it difficult to wade through this swamp of competing information to pursue a singular agenda of manipulation.

The problems with implementing a perfect society involve a series of ongoing questions. Why is it so hard for those in power to govern fairly? How does society maintain order and efficiency without stifling personal freedom? In a majority-rule type of government, ostensibly the least objectionable of any available, are there ever exceptions to allow for insight, intuition, flexibility, and the encouragement of innovation, which may initially seem counter-productive but would help to achieve the goal of a better world? And how do individual choices affect the progress of civilization? The dystopic/utopic novels carry not predictions but warnings—as if we could do nothing else but learn from books.

Notes

1. Bradbury's lifelong friend Forrest Ackerman considered it the best science fiction film ever and claimed to have watched it over a hundred times (Lozano).

2. Dick had a twin sister who died in infancy (Link 3).

3. Yet *The Martian Chronicles* also addresses topics of environmental pollution, bad stewardship, bigotry, and racism.

4. Interestingly, Faber's name also is part of the name of a publishing house and a manufacturer of writing instruments.

5. In the film, it is Poe's *Tales of Mystery and Imagination*.

Works Cited

Ashton, John. *Curious Creatures in Zoology*. London: Nimmo, 1890.

Baker, Robert S. *Brave New World: History, Science, and Dystopia*. Boston: Hall, 1990.

Bergonzi, Bernard. *The Early H.G. Wells: A Study of the Scientific Romances*. Manchester: Manchester UP, 1961.

Bouzereau, Laurent. *Fahrenheit 451, the Novel: A Discussion with Author Ray Bradbury*. Universal Studios Home Video, supplement. 2002. DVD.

Bradbury, Ray. *Fahrenheit 451*. 1953. New York: Ballantine, 1969.

Brazil. Dir. Terry Gilliam. Perf. Jonathan Pryce, Kim Greist, Robert De Niro. Embassy, 1985. Film.

Burgess, Anthony. *A Clockwork Orange*. 1962. New York: Ballantine, 1972.

Butler, Samuel. *Erewhon*. 1872. London: Penguin, 1985.

Dick, Philip K. *Do Androids Dream of Electric Sheep?* 1968. New York: New American, 1969.

_____. *The Man in the High Castle*. 1962. New York: Berkley, 1974.

_____. "Minority Report." 1956. *Minority Report*. New York: Random, 2002.

_____. *A Scanner Darkly*. 1977. New York: Houghton Mifflin, 2011.

_____. *The Three Stigmata of Palmer Eldritch*. 1965. New York: Houghton Mifflin, 2011.

_____. *Ubik*. 1969. New York: Houghton Mifflin, 2012.

_____. "We Can Remember It for You Wholesale." 1966. *The Magazine of Fantasy and Science Fiction: A 30-Year Retrospective*. Ed. Edward L. Ferman. New York: Doubleday, 1980. 245-64.

Erasmus. *The Praise of Folly*. 1509. New York: Black, 1942.

Fahrenheit 451. Dir. François Truffaut. Perf. Oskar Werner, Julie Christie, Cyril Cusack. Universal, 1966.

Fox, Alistair. *Thomas More: History and Providence*. Oxford: Blackwell, 1982.

Johnson, Samuel. *The History of Rasselas, Prince of Abysinnia*. 1759. Oxford: Oxford UP, 2009.

Lafferty, R.A. *Past Master*. 1968. New York: Garland, 1975.

Link, Eric Carl. *Understanding Philip K. Dick*. Columbia, SC: U of South Carolina P, 2010.

London, Jack. *The Iron Heel*. London: Macmillan, 1908.

Lozano, Alicia. "Forrest J. Ackerman's Scary Treasures Part of Hollywood Auction." 29 Apr. 2009. <http://herocomplex.latimes.com/uncategorized/forrest-j-ackermans-scary-treasures-go-to-the-auction-block/> 23 Sept. 2013.

Marius, Richard. *Thomas More*. New York: Knopf, 1984.

Matter, William. "On *Brave New World*." *No Place Else: Explorations in Utopian and Dystopian Fiction*. Eds. Eric S. Rabkin, Martin H. Greenberg, and Joseph D. Olander. Carbondale and Edwardsville, IL: Southern Illinois UP, 1983. 94-109.

Metropolis. Dir. Fritz Lang. Perf. Brigitte Helm, Alfred Abel, Gustav Fröhlich. UFA, 1927. Film.

Miller, Walter M., Jr. *A Canticle for Leibowitz*. 1959. Philadelphia: Lippincott, 1972.

More, Thomas. *Utopia*. 1516. Harmondsworth, England: Penguin, 1970.

Network. Dir. Sidney Lumet. Perf. Faye Dunaway, William Holden, Peter Finch, Robert Duvall. MGM-United Artists, 1976.

Orwell, George. *Animal Farm*. 1945. New York: Harcourt, 1946.

_____. *1984*. 1949. New York: New American Library, 1950.

Petri, Alandra. "For Banned Books Week, Two Reasons to Ban 'Brave New World'." 28 Sept. 2011. 5 Sept. 2013. <http://www.washingtonpost.com/blogs/compost/post/for-banned-books-week-two-reasons-to-ban-brave-new-world/2011/09/28/gIQAViSe5K_blog.html>

Platt, Charles. *Dream Makers*. New York: Berkley, 1980.

Rabkin, Eric S., Martin H. Greenberg, and Joseph D. Olander, eds. *No Place Else: Explorations in Utopian and Dystopian Fiction*. Carbondale and Edwardsville, IL: Southern Illinois UP, 1983.

Reid, Robin Anne. *Ray Bradbury: A Critical Companion*. Westport, CT: Greenwood, 2000.

Rollerball. Dir. Norman Jewison. Perf. James Caan, John Houseman, Maud Adams. United Artists, 1975.

Shandler, Jeffrey. *While America Watches: Televising the Holocaust*. New York: Oxford UP, 1999.

Spinrad, Norman. *Bug Jack Barron*. 1969. London: Granada, 1972.

Stansky, Peter, ed. *On* Nineteen Eighty-Four. New York: Freeman, 1983.

Time Machine, The. Dir. George Pal. Perf. Rod Taylor, Alan Young, Yvette Mimieux. MGM, 1960.

Umland, Samuel J., ed. *Philip K. Dick: Contemporary Critical Interpretations*. Westport, CT: Greenwood, 1995.

Warrick, Patricia S. *Mind in Motion: The Fiction of Philip K. Dick*. Carbondale and Edwardsville, IL: Southern Illinois UP, 1987.

Weller, Sam. *The Bradbury Chronicles*. New York: Morrow, 2005.

Wells, H.G. *The Invisible Man*. 1897. New York: Heritage, 1967.

_____. *The Island of Dr. Moreau*. 1896. New York: Random, 1996.

_____. *A Modern Utopia*. New York: Scribner's, 1905.

_____. *Outline of History*. 1920. New York: Macmillan, 1926.

_____. *The Shape of Things to Come*. 1933. London: Penguin, 2005.

_____. *The War of the Worlds*. 1898. New York: Airmont, 1964.

Williamson, Jack. *H.G. Wells: Critic of Progress*. Baltimore: Mirage, 1973.

Zamyatin, Yevgeny. *We*. 1921. New York: Random House, 2006.

Zipes, Jack. "Mass Degradation of Humanity and Massive Contradictions in Bradbury's Vision of America in *Fahrenheit 451*." *No Place Else: Explorations in Utopian and Dystopian Fiction*. Eds. Eric S. Rabkin, Martin H. Greenberg, and Joseph D. Olander. Carbondale and Edwardsville, IL: Southern Illinois UP, 1983. 182-98.

"The House All Burnt": Disintegrating Domesticity in Ray Bradbury's *Fahrenheit 451* _____

Andrea Krafft

At first glance, Ray Bradbury's *Fahrenheit 451* (1953) is primarily concerned with the dangers of totalitarian censorship and the encroachment of mass culture that occurred during the post-World War II era. Bradbury himself stated in a 1964 interview with *Show* that his novel functions as "a direct attack on the kind of thought-destroying force" that emerged under the leadership of Senator Joseph McCarthy ("Portrait" 19). Within *Fahrenheit 451*, such anti-intellectual threats not only stem from the State apparatus but also develop as a result of the mind-numbing entertainment technologies that ensure the continuance of the status quo. Bradbury's critical views of technology and mechanization are well-known, though often misunderstood, but "he has no simplistic anti-machine phobia" (McNelly 18). He does not demonize technology as a whole, but instead, to paraphrase Marvin E. Mengeling, critiques machines and ideologies that weaken familial and communal bonds (86). The novel accordingly traces Guy Montag's recognition of how the mechanics of mass culture pervert the domestic sphere, resulting in both the failed fraternity of the firemen and the protagonist's emotionally empty marriage. *Fahrenheit 451* ultimately signals Bradbury's yearning for a nostalgic vision of domesticity that is disintegrating within modernity, as he calls for a return to the values of the extended family found in his idealistic vision of small-town America.

The firemen who police the dystopian society of *Fahrenheit 451* visibly oppose domestic security, as they literally burn down their surrounding community rather than protect it from external threats. As David Mogen argues, the author ironically inverts "the heroic image of the community firehouse" (). The firemen thus embody the uncritical consumption of the flames rather than the expected extinguishing properties of water. Worse still, they actively enjoy their destructive power, such as how Montag takes "a

---

special pleasure...to see things blackened and *changed*" (Bradbury, *Fahrenheit* 1; emphasis Bradbury's), an impulse that Donald Watt views as quintessentially "sado-masochistic" (195). Within the world of the novel, however, the firemen do not view themselves as pyromaniacs, but as performers who, in the words of Faber, "provide a circus now and then" (Bradbury, *Fahrenheit* 83). They present burning as "a comic ritual" (Eller and Touponce 188), requiring that they adopt the "fierce grin of all men singed and driven by flame" (Bradbury, *Fahrenheit* 2). Yet the firemen's clownish attitude only further emphasizes the viciousness of their actions, as their laughter while burning down a woman's house, with her inside, appears particularly cruel in the face of her suffering. They do not ensure domestic happiness, but instead tyrannically force their will upon both the community and the individual, as Montag begins to feel that "the fiery smile still gripped by his face muscles...never went away" (Bradbury, *Fahrenheit* 2).

Although Montag becomes conscious of the discomfort resulting from the constant performance of "happiness," Captain Beatty insists upon the firemen's central function as defenders of communal stability. He touts that they are "the Happiness Boys," protecting humanity from "conflicting theory and thought," thus preserving the delicate balance of a culture of mass simplification (Bradbury, *Fahrenheit* 59). This "paste pudding norm" is not, as Beatty would claim, a great equalizer (Bradbury, *Fahrenheit* 51), but rather a "kind of narcosis" that dulls the public's awareness of the more pressing domestic threat of nuclear war (Seed 80). Distracted by the firemen's showy exploits and the colorful displays of the parlor walls, many of the characters in the novel appear oblivious to the presence of bombers and jets that fly overhead (perhaps explaining the suddenness of their later annihilation). However, the noise of imminent warfare begins to crack through Montag's own shellacked happiness, breaking him apart with "a tremendous ripping sound" and standing in for his own existential scream (Bradbury, *Fahrenheit* 11). In acknowledging the war that Beatty attempts to candy-coat, Montag begins to step away from the tyranny of happiness and recognizes that he must begin to listen and communicate in order to have a chance at recovering a healthy understanding of his surroundings.

However, Montag's world denies his desire to reclaim domestic stability, as he repeatedly encounters widespread patterns of self-destructive and nihilistic behavior. The most notable practitioners of this cultural death wish in the novel are those individuals who race cars and actively run down both animals and people on their morbid joy rides. Children especially delight in this vicious form of entertainment, as Guy Montag encounters "a carful of children, all ages," who attempt to kill him without provocation (Bradbury, *Fahrenheit* 122). If, as Lee Edelman claims, the child is "the emblem of futurity's unquestioned value" (4), then the murderous progeny of *Fahrenheit 451* speak to the decay of both familial and national longevity. Unsurprisingly, the firemen, as products of this grotesque upbringing, become cold and mechanized rather than emotionally united. The firehouse itself represents their lack of brotherly bonds, as it is "full of glitter and shine and silence," the "cold" space of disconnected automatons (Bradbury, *Fahrenheit* 30). Moreover, Captain Beatty, with his resolute command to "burn all, burn everything" (Bradbury, *Fahrenheit* 57), functions as the sociopathic father of this failed home, a figurehead whom Montag must eventually dismantle.

Just as the firehouse represents an inaccessible fraternity and a warped community, Guy and Mildred Montag's marital home, haunted by noisy gadgetry, signals the absence of romantic partnership. When Montag first enters his home, he envisions it as "a mausoleum" and "a tomb-world" occupied by his catatonic wife (Bradbury, *Fahrenheit* 9). Mildred, more machine than woman, becomes a commodified robot who plugs into her Seashells, shutting out the possibility of communication with her husband. Mildred personifies "just about every form of self-narcotization available in this society" (Eller and Touponce 188), replacing human contact with technological analogues. Montag appropriately associates her miniature radios with aggressive insects, which, "mosquito-delicate" (Bradbury, *Fahrenheit* 9), vampirically drain away the possibilities of domestic happiness. The absence of children from their home and their apparent withdrawal from sexuality further emphasize the emotional emptiness of their marriage. Guy's "open, separate, and therefore cold bed" (Bradbury, *Fahrenheit* 10) fuels his dissatisfaction with his life as a fireman, as he searches for the warm hearth that he lacks at home. Guy and Mildred, rather than offering solace to one another in the face of a totalitarian society, are virtual strangers, reduced to anonymous "street face[s]" and "newspaper image[s]" (Bradbury, *Fahrenheit* 41).

Indeed, Mildred sees little difference between her husband and the simulated warmth of the televised "family," frequently preferring her parlor wall's laughter and garish displays over his company. She insists that "my 'family' is people" (sic.; Bradbury, *Fahrenheit* 69), yet can explain neither the content of her programs nor the personalities of the characters that she obsessively watches. Her main interest as a viewer lies in the seemingly participatory nature of the "family," as the show provides her with a script and her parlor walls utilize a "converter attachment" and "special spot-wavex-scrambler" that offer the illusion of a relationship with the announcer (Bradbury, *Fahrenheit* 61). As William F. Touponce notes, Mildred participates in the "pathological narcissism" of mass culture (95) because it offers an escape into "that favorite subject, Myself" (Bradbury, *Fahrenheit* 68). Anticipating the critical perspective of Vance Packard's *The Hidden Persuaders*, a 1957 exposé of advertising culture, Bradbury makes clear the "anti-humanistic implications" of how the media manipulates the "secret miseries and self-doubts" of its consumers (Packard 57). Mildred not only becomes an echo of her television, but also begins to treat Guy as only another channel, looking "at him as if he were behind the glass wall" and referring to his voice as "junk" (Bradbury, *Fahrenheit* 62).

The Montags' marriage is not alone as an example of crumbling domesticity, as Mildred's friends, Mrs. Bowles and Mrs. Phelps, similarly embrace the culture of visual entertainment at the cost of their personal relationships. Bradbury again points to the child as a signal of failing family bonds, as Mrs. Bowles views motherhood as a chore on the same level as "washing clothes" (Bradbury, *Fahrenheit* 93). Rather than spending time with her children, she leaves them to the care of the television screen and jokes about the fact that "they'd just as soon kick as kiss me" (Bradbury, *Fahrenheit* 93). Mildred and her friends ignore such concerns about their failing families by consuming mass-produced violence, watching the cartoon White Clowns killing one another and staring at car crashes. They become dependent on these distractions, without which they would only fixate on the problems that surround them. For example, Mrs. Phelps quickly becomes anxious about her husband's role in the war when Montag turns off the parlor walls, as she obsessively repeats that she's "not worried" and giggles (Bradbury, *Fahrenheit* 91). Similarly to the firemen, with their insistence on happiness, these women plaster on "Cheshire cat smiles" (Bradbury, *Fahrenheit* 89) because they need to bury the dark reality of impending destruction. Moreover, the structure of suburbia seems to worsen their mortal anxiety. Mildred and her friends, "isolated in a world of other mothers" (Halberstam 143) and with no evident extended family structures, necessarily turn inward. Bradbury thus reflects emergent concerns during the 1950s regarding the dangers of suburban alienation, which arguably led to the "rise in the consumption of the new tranquilizer drugs such as Miltown and Thorazine" (Miller and Nowak 138).

While Guy Montag eventually breaks away from emotionally empty domesticity, Mildred demonstrates the dangers of clinging to the structures of suburbia and technological obsession. Mildred enters the novel already on the brink of death, after taking a bottle of sleeping pills. Though he does not explore her mental instability at length, Guy observes that Mildred's unhappiness stems from an internal division between her public persona and "another Mildred...deep inside this one" who is "really bothered" (Bradbury, *Fahrenheit* 49). Despite the fact that he also suffers from a similar internal division, between "two halves grinding one upon the other" (Bradbury, *Fahrenheit* 21), he seems to be desperately unable to save his wife from her suffering. Likewise, the community offers no support for Mildred's problem beyond two suicide "handymen" whose key motivation stems from a fifty dollar service fee (Bradbury, *Fahrenheit* 13). To these men, Mildred becomes an appliance to repair: They can see the problem through the "Eye" of a mechanical snake, yet they are blind to her greater distress (Bradbury, *Fahrenheit* 12). However, as Guy Montag mourns, the problem is not that they are "fused to…contraptions" (Bradbury, "Portrait" 30), but rather that "nobody knows anyone" in their society (Bradbury, *Fahrenheit* 14). The handymen "get these cases nine or ten [times] a night" (Bradbury, *Fahrenheit* 13) because, like Mildred and Guy, the majority of the people in the novel are living in a world of strangers, searching for support from the wrong "family."

Clarisse McClellan, though labeled as mentally ill and "antisocial" by the psychiatric establishment (Bradbury, *Fahrenheit* 26), represents an alternative model of domesticity that breaks away from the self-destructive and alienating tendencies of mainstream culture in *Fahrenheit 451*. The Montags' young neighbor rejects nihilistic sources of entertainment, instead delighting in nature and absorbing lessons about "a long time ago" from her uncle (Bradbury, *Fahrenheit* 27). Bradbury captures Clarisse's unique blend of nature and nostalgia when he contrasts the "soft and constant light" of her face with "the hysterical light of electricity" (Bradbury, *Fahrenheit* 5). Unlike the harsh technology of the parlor walls that deaden the senses, Clarisse elicits in Montag a hazy childhood memory of lighting a candle with his mother during "a power failure" (Bradbury, *Fahrenheit* 5). William F. Touponce aptly describes Montag's nostalgia as "a utopian…reverie" (91), as Clarisse wakens his dormant knowledge of domestic comfort. Furthermore, Bradbury links this memory of the home to, in the words of Rafeeq O. McGiveron, "very positive, lyrical nature imagery" (121), implying that the domestic situation of Montag's present is artificial and degrading. Under the light of Clarisse's gently illuminating face, Montag realizes that his fireman's smile is a fragile construct that barely covers the fact of his unhappiness.

The McClellans' house, associated with warmth and the lost art of conversation, similarly makes Montag conscious of the coldness and funereal aspects of his own home. Yet the McClellan family is not starkly anti-technological: the contrast here is not, as Wayne Johnson suggests, between "the dangerous mechanical world of the city" and "the traditional haven of the country" (87). Instead, they harness the power of electricity to facilitate their unity rather than to fuel the meaningless noise of mass entertainment, as their house is "blazing" with lights rather than with destructive fire (Bradbury, *Fahrenheit* 7). The McClellan home, "brightly lit," pulls Montag away from his suicidal wife and into its "hypnotic web" of conversation (Bradbury, *Fahrenheit* 14). Furthermore, the McClellans' "laughter was relaxed and hearty and not forced in any way," further marking their distance from the pained grimaces of the firemen and the murderous humor of the White Clowns. As a result of his brief interactions with Clarisse, Montag's own "laugh sounds much nicer than it did" (Bradbury, *Fahrenheit* 26), indicating his shift away from the artificial nature of his profession. In the process of re-educating Montag, Clarisse turns him back to long-forgotten models of the home. He even yearns for the architecture of small-town America, as he compares the "flat fronts" of the suburban houses with the lost "front porches" that formerly enabled people to talk comfortably (Bradbury, *Fahrenheit* 60). Though Clarisse ultimately becomes a victim of her generation's violence, she serves, in both David Seed and Donald Watt's term, as a catalyst that transforms Montag's view of domestic health (Seed 82; Watt 197).

Moreover, Clarisse's influence spurs Montag's interest in reading, which he explores not as an act of political defiance but because he believes it holds the secret of communal renewal. After her death, he finally retrieves his books from their hiding place because, as he explains to his wife, "their words point, one way or another to Clarisse" (Bradbury, *Fahrenheit* 68). The act of reading is only a means to an end for Montag. In Faber's words, "it's not books you need, it's some of the things that once were in books" (Bradbury, *Fahrenheit* 78). For Bradbury, books "are indifferent," as, like any other piece of technology—thinking of technology broadly construed as a manmade tool or object—they "do not 'know' but they can teach us humanism" (Bradbury, "Interview" 113). Montag treats reading as essentially a pathway back to the long-forgotten habit of conversation, since "nobody listens any more" (Bradbury, *Fahrenheit* 78). Notably, he attempts to include his wife in this act of domestic revival, believing that they might steer their marriage away from "the cliff" if they are "in this together" (Bradbury, *Fahrenheit* 63). Reading in *Fahrenheit 451* is never a solitary act, but one that unites the family and the community into a tradition of oral storytelling and mutual participation.

However, Bradbury emphasizes that the formation of domestic bonds around the act of reading requires willing participants, lest this new community simply form a new kind of totalitarian system that subjugates individual willpower. Mildred and her friends, for example, recognize that reading can crack their façade of happiness, yet they prefer to "laugh and be happy" rather than join him (Bradbury, *Fahrenheit* 97). Though their rejection of Montag ultimately condemns them to destruction, this option still is preferable to having books imposed on them, which would close off their only available act of defiance. Furthermore, Mildred's rejection provides Montag with a clean break from their failed marriage, as she and her friends turn him over to Beatty and the firemen. Burning his house at Beatty's command, he views the fire not as a punishment, but as a kind of ritual cleansing, practicing again "the purging power of the fireman" (Watt 207). He targets "everything that showed that he had lived here in this strange house with a strange woman," burning their twin beds and the parlor walls (Bradbury, *Fahrenheit* 110). Fire in this case is not a technology of State control, but an indiscriminate tool that transforms into a source of natural beauty, "one huge bright yellow flower of burning" (Bradbury, *Fahrenheit* 111).

Even Montag's killing of Beatty functions as an apparent act of purification, as the patricide of his ersatz father marks his ultimate departure from the firehouse and its failed community. The language of the novel does not see this act as dehumanizing, as Beatty, with his "phosphorescent cheeks...smiling furiously," embodies the insistent happiness of mass culture (Bradbury, *Fahrenheit* 106). He is not a fully developed person in the eyes of the narrative, but rather functions as a "personification of that authority" (Seed 83) that stands in the way of domestic health. The narrator does not mourn for Beatty's death, but instead describes him as "a jumping, sprawling, gibbering manikin, no longer human or known, all writhing flame" (Bradbury, *Fahrenheit* 113). Engulfed in flames, Beatty's human shell falls away to reveal what he always has been: an empty automaton of the system, "a charred wax doll" who fails to provide meaning (Bradbury, *Fahrenheit* 113). Furthermore, Beatty's death marks the culmination of his own nihilism, as Montag realizes that "Beatty had wanted to die," as he never tried "to save himself" (Bradbury, *Fahrenheit* 116). Beatty's downfall is that he never casts off his "fixed smile," loyal to the tyranny of happiness no matter the personal cost (Bradbury, *Fahrenheit* 113). Always the joker, he leaves the novel as he entered it, taunting Montag and grinning.

With his "house all burnt" and unable to return to mainstream society after killing Beatty, Montag necessarily flees from the city, finding shelter in the surrounding countryside (Bradbury, *Fahrenheit* 125). While Rafeeq O. McGiveron, Wayne Johnson, and Donald Watt all have noted Bradbury's privileging of nature as a site of renewal, Montag does not enter the romanticized wilderness so much as the manmade space of agriculture. Floating down the river, washed clean of the blackened grime of the firemen, he praises the pastoral scene, delighting in the herds of cows, pigs and "white sheep on a hill" (Bradbury, *Fahrenheit* 135). More importantly, he associates these farms with a nostalgic and sentimentalized view of domesticity, fantasizing about sleeping in the loft of a barn "until a very young and beautiful woman"—clearly a reincarnated Clarisse McClellan—would wake him with a plate of fruit and "a cool glass of fresh milk" (Bradbury, *Fahrenheit* 136). Montag goes on to associate the farmlands with the olfactory experience of the kitchen, imagining how the land smells "like a cut potato" while the air carries the odors of "pickles from a bottle" and "mustard from a jar" (Bradbury, *Fahrenheit* 137-38). Despite the material difficulties that Granger and the book people face as exiles from mainstream society, they carry with them all the comforts of home and recall an "appeal to the past" (Seed 87).

Similarly to the McClellan household, the book people embrace the power of light and fire, transforming it into something that is "not burning," but *"warming"* (emphasis Bradbury's; *Fahrenheit* 139). Bradbury does not, as John Huntington suggests, set up a dichotomy between "controllable" nature and "predatory" technology (137), but rather aligns the book people with humanizing tools. They still watch television, after all, but do so for the purposes of acquiring information rather than for dull entertainment. Furthermore, they live alongside the railroad track, trains being a set of machines that Bradbury has persistently praised "for keeping us in touch with humane ideas and a democratic past" (Mengeling 91). Beyond their associations with positive technologies, the book people focus on conversation, that all-important center of domestic life. Though they claim to subjugate their personalities for the sake of memorizing books, they still virtuosically produce conversations so that "there was nothing they could not talk about" (Bradbury, *Fahrenheit* 140). Inside jokes serve an important role in their conversations, as they "all laughed quietly" at the new meaning of the cliché not to "judge a book by its cover" (Bradbury, *Fahrenheit* 148). Contrasting with the noisy laughter of the firemen and Mildred Montag, who employ comedy as a distraction, the book people turn to humor to "constitute a new kind of folk culture" (Eller and Touponce 166). Bound together in their shared value of books, they affirm a new vision of the family, the main task of which is to "pass the books on to our children" (Bradbury, *Fahrenheit* 146). They reject the violent lessons of mainstream culture and embrace a vision of the future based on a sense of tradition and togetherness.

However, the book people's vision of domestic renewal cannot occur without the destruction of the old system. As occurs at the end of *The Martian Chronicles* (1950), the insufficient "way of life is…burned clean" (Bradbury, "Picnic" 267), just as the bombing of the city in *Fahrenheit 451* wipes it out almost instantaneously. The destruction here is not all-encompassing, but rather functions as a kind of slash-and-burn technique, creating space for the cultivation of new domestic forms. Just as "The Million-Year Picnic," the final section of *The Martian Chronicles*, features the exodus of family rockets to colonize Mars, *Fahrenheit 451* concludes with what Kevin Hoskinson calls the "notion of recivilization." Granger, whose name connects him with traditions of agricultural growth (Seed 87), mourns the destructive patterns of humanity, yet encourages a need to rebuild society while "remembering" past mistakes (Bradbury, *Fahrenheit* 157). Thus, Montag does not abandon his memories of Mildred as he enters the society of the book people, but mourns her loss, remembering their first meeting as she dies in the annihilated city. He carries with him not only a new community but also a sentimental memory of his marriage, embracing a nostalgic view of domesticity that might aid in "the healing of the nations" (Bradbury, *Fahrenheit* 158). Ultimately, the hope for domestic renewal in *Fahrenheit 451* lies not in the withdrawal from mass culture and technology, but in the movement toward reform. Montag and the book people trudge back toward the city, bringing with them not only their historical and literary consciousness but also, and more importantly, a sense of communal unity.

Writing during a period marked by the spread of electricity and entertainment technologies, Bradbury explores the issue of disintegrating domesticity beyond *Fahrenheit 451*, in both his short fiction and his homage to small-town America, *Dandelion Wine* (1957). While Jonathan R. Eller notes that countless Bradbury stories examine marital conflict (176), "Marionettes, Inc." (1949) and "Punishment Without Crime" (1950) in particular illustrate the author's overarching concern with how supposedly convenient inventions might dislocate romantic bonds. In "Marionettes, Inc.," the promising technology of humanoid robots comes between husbands and wives, not only because they utilize the technology to abandon their spouses but also as a result of the malicious agency of the robots themselves. "Punishment Without Crime" similarly considers the slippage between the robot and the human, as George Hill "murders" a copy of his estranged wife, Katie. Although Bradbury acknowledges that the robot mannequins might offer a kind of safety valve for the expression of domestic violence, his narratives of robotic replacement suggest that technology tends to disrupt rather than unite the family.

"The Veldt" (1950) is undoubtedly Bradbury's most famous story about how technology can shatter domestic security. Wendy and Peter Hadley take Mildred Montag's obsession with the parlor walls a step further, as they choose to murder their parents, George and Lydia, rather than shut off their glittering technological nursery. Just as the children in *Fahrenheit 451* enjoy running down pedestrians, the Hadley children embrace violence and view the savage lions as entertaining spectacles. While the influence of technology is partially to blame for the dangerous youths in both the novel and this short story, "The Veldt" more clearly points out how "the lack of parental responsibility" contributed to the Hadleys' deaths (Mengeling 93). Lydia and George Hadley passively allow their mechanical home to replace them as caretakers, up to the point where they become obsolete. As the psychologist David McClean belatedly points out to George Hadley, "You've let this room and this house replace you and your wife in your children's affections" (Bradbury, "Veldt" 24). Although "The Veldt" ends with the ultimate destruction of the nuclear family, the story conveys Bradbury's abiding investment in a model of domesticity that combines responsibly used technology and familial affection.

Unlike his short stories that feature domesticity destroyed by the impact of technology, *Dandelion Wine*, a sentimental chronicle of small-town life, is the culmination of his vision of the extended family that begins with Clarisse McClellan. In his introduction to the sixtieth anniversary edition of *Fahrenheit 451*, Neil Gaiman argues that Bradbury's vision of dystopia ultimately serves as "a love letter to the world of Waukegan, Illinois…which he immortalized as Green Town in his book of childhood, *Dandelion Wine*" (xvi). David Mogen similarly observes the intimate connection between the two novels, as the raw materials of domestic health at the end of *Fahrenheit 451* ferment within the stories of Douglas Spaulding's glorious summer. The eponymous image of the dandelion marks the transformation from domestic dystopia to utopia between the novels. While the dandelion is a solitary plant in *Fahrenheit 451*, appearing briefly in Clarisse's hands, it crowds the fields of Green Town. Furthermore, Douglas describes the field of dandelions as "molten

Critical Insights

sun," transmuting the image of destructive fire into a life-sustaining force of nature (Bradbury, *Dandelion* 12). Likewise, the evolution of technology between the two novels indicates Bradbury's privileging of domestic tranquility. While the parlor walls and Seashells fail to resolve the crisis of modern alienation, Leo Auffmann in *Dandelion Wine* teaches Douglas and his grandfather about "the *real* Happiness Machine" (emphasis Bradbury's; 63). Although he successfully builds a machine that could simulate happiness, Leo allows this narcotizing invention to burn away. Instead, he indicates that his children and wife are a successful mechanism that "patented a couple thousand years ago…still runs" (Bradbury, *Dandelion* 62).

This notion of the family as a happiness machine recurs throughout Bradbury's oeuvre, as he elevates an ideal of the home that refuses the senseless distractions of entertainment in favor of a community bound by conversation. Bradbury's repeated decision to resurrect Clarisse McClellan in the stage and musical adaptations of the novel further indicates his deep investment in the domestic promises that she represents. As he told Jason J. Marchi in a 1999 interview for *Hollywood Scriptwriter*, "she was too good a character to lose" (178), despite the fact that her death fueled Montag's nostalgic search for affectionate bonds. Within *Fahrenheit 451*, the mechanism of domesticity initially appears to be broken and in need of repair. Although he does not recover his relationship with Mildred, Guy Montag discovers a replacement family among the book people, as the community of readers becomes an extension of the logic of domesticity.

Works Cited

Aggelis, Stephen L., ed. *Conversations with Ray Bradbury.* Jackson: UP of Mississippi, 2004.

Bloom, Harold, ed. *Modern Critical Interpretations: Ray Bradbury's* Fahrenheit 451. Philadelphia: Chelsea, 2001.

Bradbury, Ray. *Dandelion Wine.* 1957. New York: Bantam, 1976.

_____. *Fahrenheit 451.* 1953. Intro. Neil Gaiman. New York: Simon, 2013.

_____. "An Interview with Master Storyteller Ray Bradbury." 1999. Aggelis 175-183.

_____. "Marionettes, Inc." 1949. *The Illustrated Man*. 1951. New York: Perennial-Harper, 2011. 211-19.

_____. "The Million-Year Picnic." *The Martian Chronicles*. 1950. New York: Perennial-Harper, 2011. 256-68.

_____. "A Portrait of Genius: Ray Bradbury." 1964. Aggelis 17-30.

_____. "Punishment Without Crime." 1950. *I Sing the Body Electric, and Other Stories*. New York: Perennial-Harper, 2001. 288-96.

_____. "Ray Bradbury: An Interview." 1982. Aggelis 112-21.

_____. "The Veldt." 1950. *The Vintage Bradbury*. New York: Vintage-Random, 1990. 13-28.

Edelman, Lee. *No Future: Queer Theory and the Death Drive*. Duke: Duke UP, 2004. Print.

Eller, Jonathan R. *Becoming Ray Bradbury*. Urbana: U of Illinois P, 2011.

Eller, Jonathan R., and William F. Touponce. *Ray Bradbury: The Life of Fiction*. Kent: Kent State UP, 2004.

Greenberg, Martin Harry, and Joseph D. Olander, eds. *Ray Bradbury*. New York: Taplinger, 1980.

Halberstam, David. *The Fifties*. New York: Villard, 1993.

Hoskinson, Kevin. "*The Martian Chronicles* and *Fahrenheit 451*: Ray Bradbury's Cold War Novels." *Extrapolation* 36 (1995): 345+. *Academic OneFile*. Web. 17 Aug. 2013.

Huntington, John. "Utopian and Anti-Utopian Logic: H.G. Wells and His Successors." *Science*

Fiction Studies 9 (1982): 122-146. *JSTOR*. Web. 17 Sep. 2013.

Johnson, Wayne L. *Ray Bradbury*. New York: Ungar, 1980.

McGiveron, Rafeeq O. "'Do You Know the Legend of Hercules and Antaeus?': The Wilderness in Ray Bradbury's *Fahrenheit 451*." *Ray Bradbury's Fahrenheit 451*. Ed. Harold Bloom. New York: Chelsea House Publications, 2001. 121-128. Bloom's Modern Critical Interpretations Ser.

McNelly, Willis E. "Ray Bradbury— Past, Present and Future." Greenberg and Olander 17-24.

Mengeling, Marvin E. "The Machineries of Joy and Despair: Bradbury's Attitudes Toward Science and Technology." *Ray Bradbury*. Eds. Martin Harry Greenberg and Joseph D. Olander. New York: Taplinger, 1980. 83-109.

Miller, Douglas T. and Marion Nowak. *The Fifties: The Way We Really Were*. Garden City: Doubleday, 1977.

Mogen, David. *Ray Bradbury*. 504. Boston: Twayne, 1986. N. pag. *Literature Resource Center*. Web. 17 Aug. 2013. Twayne's U.S. Authors Ser.

Packard, Vance. *The Hidden Persuaders*. New York: McKay, 1957.

Seed, David. "The Flight from the Good Life: *Fahrenheit 451* in the Context of Postwar American Dystopia." Bloom 75-88.

Toupence, William F. *Ray Bradbury and the Poetics of Reverie: Fantasy, Science Fiction, and the Reader*. Ann Arbor: UMI, 1981.

Watt, Donald. "Burning Bright: *Fahrenheit 451* as Symbolic Dystopia." *Ray Bradbury*. Eds. Martin Harry Greenberg and Joseph D. Olander. New York: Taplinger, 1980. 195-213.

"Where Ignorant Armies Clash by Night": Love, War, and the Women of *Fahrenheit 451* _____

Timothy E. Kelley

It is easy to read the women in *Fahrenheit 451* as stock, one-dimensional characters, set up only to illustrate the opposite poles between which Montag struggles. Donald Watt correctly points out that, while Faber and Beatty present the intellectual arguments for the two positions, Clarisse and Mildred live those positions (197). Dismissing the women in *Fahrenheit 451* as just one-dimensional representations of the sides of an intellectual conflict, however, misses the important role they play in advancing not only the plot but a basic philosophical argument about the nature of human love and happiness. "The good writers touch life often," Faber tells us (83). And it is in the characters of Montag and the women that Bradbury most often touches life. In the relationships with these women, we see his search for happiness and love in his own life turn into a battle against the government of a society, in which love and happiness are impossible.

"Are You Happy?"

Kathryn M. Grossman describes Clarisse as a "benevolent femme fatale" who both allures Montag and awakens him to the realities of their dystopian society. "Instead of merely seducing the male protagonist out of his earthly paradise," says Grossman, this new archetype of the dystopian temptress "charms him into seeing it in a new manner. In other words, she does not just enchant him; she also disenchants him, for it is through her that he comes to know his world for what it really is—an inhuman monstrosity" (135). Although the thought of Clarisse seducing Montag might be a bit of a stretch, she does "charm him into seeing" his world differently, she does enchant him, and she does at least contribute to his disenchantment. Their relationship might be as hard for the reader to pin down as it is for Montag, but she is unquestionably the greatest influence on his development. Beyond simply awakening him to the "inhuman monstrosity" of his America, she awakens him to himself and shows him how to become human again.

The women in the novel do, as Watt suggests, live the theories of Faber and Beatty. In "The Sieve and the Sand," Faber lays out his three-part process for changing the path of their society: we need "quality of information," "leisure to digest it," and "the right to carry out actions based on what we have learned from the interaction of the first two" (84-85). Before Montag can begin to recognize his connection to others and to his inhuman society, however, he needs to reconnect with himself, to reestablish his relationship with the world. Clarisse, in their first two meetings, lives Faber's formula, showing Montag how the plan works on an individual level.

In their first two meetings, Bradbury carefully uses Clarisse to establish the role of sensory experience and memory, the primary source of all quality information and the tool we need to begin processing that information. Montag leaves the fire station with an unconscious confidence and grace, whistling his way home while "thinking little at all about nothing in particular" (4). But when he reaches that corner, everything changes. He becomes suddenly engaged with his own sensory experience. As Clarisse appears before him, white, floating almost ethereally, he is recognizing his own sensations. This is her influence. As he looks at her face for the first time, he recognizes immediately that "gentle hunger," that "tireless curiosity," and though he finds her unsettling, those qualities already are beginning to encroach on his mindless, whistling complacency (5). Bradbury, in this first meeting of the two, significantly weaves in detail about sight, scent, and hearing, and in their second encounter, he adds taste when Clarisse drinks in a few drops of rain (21) and touch when she rubs the dandelion on his chin and then touches his arm to comfort him when he becomes upset (22). Through her curiosity and active engagement of her senses, Montag is being reintroduced to his own. He is learning, or relearning, that information is all around him if he just allows himself to be aware. Even Faber will tell him later that books are not the only source of quality information. Look for it "in old friends," he says; "look for it in nature and look for it in yourself" (82).

Bradbury also uses Clarisse to introduce memory as the essential secondary element necessary for processing sensory experience. In order to put observations about our sensory experience together, we must have memories against which to juxtapose those observations. Memory is as important as empirical observation in gaining quality of information. Memory provides the texture. Beyond paying little active attention to sensory experience for some time, Montag has failed to commit even the simplest of observations of that experience to memory. He cannot remember if he ever knew about the dew on the grass (9), for example. When Clarisse asks him later if he had looked at the giant billboards, he says, "I think so. Yes" (29), either having a hard time remembering or guessing because he cannot remember at all. He has been content behind that smile, content for too long to have all other memory blocked out by the flame that feeds the smile.

Montag is not, however, without any memory, even in the first scene with Clarisse. Looking into her eyes for the first time rekindles a memory from his childhood, when his mother lit a candle during a power outage and "there had been a brief hour of rediscovery, of such illumination that space lost its vast dimension and grew comfortably around them, and they, mother and son, alone, transformed, hoping that the power might not come on again too soon" (7). The description of this memory seems almost out of place, and it is dropped abruptly when Clarisse cuts him off with a question. However, the recollection is important in establishing not only that Montag has some memory against which to juxtapose the information she is awakening within him, but also that he has the memory of a loving bond to another human being and that he remembers a comfort in the company of that other person powerful enough to shrink the vast dimension of space.

Just as Clarisse reintroduces him to the power of his own observation and memory to provide quality information, she introduces him to the second and third phases of Faber's formula long before we meet Faber. Montag is fascinated by the idea of a house with all the lights on at night, a house in which people actually sit and talk. Clarisse does not spend her time in front of the "parlor walls" or engage in the frivolous and mind-numbing activities pushed on the majority in this society. Her family has created "leisure to digest" the information. She has "time for crazy thoughts" (9). Yet those thoughts do not come without a price. Through her, Montag and the reader also get a glimpse of the obstacles to Faber's third element. Acting on the results of observation and thought create problems for the individual. Her uncle has been arrested twice, once for being a pedestrian and again for driving slowly enough to actually see what he was passing. She is forced into regular visits with a psychiatrist, and the entire family, Montag will find out later, is under Beatty's scrutiny.

At the end of their first encounter, Clarisse sets up a search for his own happiness that gradually will become his struggle for the freedom and happiness of his dystopian society when she leaves him with that annoying question: "Are you happy?" (10). Although Montag's initial response is to laugh the question off, it takes him just a moment, after opening the bedroom door to enter the "mausoleum" he shares with his wife, to realize that he is not happy (11). That smile that allowed him to whistle his way complacently home from the firehouse had been just a mask, "and the girl had run off across the lawn with the mask" (12). When Clarisse first awakens him from the sleep-like state, in which he has existed behind that smile, the "gentle hunger" and "tireless curiosity" he sees in her face arouse his suspicion that there has been something missing in his life (5). Burning has been a pleasure that fed the smile only "as long as he remembered" (4), and now, in one short encounter, she has managed to make him forget for long enough to steal it away from him. Now he is forced to question whether there was any real happiness behind the pleasure of burning.

The difference between pleasure and happiness is central to the book and to the problems of its dystopian society, and although Beatty artfully avoids addressing the difference by blurring the two in his sickroom lecture to Montag, it is in this lecture that we see the distinction most clearly. "People want to be happy," Beatty tells him. "Well, aren't they? Don't we keep them moving? Don't we give them fun?" (59). In a sort of verbal sleight of hand, he reduces happiness to fun, to "pleasure" and "titillation," and Montag, not yet ready to recognize the distinction, lets the trick pass, allowing Beatty to make yet another shift. In accepting the idea that fun is synonymous with happiness, he accepts the Fire Chief's assumption that the mindless masses are indeed happy, and the remainder of the lecture defends the firemen, the "Happiness Boys," not as protectors of happiness, but as protectors against unhappiness. The books they burn, the meaningful thought against which they fight, threaten the mindless complacency that allows people go on believing they are happy. Clarisse is a threat because she is inquisitive. "You ask why to a lot of things," says Beatty, "and you end up very unhappy indeed" (60). The books are a threat for much the same reason. People need to be left to their pleasure, they need to be fed "noncombustible data," they need to be entertained and kept busy (61). Books raise questions, questions that often cannot be answered. "You come away lost," Beatty concludes (62). If people are happy, leave them alone. The "Happiness Boys" merely defend them from any thought that might encroach on their pleasure.

Although Montag has not yet recognized the problem with this reduction of happiness to a step below hedonism, a kind of vicarious hedonism, in which even sensation is often artificially provided, Beatty seems aware of it. There is hint of disdain in his words when he talks about the minorities who led the gradual decline of thought and a hint of sarcasm when he says, "if the play is hollow, sting me with the theremin, loudly. I'll think I'm responding to the play, when it's only a tactile reaction to vibration. But I don't care" (61). He recognizes Mildred for the fool she is, acknowledging her only to command her to "[s]hut the 'relatives' up" (53), and to suggest that she might know the title of *Hamlet* only as "faint rumor" (55). Defending the complacency of the billions is certainly in the interest of the unseen government paying the Fire Chief, but he seems to be playing a game, and he sees nothing worth defending in the mindless billions. He knows that the "happiness" they enjoy is empty and meaningless.

Although he has still not consciously acknowledged this distinction, Montag has been struggling with it. "He's right," he tells Mildred after Beatty leaves. "Happiness is important. Fun is everything. And yet I kept sitting there saying to myself, I'm not happy, I'm not happy" (65). He is still here at the level of "I," trying to understand why others can be happy while he cannot. But he knows, at some level, that he is not alone in his unhappiness. Guy knows that despite her response that she *is* happy, there is somewhere inside her another Millie—the Millie of the sleeping tablets and the high speed car rides, during which she takes pleasure in running over rabbits and dogs—a deeply unhappy person. She is not happy. No one in this society is happy. The entire culture suffers from this buried unhappiness, split between hours of self-indulgence and moments of vicious despair, vented in beating one another and making sport of running people down on the highway. School children murder one another, people are jumping off buildings, and the stomach-pumping "handymen" are even busier than the firemen. Trying to avoid unhappiness has not worked. Trying to achieve happiness through indulging themselves with pleasures has not worked. No, he is not happy. None of them are.

"What a Shame. You're Not in Love with Anyone."

When Clarisse tells him this after rubbing that dandelion under his chin, Montag's protest sounds almost like that of a little boy offended on a playground. "Yes I am!" he exclaims. "You've used it all up on yourself. That's why it won't work for me" (22). He wants to believe he is in love, yet he is unable to come up with the face of a lover to support his claim, and the accusation haunts him. That evening at the firehouse, when Captain Beatty tells him the Mechanical Hound thinks nothing but what it has been taught to think, Montag responds with Clarisse's words: "What a shame" (27). He recognizes the similarity of this mechanical creature's mentality to his own. If he cannot love, he is no better than this live but lifeless creation. He thinks only what he has been taught to think. He wants to believe he loves Millie, but we have already witnessed evidence of their loveless existence together. They sleep in separate beds, and Millie has rendered herself near-comatose with the sleeping tablets every night for the past two years. There is no romantic love here, and Bradbury's dark imagery of the cold "mausoleum" and Millie's body lying there as if "displayed on the lid of a tomb" confirm that the marriage has offered Guy no warmth or comfort for a long time (12).

Yet Montag is not without feelings for the woman who lies there, and when he realizes that Mildred is near death from an overdose of sleeping pills, he goes into a panic, a panic purposefully mirrored by the first appearance of the jet bombers ripping through the sky tearing "ten thousand miles of black line[n][1] down the seam" (13). While we might read this as just a symbolic representation of the rift Montag has begun to feel in himself and the line separating the living world of Clarisse from the death-like trance in which Millie lives, we should not be too quick to dismiss the more immediate effect this sudden appearance of the planes has on the reader. Death is tearing through the sky above, shaking the house as Montag faces the reality that his wife is about to die. Their screams become his, and he does not just reach for the phone, but feels "his hand plunge" for it (14). Unlike Millie, who later cannot escape her own distractions long enough even to bring him an aspirin, he cares for her. His rage at the impersonal treatment she receives from the emergency "handymen" who come to snake her out shows us that he feels something more than mere responsibility for her. While she feels not even any sense of responsibility for him, he genuinely cares about her.

Montag cannot, however, convince himself that he is in love with her. Too many walls stand between them, too many "family" members, too many sleeping pills and years of drifting away to the sound of her Seashell ear radios. Any real connection with her is impossible. When she inevitably dies, he knows he will not cry, because she is a stranger to him, because she has no identity to mourn. "And that awful flower the other day," he thinks, "the dandelion! It had summed up everything, hadn't it? 'What a shame! You're not in love with anyone!' " (44).

Yet Guy does not give up on Mildred. "Let me alone," she tells him as he tries to explain how seeing the woman burn with her books had changed him. "We need not to be let alone," Montag responds.

"We need to be really bothered once in a while. When was the last time you were *really* bothered? About something important, about something real?" But he stops himself, remembering her attempted suicide, "the two white stones staring up at the ceiling and the pump snake with the probing eye…" Just as there was another Montag hidden behind the smile, he realizes there is another Mildred, but that she is buried "so deep inside this one, and so bothered, so really bothered, that the two women had never met" (52). As harshly as Millie's character is depicted in this satire, it is hard to sympathize with her or even take her seriously. Her accusation that the old woman with the books "was simple-minded" (51) is laughable in its irony, and in the bedroom scene with Beatty, she borders on comical, bouncing back and forth, around, and in and out of the room like a pinball. Comically foolish as she is, however, her character becomes a little more real and a little more sympathetic when we think of her as a narcotics addict rather than just a fool. Montag's fear of what might happen to her if he forces her to face that other self is the same fear faced by anyone who has cared for a long-term drug addict. He backs away, a co-dependent, afraid that the darkness she needs to get through before finding any light will be too much for her. But he will try again.

After showing Millie his hidden books, after restraining her, slapping her, shaking her to try to get her to listen, Guy begs her to understand. "We've got to start somewhere here," he says, "figuring out why we're in such a mess, you and the medicine nights, and the car, and me and my work. We're heading right for the cliff, Millie. God, I don't want to go over. This isn't going to be easy. We haven't anything to go on, but maybe we can piece it out and figure it and help each other. I need you so much right now, I can't tell you. If you love me at all you'll put up with this…" (66). He wants to include her. He wants to help her, but she will cooperate for a very short time, and, of course, betray him in the end. As Montag concludes his speech, he tells her, "if there is something here, just one little thing out of the whole mess of things, maybe we can pass it on to someone else" (67). Here he is making that next step, moving from responsibility for another person to his responsibility to the society.

Before he leaves to visit Faber, Guy takes one last shot, asking Millie without looking at her if the White Clown loves her. When she doesn't answer, he asks, "Does your 'family' love you, love you *very* much, with all their heart and soul, Millie?" Of course, she does not understand why he would ask such a question, but the reader does. Montag is desperately trying to find something that might lead her to that other Mildred, the one who might have been capable of love and worthy of loving. At this moment, as he stands there, feeling "her blinking slowly at the back of his neck" (77), we can see that now he is giving up on her. There is no freeing Millie without freeing their entire society.

Montag does, however, at least for a short time, have Clarisse, and although their relationship might be nothing but a friendship, she does not need to be read as a seductress to draw the conclusion that he does love this girl. Immediately after their first meeting, he seems very much like a man falling in love describing her face as "beautiful...astonishing, in fact" and imagining the shadow of her "slender body" on the wall (10,11). He has already begun to think of her as a part of him, or even as one with him, feeling "that if his eye itched, she might blink. And if the muscles of his jaws stretched imperceptibly, she would yawn long before he would" (11). But we cannot forget that first time Montag looked into her eyes, he was reminded of a comforting childhood experience with his mother, and in a later scene, he tells her that she makes him "feel very old and very much like a father" (28). When he is with Clarisse, Montag feels at times like a child, at other times like a parent, and at other times just confused about why he likes this person so much.

Regardless of what kind of love he feels for her, in these few meetings, we see a Montag growing more comfortable with Clarisse, more open, and less suspicious. She tells him that his laugh sounds "much nicer" and "more relaxed" (29). We see a Montag who seems to be happy. When she fails to show up on that eighth afternoon, we sympathize with him as a man who has just lost a person he loved. The emptiness of his world and those "vague stirrings of dis-ease" haunt us as they do him (32), and as he sits later in the firehouse, still struggling with those stirrings, the radio announces that the war is imminent, and the jets strike "a single note across the black morning sky" (33), reminding us again that death hangs over love.

Clarisse, on the other hand, seems almost to be courting him, showing up at the right time every day to walk him to his train, sharing the details of her life with him, leaving him little gifts. And perhaps she had been out there waiting for him that first night. Perhaps she had watched him and chosen him because she recognized that he was not like the other firemen. Perhaps she had chosen him to take the quality information she helped him discover, think about it, and act on it.

By the time he reaches Faber, Montag has made the leap from "I" to "We," and from seeking to free only himself and his wife to seeking to free his entire society. "We have everything we need to be happy," he tells the professor, "but we aren't happy. Something's missing. I looked around. The only thing I positively *knew* was gone was the books I'd burned in ten or twelve years. So I thought the books might help" (82). Now he recognizes that the problem is not his alone, and he is ready to accept responsibility not only for himself but for all the inhabitants of his "inhuman monstrosity" of a world.

"On a Darkling Plain"

Montag's reading of "Dover Beach" when he returns from his visit with Faber is his first attack on the state of his world itself. The lover's plea in the Matthew Arnold poem—a selection ironically made by Mildred, who remembers only that it goes "umpty-tumpty-ump" (99)— suggests that in a world that offers no hope for happiness, their only choice is to turn to one another. Love here is a response not only to the darkness and hopelessness of this world, from which "The Sea of Faith" has receded, but also to the war reminding them of their mortality. While Mildred seems still unaffected and Mrs. Bowles is simply angered at the affront, Mrs. Phelps is saddened by the poem, though she does not understand why. She might be just affected by Arnold's bleak language, or perhaps, somewhere deep down, the other Clara has recognized that she lives in this dark world "[w]here ignorant armies clash by night" (100).

This connection of love and war has been foreshadowed in Bradbury's imagery up to this point, with the first jet passing over as Montag realizes his wife is near death. They appear again, striking "a single note across the black morning sky" as he sits in the firehouse still feeling those stirrings of dis-ease after Clarisse's disappearance (33). When he is imploring Mildred to feel some kind of compassion, something of the loss he feels, they cross the sky for the third time. "What about Clarisse McClellen," he asks, "where do we look for her? The morgue!" And the bombers again circle over the house (73). Love and death, love and loss, love and war are connected by this imagery throughout the first part of the book.

Even in the idyllic scene Montag imagines as he emerges from the river near the end of the book, he includes the bombers. In the world he fantasizes about from a childhood memory, Clarisse braids her hair in the window of the farmhouse while he watches from the loft of a barn. The distance between them offers little clarity about exactly what kind of love he feels for her, but the fantasy leaves little doubt that he loves her. She has succeeded in awakening him, in showing him that awareness and curiosity lead us to both happiness and a connection with others, and she shows him that he is still capable of loving someone. Yet even in this idyllic fantasy, Montag imagines the jets flying over. Yes, there is some hope in the way he imagines "those strange new stars…fleeing from the soft color of dawn" (143), but the darkness always returns, and the presence of death and war, even in this blissfully imagined scene, reinforce the idea that love is the proper response to pain and death, for both love and happiness are possible only when we have the strength and desire to live beneath the full weight of mortality and uncertainty. And in the morning, he is rewarded with an act of love. The fruit and the milk left for him, like the other little gifts Clarisse had left for him earlier in the story, remind him that he is loved, that this other person cares for him and wants to provide for him.

In the world he has left behind, however, this kind of love cannot exist. In the world protected by Beatty and the firemen and inhabited Mildred and billions of others like her, no one can find love because no one is willing to face the pain that might come with loss. In an effort to protect their "happiness," the mindless state of pseudo-pleasure in which they exist, any thought, any feeling that might lead to discomfort, is simply denied. In this world, "It's always someone else's husband dies" (94). The chaff women, Mildred's friends, cannot be bothered with any human connection that might make the death of another unpleasant. Hedonism is opposed to pain as much as it is attracted to pleasure, and love does not come without pain. As they stand outside Montag's house after the alarm has been turned in on the books he has stolen, Beatty points out the pain Clarisse has caused him. "She chewed you around, didn't she?" Beatty asks (114). And she did. Love chews us around. She pulled Montag out from behind that idiotic smile and introduced him to the loss that comes with love and the pain that comes with consciousness. She encouraged him to think the kind of thoughts that Beatty claims are good only for "making a man feel bestial and lonely" (61). And this is the problem with Beatty's world. Until we are made to feel "bestial and lonely," we have no need for others, no need for love. Until we accept all the uncertainty and pain that come with awareness, we cannot be fully human.

"Half a Smile"

In a way, the resolution of Montag's love story seems more satisfying than that of the broader story about the battle for the freedom to think. Although he has lost Clarisse, Montag did at least have love for a while. When he awakens in the loft in that fantasized scene, he imagines his mouth would be "half a smile." He would, he imagines, be "so fully aware of the world that he would be afraid" (143). It is still just half a smile, but it is not a mask, and although he knows there is reason to fear the world, he is prepared by the night, by the comfort of the loft, by the beauty and kindness of the girl, and by the love and gratitude he feels for her to step into the day despite the fear.

When Montag leaves his fantasy and emerges from the river, that fear is upon him. The vast darkness of the land comes down on him like "a tidal wave," and he is "crushed by darkness" (142). "It is difficult to read this description as majestic or inviting," writes

Rafeeq O. McGiveron, "for the land's nightmarish darkness, its vast size, and its 'waiting' make it seem brooding and ominous instead. When Montag finally steps ashore, the enormity of the wilderness is humbling" (73). The blackness here is no less ominous than the blackness used in the war imagery, and rightly so. The wilderness can take us out as easily as the atom bomb, "as easily as blowing its breath on us or sending the sea to tell us we are not so big" (157). This is no retreat for any man who believes in an "understandable and rightful dread of being inferior" (59). This is a place that calls on us to recognize our inferiority, our vulnerability. Here, we get another reminder that genuine happiness always exists only under the weight of mortality, the weight of knowing that it is only temporary. Yet Montag, strengthened and taught by Clarisse, perseveres. His senses come alive as he steps into the woods, and as he samples the smells and feels the weeds rise up and brush by him, we are reminded of that first meeting when she awakened him to an active engagement of his senses.

It would be nice to have Clarisse back with him at the end. Bradbury acknowledges as much in his 1982 Afterword, saying that he received enough mail from readers about Clarisse that in his 1979 two-act play, he brings her back "to welcome Montag and give a somewhat happier ending to what was, in essence, pretty grim stuff" (172). Even without her there, however, we recognize the strength he has drawn from her and the value of their brief relationship. The book's resolution might, in fact, be the better one, leaving us with a Montag who has loved and suffered the pain of loss while becoming stronger for both. The happiness love brings may be fleeting, but the strength we draw from sharing our thoughts, our fears, our lives with another is more lasting.

The warning in Bradbury's satire is not as much about a repressive government as about a society of people who willingly give up their right to be happy in favor of protection from ever being unhappy, their right to love in exchange for protection against the pain of loss, and not just their right but their desire to exercise the innate curiosity that makes us human. Unwilling to face the black reality of the pain and uncertainty that comes with consciousness, they have denied themselves the light of genuine happiness, visible only when we accept and embrace that blackness. They exist "like gray animals peering from electric caves, faces with gray colorless eyes, gray tongues, and gray thoughts looking out through the numb flesh of the face" (139). Montag, through his interaction with Clarisse and Mildred, gradually comes to understand this and moves from seeking his own happiness to recognizing his connection to and responsibility for the others around him, his society, and his world at large. As he leads the book memorizers toward the city, we are indeed faced with "pretty grim stuff." We do not know who won the war, there is no certainty that the collective memory of the book memorizers will lead to a better future, but Montag's transformation is complete; he will not return to a world of gray, and half a smile is at least better than no smile at all.

Notes

1. In the error-strewn 1991 printing, this word appears as lines, but, of course, earlier printings show it as linen.

Works Cited

Bradbury, Ray. *Fahrenheit 451*. 1953. New York: Ballantine, 1991.

Grossman, Kathryn M. "Woman as Temptress: The Way to (Br)Otherhood in Science Fiction Dystopias." *Women's Studies* 14.2 (1987): 135-145. Rpt. in *Contemporary Literary Criticism* vol 168. Ed. Janet Witalec. Detroit: Gale, 2003. *Literature Resource Center*. Web. 20 Aug. 2013.

McGiveron, Rafeeq O. "The Power of the Wilderness in *Fahrenheit 451*." *Readings on Fahrenheit 451*. Ed. Katie de Koster. San Diego: Greenhaven, 2000. 66-75. Greenhaven Literary Companion Ser.

Watt, Donald. "Burning Bright: *Fahrenheit 451* as Symbolic Dystopia." *Ray Bradbury*. Eds. Martin Harry Greenburg and Joseph D. Orlander. New York: Taplinger, 1980. 195-213. Writers of the 21st Century Ser.

Knowledge and Masculinity: Male Archetypes in *Fahrenheit 451*

Imola Bulgozdi

Meet Guy Montag, fireman, member of the happiest bunch in a society hell-bent on happiness, so much so that any cause for upset is quickly eliminated with the help of the incinerator. Consequently, firemen are considered "custodians of our peace of mind,…official censors, judges, and executors" (Bradbury 77). In other words, they are book-burners hailed as heroes, "stand[ing] against the small tide of those who want to make everyone unhappy with conflicting theory and thought" (81). Our first glimpse of Montag shows him absorbed in the pleasure of burning, in a scene that operates with the macho imagery of man in control of fire and a dangerous beast at the same time: he pumps venomous kerosene from a great python, "his eyes all orange flame" (9) and a fierce grin on his face. Bradbury's description of all firemen as characterized by the "continual smell of burning from their pipes" and the "charcoal hair and soot-colored brows and bluish-ash-smeared cheeks" (46) points at an existential relationship with fire, but it is Montag's ever-present fiery smile that betrays how strongly he is influenced by the experience of burning.

The image of the contented hero soon crumbles, though, when probed by seventeen-year-old Clarisse, whose simple question of "Are you happy?" (Bradbury 17) is the final push to get Montag thinking, to feel his perpetual smile fade, and to realize that his happiness is only a mask, far from genuine. In the novel's bleak society, people are programmed to remember facts but are strongly discouraged from thinking, thus losing not only their decision-making ability but also the capacity for genuine human relationships, and Montag's search for a meaningful existence compels him to find a teacher who will help him make sense of the books he used to burn. Since he has to face the sobering fact that his identity as a macho fireman is built on lies, while he finds a mentor in the person of Faber, an old and frail English teacher, the relationship between masculinity, maturity, and knowledge calls for a closer look.

The society of *Fahrenheit 451* does not allow for a variety of subject positions—defined by Chris Barker as "empty spaces or functions in discourse from which the world makes sense" (450)—which can be taken up by the individual. The authorities keep the masses happy with unsophisticated entertainment: clubs, parties, acrobats, magicians, jet cars, motorcycle helicopters, sex, and heroin, thus encouraging "everything to do with automatic reflex" (80). In order to create individuals who will kill time happily in this manner, the state practically snatches children from the cradle, and everyone is "*made* equal. Each man the image of every other; then all are happy, for there are no mountains to make them cower, to judge themselves against" (77). By this means, the state creates the discourse of happiness, defining the ideal subject position of the 'happy person,' as well as that of the enemy of the system—no wonder "the word 'intellectual'…became the swear word it deserved to be" (76).

Fire Captain Beatty's lecture on the history of firemen is the perfect example of the workings of the power of discourse. His explanation reveals that since houses all had been fireproofed, there was no need for firemen anymore, and therefore they were given the new job of guarding the happiness of the masses. They were given power; the firehouse "full of glitter and shine and silence, of brass colors, the colors of coins, of gold of silver" (Bradbury 45), is a display of prestige, and the subject position of the heroic fireman working for the good of the community was created. At the beginning of the novel, Montag happily fills in this subject position, enjoying the experience of burning. It is only later that he realizes he did not really have a say in his choice of a profession, having blindly followed in the footsteps of his father and grandfather.

Montag's conversations with Clarisse raise his awareness of the discrepancies between the past as remembered and official history, and later Beatty himself also reveals the fabricated nature of the discourse of happiness: "If you don't want a man unhappy politically, don't give him two sides to a question to worry him; give him one. Better yet, give him none" (Bradbury 80). Nevertheless, the subject positions—the obedient happy citizen who reports anyone in possession of a book, the fireman who solves the problem, and the intellectual branded as the enemy of the system—are produced by this discourse, and people "must submit to its rules and conventions" (Hall 55), regardless of truth value or fairness. This discourse, however, provides such a superficial basis for constructing a subjectivity—"the condition of being a person and/ or the processes by which we become persons" (Barker, *Sage Dictionary* 194)—that those who unthinkingly submit, like Guy's wife Mildred, end up without possessing a single original thought or meaningful relationship.

Bradbury makes this clear by contrast: Mildred by night is "stretched on the bed, uncovered and cold, like a body displayed on the lid of a tomb" (20) and by day is engrossed in the three giant parlor walls, watching television shows that do not make sense, while Clarisse, labeled antisocial, is characterized by tireless curiosity, dark eyes "shining and alive" (12), and a face lit as if by the soft light of a candle. Thirty-year-old Mildred is the uncomplaining product of the system, an idle housewife, whose grotesque appearance puts one in mind of a puppet: "her hair burnt by chemicals to a brittle straw, her eyes with a kind of cataract unseen but suspect far behind the pupils, the reddened pouting lips, the body as thin as a praying mantis from dieting, and her flesh like white bacon" (65). The impression of a dummy-like existence is heightened by Montag's wish that her mind could be cleansed from poison just like her blood after her involuntary sleeping pill overdose.

Clarisse, on the other hand, comes from a family, which, despite some degree of outside conformity, refuses to take up "a pre-existent subject position and to be subjected to the regulatory power of that discourse" (Barker, *Cultural Studies* 229). She has learned to observe the world, to enjoy conversation and the life of the mind, and to realize how detrimental the system is for children, admitting she is afraid of people her own age, whose thrill-seeking irresponsible behavior leads to numerous lethal accidents. Clarisse, a stranger, asks Montag upsetting personal questions out of genuine interest, whereas he can hardly speak to his wife of ten years either because of the blaring TV walls or the radio earplugs to which she listens in a trance by night.

The dominant discourse of the future society Bradbury envisions is very restrictive. However, not all individuals fit the mold, because the construction of personhood entails the continual acceptance and rejection of certain subject positions that are available at a given historical place and time. For instance, even the traditionally highly regarded subject position of the caring mother is denied the female characters in a society that regards children as a nuisance to be sent to school nine days out of ten. The rest of the time they are sat in the parlor to watch the walls: "It's like washing clothes; stuff laundry in and slam the lid" (Bradbury 125), says a mother, who betrays no emotional attachment to her children at all. Yet the existence of a person like Clarisse testifies to a loving and caring home environment and a real family, which, in Beatty's words, "had been feeding her subconscious" (79).

Nick Mansfield explains that, contrary to earlier essentialist theories, subjectivity in Michel Foucault's view "is not the free and spontaneous expression of our interior truth. It is the way we are led to think about ourselves, so we will police and present ourselves in the correct way, as not insane, criminal, undisciplined, unkempt, perverse, or unpredictable" (10). It is this socially constructed nature of subjectivity that explains how such a sudden change could take place in Montag, who goes from enthusiastic fireman fulfilling a prestigious subject position to killer on the run in a matter of days.

It turns out that Montag has been stealing and stashing books for about a year, since his meeting with an old English professor, Faber, but it was the shocking discovery of his own unhappiness, followed by Mildred's accidental near-suicide, that acted as a catalyst for the admission "I don't know anything anymore" (Bradbury 27). In retrospect, he pinpoints this event as the disappearance of his burnt-in smile, without which he feels lost and numb (101). At the same time, Clarisse's observation that his choice of a job does not seem to be right for him causes a split in Montag: "He felt his body divide itself into a hotness and a coldness, a softness and a hardness, a trembling and a not trembling, the two halves grinding one upon the other" (34-35). Witnessing an old woman refuse to leave her house and burn along with her beloved books makes him conclude that there must be something in them, something he could use to change the lives of the "silly empty man" living along with "a silly empty woman" he realizes is scarcely his wife but instead merely "an unknown, a street face, a newspaper image" (59).

Montag's quest for a new self is interwoven with books and the search for knowledge from the very first step. Lacking any training in literature, however, he is unable to make sense of his odd assortment of looted books and contacts Faber. He expects to find himself with Faber's help, for otherwise "someone somewhere will give me back the old face and the old hands the way they were" (101), but first he has to face the truth about his profession: "Those who don't build must burn. It's as old as history and juvenile delinquents" (116). Yet this refers not only to Montag and the firemen, but to all the population, for Bradbury describes a society that does not require its members to grow up and take responsibility for their actions. Teenagers running over the rare pedestrian for fun is condoned, provided that the drivers have good insurance, for instance. And human relationships have lost any intimacy: Montag's bedroom is a "cold marbled room of a mausoleum" with windows tightly shut, where he gropes about in the complete darkness of "the chamber of a tomb-world" (19) toward "his open, separate, and therefore cold bed" (20). The lack of any commitment in relationships could not be more brutally presented than in the scene prior to Montag burning his own house. Mildred, after reporting her own husband to the fire brigade, flees the house in a puppet-like, stiff run, not even looking at him, but muttering "poor family" (148), the name by which Guy referred to the characters in her favorite television programs.

Bradbury's dystopian vision is eerily similar to the state of affairs, which Robert Bly, poet and founder of the first men's movement, laments forty years later in his introduction to *The Sibling Society*:

we navigate from a paternal society, now discredited, to a society in which impulse is given its way. People don't bother to grow up, and we are all fish swimming in a tank of half-adults. The rule is: Where repression was before, fantasy will now be; we human beings limp along, running after our own fantasy. We can never catch up, and so we defeat ourselves by the simplest possible means: speed. Everywhere we go there's a crowd, and the people all look alike. (vii)

Stephen Wicks's historical overview of the concept of masculinity in *Warriors and Wildmen: Men, Masculinity, and Gender* demonstrates that the main underlying reason for the present crisis of masculinity is the relocation of the workplace outside the home in industrialized societies, which drastically reduced the time fathers spent with their children, and consequently, their influence as well. "Boys were beset with the task of forging their masculine identities at a distance from their fathers, and the industrial-age father sought new ways to retain his position in the family as a moral model and authority figure" (33-34). Although Montag is only thirty years old, his own father is but a distant memory, and all we find out about him is that he was a fireman. Bradbury's future sorely lacks authority figures with the exception of Fire Captain Beatty, but all he offers Montag is the advice to conform, based on the official views on books and the sociological changes that made the existence of the fire brigade necessary.

Montag's search for identity after his disenchantment with his job is further complicated by the fact that families have become dysfunctional. Since identity "represents the processes by which discursively constructed subject positions are taken up...by concrete persons' fantasy identifications and emotional 'investments' " (Barker, *Sage Dictionary* 93-94), he has run out of subject positions constructed by the official discourse of happiness. On the one hand, he refuses to be one of "the Happiness Boys, the Dixie Duo" (Bradbury 81), thus losing not only his identity as breadwinner but also the subject position of dominant masculinity, which sociologist Robert W. Connell defines as "hegemonic masculinity, the culturally idealized form of masculine character (in a given historical setting)" (69). On the other hand, Mildred and her friends represent the brainwashed woman of the future, who is impossible to relate to, thus denying Montag the adult male identity of lover, husband, or father.

Bradbury does indeed describe a "sibling society" in the novel. "Out of the nursery into the college and back to the nursery; there's your intellectual pattern for the past five centuries or more" (72), admits Beatty, and Montag finds himself in the only other role the dominant discourse has scripted, that of the enemy of the system, simply because he wants to think for himself and not be ordered about like he was all his life. Significantly, Bly argues that the sibling society is prone to sliding into primitivism since children are credulous, will follow a leader, and easily become members of a pack (viii), characteristics all typical of the vast majority of people in *Fahrenheit 451*. Montag, setting about the task of growing up by trying to find the cause of his unhappiness, first hopes that his wife will be his partner in reading books to find a way out from the mess their life has become, but screen addict Millie is unable to grasp this need.

It is at this point that Montag turns to Faber, the only person he knows who understands books, and tries to persuade the professor to make a copy of the Bible he had saved from the fire. With this step he comes into contact not only with cultural tradition, but also with someone whose mind has not been manipulated and who can expose Beatty as the spokesman of "the most dangerous enemy of truth and freedom, the solid unmoving cattle of the majority" (Bradbury 140). Via their private radio connection, he listens to Faber read and feels "he was two people, that he was above all Montag, who knew nothing" and "he was also the old man who talked to him," while his mind absorbs knowledge so that at a certain point "he would be Montag-plus-Faber, fire plus water, and then, one day, after everything had mixed and simmered and worked away in silence, there would be neither fire nor water, but wine. .... Even now he could feel the start of the long journey, the leave-taking, the going away from the self he had been" (133).

While the most general definition of being a "man" is constructed in opposition to being a "woman" (think of the Freudian theory of gender formation), Judith Kegan Gardiner draws our attention to the fact that masculinity also can be conceptualized from a developmental aspect: in opposition to being a boy. By understanding gender developmentally, that is, "in terms of change over the life course and in history rather than in terms of a static and binary opposition between masculine and feminine" (91), Bradbury provides Montag with the opportunity to reach the next developmental step: he is initiated into a secret society of educated elderly men who, despite having become superfluous in the bookless society, devote themselves to the preservation of knowledge.

In Bly's view, the social problems typically attributed to men, such as violence, sexism, anger, or personal unhappiness, can be traced back to "men losing touch with their bonds to nature, or an inner self that reflects a kind of male gender heritage or archetype" (Wicks 64). He also places great emphasis on the process of male initiation, which must be completed with the help of an older man or group of men in a positive, encouraging—rather than humiliating—way (67). Montag, though definitely not in touch with nature—he does not remember if he knew there is dew on the grass in the morning or what rain tastes like—possesses some of the instincts of the hunter, which, according to Wicks, is the longest-standing personification of manhood in history (25). Before he bumps into Clarisse, for example, Montag senses someone has been there: "Perhaps his nose detected a faint perfume, perhaps the skin on the back of his hands, on his face, felt the temperature rise at this one spot" (Bradbury 11). The fact that the firemen deploy a robot called the Hound to sniff out suspicious individuals reinforces this imagery, and later they find the presence of the old woman disturbing during the burning because she "was spoiling the ritual" (50), the ancient all-male ritual of the hunt, where the magazines "fell like slaughtered birds" and "the books lay like great mounds of fishes left to dry" (51-52).

Nevertheless, there is nothing manly about what they accomplish: they batter down unlocked doors with their silver hatchets, tumble through like boys rollicking, and try to drown out the old woman's accusing silence with jokes, laughter, and too much noise. The fact that the police have failed to adhesive-tape the victim's mouth and cart her away before the arrival of the firemen fills Montag with unease, and makes him rationalize that the fire brigade does not hurt anybody, only things, and is simply part of the cleaning process. "Janitorial work, essentially" (Bradbury 50), argues Montag to quiet his conscience, stripping the Happiness Boys of macho glamour. What is more, when the old woman flourishes a match in hand in the house soaked with kerosene, only Beatty backs out slowly to save face, while all the rest simply flee. This is not a real hunt, and the participants are not real men either. They are boys pretending to be men, without assuming the duties and responsibilities of an adult.

In *King, Warrior, Magician, Lover—Rediscovering the Archetypes of the Mature Masculine*, Robert Moore and Douglas Gillette describe male psychological development based on their study of ancient myths and modern dreams, coupled with years of clinical practice of psychotherapy. Jungian archetypes—defined as blueprints similarly embedded in the human mind as the instincts of animals—are stored and passed on by heredity in the collective unconscious, which "contains the cumulative history of the human race, and its influences are universal and identical in every individual" (Wicks 71). However, the deep unconscious of each individual contains "an enormous variety of archetypes, that surface according to cultural, social, and personal conditions" (Wicks 71), which can explain why Montag is the only one to try to persuade the old woman to leave the house. He knows something has been brewing in him and needs to change: "I'm so damned unhappy, I'm so mad…. I feel like I've been saving up a lot of things, and don't know what" (Bradbury 84). He sets off, therefore, in search of a teacher and a purpose: "'I'm going to do something,' said Montag. 'I don't even know what yet, but I'm going to do something big'" (85).

At this stage, we hear the most advanced form of Boy psychology, the Hero archetype speaking through Montag, which, according to Moore and Gillette, is generally assumed to be the noblest approach to life or a task, although its immaturity is apparent from the fact that the hero begins by thinking that he is invulnerable (37-38). Montag upsets Millie's two brainwashed friends by reading "Dover Beach" by Matthew Arnold, and yet stares with disbelief later when the fire brigade, including himself, arrives at his own house. He feels petrified, his face "entirely numb and featureless" (Bradbury 147), until he is told to burn his own home with a flamethrower, which he turns into the opportunity "to change everything that showed that he had lived here in this empty house with a strange woman…, who had gone and quite forgotten him already…" (151).

This is how the real initiation ritual begins. Self-preservation compels Montag to kill Beatty and knock two of his colleagues unconscious before facing the Hound, which he also manages to burn, but not before being briefly stung. When one of Montag's legs is incapacitated by the anaesthetic and causes him excruciating pain, his situation recalls ancient and often painful rites of passage, which here turn into a manhunt. In order to reach Man psychology, a symbolic, psychological, or spiritual death is required and forms a vital part of any initiation ritual (Moore and Gillette 6), and now "[t]he big game, the hunt, the one-man carnival" (Bradbury 173), is on. This time, however, Montag is the prey chased by another Mechanical Hound and dies several symbolic deaths: he is almost killed by joyriders, dives into the depths of the dark river, and finally witnesses the death of a person declared by the voice on television to be Montag himself, followed by the reassurance that "a crime against society has been avenged" (192).

While on the run, Montag is aware of the power of the official discourse that attempts to constrain him into the subject position of the criminal. He knows that in all TV parlors, he could "see himself dramatized, described, made over,…a drama to be watched objectively,…large as life, in full color, dimensionally perfect" (173). Montag now struggles to rewrite his own story and to create a new subject position for himself in order to survive both physically and spiritually, and the only person to whom he can turn is Faber. Even though his chances are very slim, the psychology of the Hero "encourages him to dream the impossible dream that might just be possible after all, if he has enough courage. It empowers him to fight the unbeatable foe" (Moore and Gillette 40), but he needs the help of a ritual elder to complete the initiation.

Old and frail Faber cannot boast of many of the values traditionally associated with masculinity, such as "strength, power, stoicism, action, control, independence, self-sufficiency, male camaraderie/mateship and work" (Barker, *Cultural Studies* 301). He is a recluse and admits having been too cowardly to raise his voice against the process that demonized books, but for Montag he represents both the freedom of thought and the moral support human contact can provide: "Faber's would be the place where he might refuel his vast draining belief in his own ability to survive. He just wanted to know that there was a man like Faber in the world" (Bradbury 161).

In a society that does not respect wisdom and knowledge, or considers them outright dangerous, mature masculinity as identified in the archetypes of the King, the Warrior, the Magician, and the Lover is hard to achieve (Moore and Gillette 43). While these archetypes ideally overlap and enrich each other, the embodiment of the Magician can be recognized clearly in the person of Faber:

> The Magician is the knower and he is the master of technology. ....
> He is the "ritual elder" who guides the processes of transformation, both within and without.
> The human magician is always an initiate himself, and one of his tasks is to initiate others. The Magician is an initiate of secret and hidden knowledge of all kinds. .... All knowledge that takes special training to acquire is the province of the Magician energy. (Moore and Gillette 98)

Even though Faber seems more pitiful than masculine, introversion and lack of the capacity to act are typical of this mature archetype.

Action is the specialty of the Warrior (Moore and Gillette 108), who seems to be embodied by Beatty in the novel, although he also betrays considerable knowledge of books and insight into the workings of the system. A closer look at this character reveals his immaturity, though; the description of the Magician archetype when failing to reach its fullness is a perfect summary of Beatty's attitude towards Montag. He is the Manipulator, who does not guide or initiate but "maneuvers people by withholding from them information they may need for their own well-being" (Moore and Gillette 111). The negative influence of this archetype is compounded by the fact that he uses his learning not for the benefit of others but to intimidate and demonstrate his superiority, while he also hurts others "with his cynical detachment from the world of human values" (Moore and Gillette 114).

Montag, governed by the self-centred Hero archetype, originally sets out in search of personal happiness, but in the course of the initiation process, his scope widens: he recognises the inherent wrongness of the system that prevents people from growing up. He manages to get rid of the false mentor and also admits that it was his pride and temper that made him rashly read poetry to the women and precipitate the events. However, by the time he stops at Faber's and realizes the hunt is broadcast, he tries to come up with the right word or sentence "that would sear all their [viewers'] faces and wake them up" (Bradbury 174) in case he is overtaken by the Hound. Cutting all ties with his previous life has freed a new Montag, who can focus and access the Warrior energy "concerned with skill, power, and accuracy, and with control" (Moore and Gillette 83) of body and mind in order to survive the chase. When reaching the river, he strips naked, and drowns his own smell in whiskey, and while wearing Faber's old clothes, he watches the Hound fooled from the comfortable embrace of the river. He is preparing for a new life, "moving from an unreality that was frightening into a reality that was unreal because it was new" (Bradbury 180), and he defines his new purpose: "someone had to do the saving and keeping…, in books, in records, in people's heads…, free from moths, silver-fish, rust and dry-rot, and men with matches" (181).

Bradbury's description of Montag wading "alone in the wilderness" (185) and later admiring a strange fire with the "foolish and yet delicious sense of knowing himself as an animal come from the forest" (187) shows him in harmony with nature, without which, as noted earlier, the construction of a masculine identity is in Bly's view impossible. He is the Wildman, the archetype standing for uncivilized but inherently good masculinity, the animal "drawn by the fire," finally joining the group of elders waiting for the successful candidate. Montag's whole worldview is altered, as symbolized by his new relationship with fire: "It was not burning. It was *warming!*" (Bradbury 187). The death of the Boy and the birth of the Man become all the more emphatic in Granger's words: "Welcome back from the dead" (192).

So what has really happened to Montag? M. Keith Booker considers rather questionable Granger's hopeful assumption that humanity will manage to avoid making the same mistakes over again by picking up "a few more people that remember, every generation" (209). Booker points out that "learning from the past, especially the distant past, requires more than individual memory, and Bradbury's individualist approach fails to account for the ability of those in power to distort official history" (84). In my opinion, Booker has taken Granger's words and strategy too literally. After all, as Tom Moylan—drawing on several works ranging from *Brave New World* to the cyberpunks—demonstrates, despite the fact that the dystopian protagonist is generally prohibited from using language in a meaningful manner—think of Clarisse's complaint about the superficiality of all human interaction—"control over the means of language, over representation and interpellation, is a crucial weapon and strategy in dystopian resistance" (149).

In this case, however, it is not the loosely organized network of book-savers that constitutes the main line of defence. Although they provide a purpose with which to identify, it is exactly Bradbury's individualist approach that makes the difference: Montag falls under the thrall of real conversation as soon as he first meets Clarisse, and it is his craving for a meaningful relationship that leads to his creating a new discourse and a new subject position, that of the mature adult. His journey from an easily manipulated representative of a malevolent authority to a responsible individual is the bedrock of any resistance, and the importance of self-examination to avoid self-destruction is amply detailed by Rafeeq O. McGiveron in his analysis of the mirror-imagery in the novel.

While Booker dismisses individual memory as a valid means to learn from the past, he does not take into account the collective unconscious, whose archetypal images are part of every human. As Bradbury shows, what is crucial is not the books themselves but what they store. "[Q]uality of information," "leisure to digest it," and "the right to carry out actions based on what we learn from the interaction of the first two" (110) are the necessities to become a mature human being. Maturity and knowledge go hand in hand, but the presence of male archetypes and the initiation ritual in *Fahrenheit 451* proves that it is not book-learning but the ability to think and make choices that makes a man out of a boy. Montag's story, on the one hand, demonstrates the fact that mature masculinity is learned and cannot be achieved without the help of a mentor, and, on the other hand, it points to a more fundamental and deeper level of remembering than the memorization of books: the blueprint of how to be a human being.

Works Cited

Barker, Chris. *Cultural Studies—Theory and Practice*. 2nd ed. London: Sage, 2003.

_____. *The Sage Dictionary of Cultural Studies*. London: Sage, 2004.

Bly, Robert. *The Sibling Society*. Reading, MA: Addison-Wesley, 1996.

Booker, M. Keith. *Monsters, Mushroom Clouds, and the Cold War: American Science Fiction and the Roots of Postmodernism, 1946-1964*. Westport, CT: Greenwood Press, 2001.

Bradbury, Ray. *Fahrenheit 451*. 1953. London: Harper Voyager, 2008.

Connell, Robert W. *The Men and the Boys*. St. Leonards, N.S.W.: Allen and Unwin, 2000.

Gardiner, Judith K. "Theorizing Age with Gender: Bly's Boys, Feminism, and Maturity Masculinity." *Masculinity Studies & Feminist Theory: New Directions*. Ed. Judith Kegan Gardiner. New York: Columbia UP, 2002. 90-118.

Hall, Stuart. "The Work of Representation." *Representation: Cultural Representations and Signifying Practices*. Ed. Stuart Hall. London: Sage, 1997. 13-74.

Mansfield, Nick. *Subjectivity: Theories of the Self from Freud to Haraway*. St. Leonards, N.S.W.: Allen & Unwin, 2000.

McGiveron, Rafeeq O. "'To Build a Mirror Factory': The Mirror and Self-Examination in Ray Bradbury's *Fahrenheit 451.*" *Ray Bradbury's* Fahrenheit 451. Ed. Harold Bloom. New York: Infobase, 2008. 163-69. Bloom's Modern Critical Interpretations Ser.

Moore, Robert and Douglas Gillette. *King, Warrior, Magician, Lover—Rediscovering the Archetypes of the Mature Masculine*. San Francisco: Harper, 1990.

Moylan, Tom. *Scraps of the Untainted Sky: Science Fiction, Utopia, Dystopia*. Boulder, CO: Westview, 2000.

Wicks, Stephen. *Warriors and Wildmen: Men, Masculinity, and Gender*. Westport, CT: Bergin and Garvey, 1996.

Reading Montag as a Postmodern Don Quixote _____

Guido Laino

"There must be something in books, things we can't imagine" (58), Guy Montag says, thinking back to the old woman who died staying in her burning house with her books. There must be so much in books that people struggle, kill, and die for them, while others rebel, as Montag will. The whole idea of the *Fahrenheit 451* world seems to be built on books, that is to say, on the project of their complete destruction or on the mission of their salvation.

Bradbury's dystopian architecture is barely sketched, and it is defective in many of its parts. As readers, we ignore many details of this society, such as the power machine that dominates it, the type of government it has (we just know that citizens choose between two body doubles who run for presidency), or its main social, economical, and political apparatus. We could define it a *cultural dystopia* because it is entirely grounded on media and cultural hegemony, assured by the suppression of any form of written culture and knowledge in favor of the spectacle, which is mostly spread by a technologic evolution of the TV screen. On the other side, the novel's final utopian perspective is even blurrier. It does not include a project for the future but keeps its gaze pointed, nostalgically, toward the past. The new foundation of the world destroyed by the bomb, the rebirth of the phoenix, will rest on memory; it will look backward, not forward. In this sense, *Fahrenheit 451* looks more like a bibliophile's dream/nightmare, than a classic utopian/dystopian novel with an organic view of an alternative world. *There must be something in books* and *Fahrenheit 451* explores all those things that otherwise, as Montag says, *we can't imagine.*

From Big Brother to the Relatives

What kind of nightmare world does Montag live in? And why does the totalitarian power in this world hate not only subversive books, but any kind of books? Captain Beatty has the assignment of describing the society of *Fahrenheit 451* from the point of view of the establishment; his "lesson" on how this world works is part of the history of firemen and the origin of the book burning system he tells to Montag. Beatty explains that, in the early twentieth century, "things began to have *mass*" and that "because they had mass, they became simpler" (54). He talks about a sort of acceleration and heavy compression of things to "fling off all unnecessary, time-wasting thought" (55). The final result is a flattening of human beings into a state of indefinite void, a paradoxical nirvana made of a permanent rest from any intellectual or emotional activity.

It is not difficult to track down the outline of this near future in the 1950s in America. As a matter of fact, apart from some technologic peculiarity mostly tied to the dimension of things—cars are faster, billboards are larger, TVs are bigger and much more intrusive—everything appears as it was in that capitalist society that was at its peak expansion in the United States after the Second World War. Bradbury's cultural dystopia appears as the anatomy of the origin of Postmodernity, as the rise of market to a dogma and the definitive subjugation of society and culture to mass media are generally considered its founding elements. In some ways *Fahrenheit 451* can be seen as the allegorical version of many critical works of the 1950s, depicting a picture of society in an increasingly bleak and apocalyptic outlook.

If the future of *Fahrenheit 451* is that of the 1950s, we should consider Marshall McLuhan's *The Mechanical Bride* a sort of sketchbook composed by a time traveler (maybe coming from a Ray Bradbury short story). Actually, two years before the publishing of *Fahrenheit 451*, McLuhan asks his readers, "Are ads themselves the main form of industrial culture?" (129). As a matter of fact, Bradbury's literary nightmare of an American mass culture, where books are burned and replaced by ads and TV spectacle, is widely depicted in McLuhan's analysis, almost as an accomplished process. In Beatty's "lesson" can be recognized that self-imposed flattening and disintegration of American culture, as described in *The Mechanical Bride*:

Enfolded in its jovial, optimistic, and self-satisfied version of the higher things, the reader soon hardens into a man who 'knows what he likes' and who resents anybody who pretends to like anything better. He has, unwittingly, been sold a strait jacket. And that is really as much as need be said about any of the effects of commercial formula writing, living, and entertainment. It destroys human autonomy, freezes perception, and sterilizes judgment. (McLuhan 160)

So the phenomena in American culture and, in a more specific way, in the American audience, which Bradbury observes and re-projects in his version of the future, portray an undeniable drift widely denounced in those years by many critics, intellectuals, and philosophers. Mildred's character, who could be easily identified as a "mechanical bride," represents the way in which people have been transformed from individuals into consumers by unremitting exposure to mass media. Something very similar to what happens to Mildred in *Fahrenheit 451* is described by the German philosopher Günther Anders in *Die Antiquiertheit des Menschen*, a work published in 1956 and never translated into English, whose title sounds like "The Obsolescence of Human Beings." Its only part published in the U.S. speaks exactly about the possession of human beings by mass media and their mutation into phantoms. Here is how Anders seems to describe precisely what has happened to Mildred in *Fahrenheit 451*:

when the conditioning is carried out separately for each individual, in the solitude of his home, in millions of secluded homes, it is incomparably more successful. For this conditioning is disguised as 'fun'; the victim is not told that he is asked to sacrifice anything; and since the procedure leaves him with the delusion of his privacy or at least of his private home, it remains perfectly discreet. (16)

This is exactly what Beatty says: "People want to be happy, isn't that right? …. Don't we keep them moving, don't we give them fun?" (Bradbury 59).

So, to return to the despotic power system in Bradbury's cultural dystopia, it is clear that a totalitarian state has come about through the work of complete eradication of any individual conscience by the pervasive allure of mass media. What is presented as a completed process in Mildred's character is described by McLuhan in these terms: "When men and women have been transformed into replaceable parts by competitive success drives, and have become accustomed to the consumption of uniform products, it is hard to see where any individualism remains" (67). Not individuals but consumers, completely unemotional, isolated in their houses, with their bodies and minds possessed by TV shows, the Mildred-like human beings become what Anders calls *mass-produced hermits*, who are "cut off from each other, yet identical with each other remain in the seclusion of their homes. Their purpose, however, is not to renounce the world, but to be sure they won't miss the slightest crumb of the world as image on a screen" (15).

This is the main point of Bradbury's cultural dystopia: the substitution of reality and human beings with their spectacular simulacra. With his 'lesson', Beatty simply anticipates the origins of what Guy Debord will perfectly describe as *The Society of the Spectacle* in his 1967 book of the same name. Its first principle is this: "The whole life of those societies in which modern conditions of production prevail presents itself as an immense accumulation of spectacles. All that once was directly lived has become mere representation" (5). The domination of the spectacle implies, among other things, the substitution of reality with image, the reduction of the individual to a mere consumer, and the perception of the spectacle as the only true form of authenticity, all of which are elements that can be easily found in *Fahrenheit 451*.

The cultural dimension depicted in *The Society of the Spectacle* shapes the very tyrannical principle of the world based on book burning. Debord describes it as "a *weltanschauung* that has been actualized…, a world view transformed into an objective force" (5), that is to say, an indisputable truth, perceived as the only possible value system. This is clear to Faber when he explains to Montag what has happened to their world: the spectacle, through TV, "is an environment as real as the world. It *becomes* and *is* the truth" (Bradbury 84). This way, the society of the spectacle creates a

---

depleted human being, deprived of his or her individuality, unable to think or choose, or even love and hate. In this framework, the power system modifies itself, its tyranny takes other forms, and the means of control and oppression evolve. Therefore, the concept of *cultural dystopia* is very substantial, as the dynamics of power and control in *Fahrenheit 451* are an issue of *hegemony*, as Gramsci has put it. As Tom Moylan observes, "as the hegemony of the dominant class increases within the cultural apparatus of the society, the need for overt coercive power decreases" (17). In this sense, here the despotic power acquires the main characteristics of Michel Foucault's theories: It is no longer a dynamic of repression, but a ubiquitous force, able to shape things, to pass through bodies, to induce pleasure, to produce discourses (13). The *iron heel* of a violent and oppressive power culminated with the pre-WWII fascist regimes, and in *Fahrenheit 451*, a new form of power made of consensus and consumption takes place.

In his analysis of the rise of the mass media era, Anders states that "the family has been re-structured into a miniature audience, and the home into a miniature theater modeled on the movie house" (17); this is exactly what goes on in Guy and Mildred's home. In terms of dystopian fiction history, we could say that in *Fahrenheit 451*, we leave the Orwellian Big Brother to get to the "relatives," as this is how they call the characters of the TV series to which Mildred is addicted. This passage is quite substantial, as the paternalistic figure of the Big Brother in *1984* still owes his pervasive force to violence and police control, while the "relatives" in *Fahrenheit 451* carry out, in many ways, those same functions by hidden persuasion and manipulation. In this case, too, McLuhan explains, in a very clear way, this same concept:

it is observable that the more illusion and falsehood needed to maintain any given state of affairs, the more tyranny is needed to maintain the illusion and falsehood. Today the tyrant rules not by club or fist, but, disguised as a market researcher, he shepherds his flocks in the ways of utility and comfort. (vi)

That is clearly not something absolutely new, as the fascist power system, for example, needed a huge work of propaganda as well (as in *1984*), but what it is particularly notable in *Fahrenheit 451* is that this smooth, persuasive process has almost reached its final focus. In Mildred's character we can see, perfectly operating, what Saul Morson calls a system of *preventive epistemology*: "having a ready-made answer for all questions, [dystopian rulers] imply, may not be enough to secure the kingdom forever against rebellion. For that it would be necessary to make sure the questions were not asked in the first place" (128). Actually, the core of Montag's rebellion is precisely to start asking questions.

We therefore could place *Fahrenheit 451* in the dystopian fiction genealogy closer to Zamjatin's *We* or Huxley's *Brave New World*, than to *1984*. Through Mildred's character, Bradbury shows the eradication of any individuality, like the "I" that becomes "We" in Zamjatin and the total consensus of an always-happy population in Huxley. What seems a novelty is that everything happens using the pervasive weapons of the spectacle instead of the panoptic control of *We* or the mix of genetic planning and massive drug use of *Brave New World*. But here we get to our first question: why does the totalitarian power in the world of *Fahrenheit 451* hate not only subversive books but all kinds of books? If the process of cultural hegemony has been completed, why are firemen still chasing and punishing rebels who keep books in their homes? And furthermore, why do they punish them to death even though they are so scarcely dangerous for the *status quo*? I think that to answer these questions we have to read *Fahrenheit 451* much more as a theoretical allegory than as an actual hypothesis of a concrete alternative world.

Orthodoxy as a Lack of Imagination

In its repressive dimension, the *Fahrenheit 451* police state could appear rather contradictory. Faber tells Montag that "firemen provide a circus now and then…, but it's a small sideshow indeed, and hardly necessary to keep things in line" (87). Maybe the easiest explanation lies in the influence of the likewise contradictory America of the 1950s, in which Senator McCarthy plays, in McLuhan's words, the role of the "successor to the little-man dramas of early Chaplin" (28), showing at the same time dark resemblances with a fool dictator and the clownish manners of a con artist. Nevertheless, looking deeper, the obsession for book burning could hide a much more elaborated sense, in line with the concept of cultural, rather than political, dystopia. Montag himself supposes that "maybe the books can get us half out of the cave. They just might stop us from making the same damn insane mistakes. I don't hear those idiot bastards in your parlor talking about it" (74). His reflection could appear as a declaration of rebellion that in some sense sets, one against the other, books and "relatives" as the high priests of society's preventive epistemology. Montag probably looks for an alternative to his anesthetized world inside books, but he himself is the living evidence that the subversive force of books is not in their contents, but in their potentialities. Actually, his rebellion begins not when he reads his first book, but in the very moment in which he saves it from fire because it is then that he recognizes his doubts and his questions, which imply the crisis of his orthodoxy.

Basically, firemen's task is not to intervene against those who dissent and oppose the government; as a matter of fact, we know almost nothing about laws and principles of this ghost structure. They do not have to destroy *subversive* books—that is to say, those books whose contents contradict the dominant voice of power—but to burn *any* existing book so as to eradicate any possible question, doubt, curiosity, or alternative possibility that not only a book could contain, but that are represented by the book in itself, as an object and a symbolic element. In a world dominated by the spectacle and organized around a monolithic concept of people as audience and consumers, any kind of book becomes an intolerable contradiction, an element of irreducible crisis, a pleating on a smooth and uniform surface. Montag feels distinctly the "contamination" of the book he saves from fire (41) without opening or reading it. His curiosity forces him to hide it, and the doubt raised by its possession, together with the infinite possibility contained in a closed book, are sufficient elements to declare him in rebellion. That is because in a world leveled on spectacular models, books represent what Louis Marin calls "the free force of unlimited contradiction" (xxii), an element on which he bases his whole concept of utopia.

So the book itself becomes a space open to rebellion and resistance, not for what it contains, but in itself, in its potential dimension of difference. While the *immense accumulation of spectacles* has overfilled the collective imagination, and while everything has become predictable as a déjà-vu in the repetitive narrative of the spectacle, books threaten to open up different horizons and to take readers back to a world that has been declared obsolete—that is, the world in which Montag takes shelter after his escape. This threat is precisely what is refused by an undifferentiated mass that views, thinks, and says the same things. Beatty explains it in these terms:

> No wonder books stopped selling, the critics said. But the public, knowing what it wanted, spinning happily, let the comic book survive. .... It didn't come from the Government down. There was no dictum, no declaration, no censorship, to start with, no! Technology, mass exploitation, and minority pressure carried the trick. (57-58)

Once every book is burnt, nothing will interrupt anymore the continuous flux of images and controlled thinking produced by the society of the spectacle. The assignment of the firemen thus is to watch over the emotive and intellectual sleep of the population, which wants to feel protected from their own humanity. Orthodoxy, in this sense, is basically a lack of imagination: to dream a common dream, to live a mass-produced life, to lose individual fantasy and the ability to imagine something different, so as not to risk, not to suffer, and to avoid any possible concern. Books are the unlimited contradiction to the spectacle as "enormous positivity, out of reach and beyond dispute" (Debord 6), not because they necessarily dissent from it, but because they allow people to imagine their own world. That is why they are always transgressive: they deny the passivity imposed by the enjoying of TV spectacle.

Lack of imagination is the primary feature of the perfect human gear in the society of the spectacle consumer-machine. In

Fahrenheit 451, the game is almost over, but still the complete elimination of books has, on the allegorical level, great significance. Actually, we could see firemen as the heirs of those who bring on the worldwide bonfire of Nathaniel Hawthorne's parable "Earth's Holocaust," where "this wide world had become so overburdened with an accumulation of worn-out trumpery, that the inhabitants determined to rid themselves of it by a general bonfire" (Par. 1). The words by which a "modern philosopher" proposes to burn "books and pamphlets" (Hawthorne) are quite close to the ones of Captain Beatty's lesson: "'Now we shall get rid of the weight of dead men's thought, which has hitherto pressed so heavily on the living intellect that it has been incompetent to any effectual self-exertion'" (Hawthorne). It is no surprise that the last thing burned, just after every literary work, is what is concerned with religion, an interesting parallel with the only book Montag saves from fire being the Holy Bible. But here, in Hawthorne's parable, arrives the revelation of the inadequacy of the whole bonfire idea, with the words of a devilish "dark-visaged stranger": "There is one thing that these wiseacres have forgotten to throw into the fire, and without which all the rest of the conflagration is just nothing at all; yes, though they had burned the earth itself to a cinder. …. What but the human heart itself?" (Hawthorne). In what happens to Mildred, there is the Hawthornian earth's holocaust done, but to get rid of the human being, it is still necessary to burn any living trace of him, just as books have been.

Utopian Endeavor of Being a Book

Books in *Fahrenheit 451* are, at the same time, the means to reacquire one's own humanity and also the proof that the human heart has not been burned so far. Thus, their subversive power does not refer to the kind of opposition produced, for example, by Emmanuel Goldstein's book in *1984*, an essay written to refute each and every point of the theoretical and political bases of the Party's ideology. As elements of *unlimited contradiction*, their effect on what has been defined as reality by the dominant power is similar to the one produced by the book *The Grasshopper Lies Heavy* in Philip K. Dick's *The Man in the High Castle*. In Dick's novel, the book represents the opening on another world, in which history has taken a different path. It shows that the world could be different from what it is, something highly menacing for a totalitarian power that needs to appear as the only possible and unavoidable reality. In *The Man in the High Castle*, the presence of the book is integrated into a patchwork of other proofs that demonstrate the actual existence of other simultaneous dimensions: there is the world where the fascist Axis Powers won the Second War World and occupied the United States, and there is the world in the book's dimension where history has taken the path the readers recognize as theirs. The force of *unlimited contradiction* lies in the revelation of the possibility of different power relations: in *Fahrenheit 451*, this means that people, through books, find out the possibilities of imagination outside the narrow, inhuman limits of the "truth" of the society of the spectacle.

In Montag's mind, to come across books is the epiphany of difference. Its liberating effect can be seen in his reaction against the intrusive advertising of Denham's Dentifrice. In the subway, people seem to be totally possessed by the pervasive voice of the advertising, while Montag tries to escape its hypnotizing mantras by reading his book:

> Montag found himself on his feet, the shocked inhabitants of the loud car staring, moving back from this man with the insane, gorged face, the gibbering, dry mouth, the flapping book in his fist. The people who had been sitting a moment before, tapping their feet to the rhythm of Denham's Dentifrice, Denham's Dandy Dental Detergent, Denham's Dentifrice Dentifrice Dentifrice, one two, one two three, one two, one two three (79).

It is a war of words against words, the written ones versus the sly, spellbinding voice that compels people to buy and consume. No matter what Montag reads in the book, he does not look for any anti-consumerism content but instead just needs to oppose the mass manipulation by finding alternative words.

The struggle is not political—it is philosophical and metaphysical. Books are not an instrument of ideological conflict,

---

but the means to claim one's own being human. From this point of view, it is not surprising that the book Montag saves and takes to Faber is the Bible, as a symbol of humanity's spiritual essence. Reduced to mechanical consumer, humanity has sold its soul and has forgotten the necessity of doubt. The Bible here contradicts the role that human beings play in the society of the spectacle, and it makes them quit their orthodox and blind participation to the capitalist role-playing game. That Montag's rebellion through books is a direct metaphysical answer to the annihilation of humanity is clear when he decides not simply to become any book but to become the Book of Ecclesiastes, that is, exactly that part of the Bible which interrogates the question of Good and Evil, and meditates on knowledge, contradiction, and faith. Just where the new dogma of spectacle prevents any doubt opposing the complete takeover of individuality, the book Montag becomes shows the fragile and contradictory human quest for metaphysical and religious answers.

At the end of the novel, we have the final evidence of the effective liberation of Montag through the words of the book he has become:

> Book of Ecclesiastes. Here. He said it over to himself silently, lying flat to the trembling earth, he said the words of it many times and they were perfect without trying and there was no Denham's Dentifrice anywhere, it was just the Preacher by himself, standing there in his mind, looking at him... (161; ellipsis Bradbury's)

In becoming a book, Montag is able to rediscover his individuality and to free himself from the ubiquitous message of the society of the spectacle. He has become the book, which human beings have forgotten, conquering back his memory, his mind, his freedom. The utopian planning of the future, therefore, is not based on a concrete political project, but on the simple re-appropriation of one's own humanity. In this sense, to become a book is a utopian endeavor, a way to salvation. To become a book is to be human again.

But is the Book of Ecclesiastes the only book Montag becomes? The third part of the novel begins with the firemen in front of his house and Montag forced into a corner. He looks doomed, about to be burned alive with the books he hid away. But the plot here has a sudden turning point, when Montag overcomes his nightmares and flees to achieve his utopian dreams. He kills Beatty, who is the personification of this world's evil; succeeds in escaping from the Hound, which is the thing he fears most of all; and joins the utopian community of book-savers, who will found a new society upon the ashes of the old one that is wiped out by the Bomb. Actually, Montag, as the phoenix, rises twice from his ashes. Once an orthodox member of the society of the spectacle, he now is born again from the ashes of his own dehumanization through the epiphany contained in books (in saving, reading, and memorizing them); as a doomed man, he is born again from the ashes of his death warrant, succeeding in a miraculous getaway. Everything looks like the granted dream of a desperate man.

In its substantial allegorical naivety, the third part of the novel could be read as the very book Montag becomes, a self-written adventure to salvation. We could imagine him as a Philip K. Dick character, who cannot discern anymore reality from dream, truth from fiction. What if Montag's reveries create his own heroic adventure, as happens to Douglas Quail, the protagonist of the short story "We Can Remember It for You Wholesale"? To grant his wish to visit Mars, Quail buys at REKAL, Inc., the implantation of the "extra-factual memory" of a trip to Mars as a secret agent. From that point, reality and his dreams get so intertwined that it becomes impossible to say what his real past is: Did he ever go to Mars? Is he a secret agent with his memories erased? Or does he simply have that false memory he purchased? Does Montag dream his getaway when he is about to die? Is it his final, desperate hallucination? Or maybe, it is something similar to what happens to Jaromir Hladík in Jorge Luis Borges' short-story "El milagro secreto"? Hladík is a poet who gets arrested by the Gestapo and is sentenced to death, but the night before his execution, he dreams of meeting God in an immense library and asking him to be granted the time to end

Critical Insights

his last poem. God concedes him one year's time, and one moment before he gets shot, everything is suspended as to permit him, in the motionless wait for the fusillade that will kill him, to imagine the last words of his poem before dying.

From a passive spectator to a reader, from a reader to a keeper of the memory of a book, now Montag can become the creator of his own utopia. He is like an author doomed to disappearance, who tries to write, by himself, his own survival. His imagination—that imagination he was able to recover through the "contamination" with books—dilates time so as to permit him to figure out his salvation. Montag becomes the book where his story is told, the diary of his double rebirth. It is a diary similar to the ones of Winston Smith in Orwell's *1984* and the protagonist of Zamyatin's *We*, texts they write to affirm their survival as human beings and, at the same time, the confessions of their desertions—that is to say, consequently, the origins of their convictions. If the world of *Fahrenheit 451* is an impending future where the human heart is destroyed through book burning, the supreme act of resistance is to write a book that can be saved from fire and then to become that book. In his survival, Montag becomes the last man alive, as it is Winston Smith in the torture room with O'Brien, in front of a mirror: "Do you see that thing facing you? That is the last man. If you are human, that is humanity" (Orwell 224).

Montag as a Postmodern Don Quixote

Don Quixote is the one who becomes his books—he is able to become a whole library—to flee from a world he does not recognize as his own. He is the author of his own utopia by melting objective and subjective plans, by confusing the reader's world and the book's world, as Borges explains in his "Magias Parciales del Quijote." In the utopian meta-fiction of his own life, Don Quixote defies his present day, making a masterpiece of himself and reinventing the world as a chivalric novel background through his gaze and his actions. Montag does almost the same: he escapes the society of the spectacle by writing himself as a romantic hero, the literary protagonist who saves humanity by remembering his own happy-ending adventure. In the utopian community he joins, every member introduces himself as the book he has become. Montag is not only the Book of Ecclesiastes, for he could say *I am Fahrenheit 451, I am Montag, I am the last man, and I am alive.*

Don Quixote literally writes himself his own survival in an intolerable world: he dies when he comes back to his real identity, when he stops projecting the character of himself in another realm. He lives as Don Quixote and dies as Alonso Quijano. He lives through the stories he is able to tell: the memory of his library gives him a whole universe to live in and to explore. His survival as a narrator sends us back to the Scheherazade character in *One Thousand and One Nights*, who offers herself to the vengeful King Shahryar, who marries a succession of virgins only to execute each one the next morning. But every night, to avoid death, Scheherazade begins to tell a different story without finishing it at dawn, so that the king, to know how it ends, cannot kill her. Scheherazade is a living library too, and has the strength of knowledge by her side. In the words of *One Thousand and One Nights*, she:

> had read many books and histories and chronicles of ancient kings and stories of people of old time; it is said indeed that she had collected a thousand books of chronicles of past peoples and bygone kings and poets. Moreover, she had read books of science and medicine; her memory was stored with verses and stories and folk-lore and the sayings of kings and sages." (first chapter)

As for Montag, like his eminent literary ancestors Quixote and Scheherazade, his secret and his only way to survive are to address his memory and to become a library, in order to project other worlds upon the world he refuses. The possibility to live lies in keeping a collective memory that no one could be successful in erasing. Neither time nor any kind of tyrannical power will ever burn past and knowledge—and with them, the *human heart*—since there will be someone remembering and keeping them.

There is one last word that keeps human beings alive in front of that irrevocable conviction—that is to have no more words.

A speechless person is a dead person. A human being with no memory is not a human being anymore. In the same way, in more political terms, we could say that this last word is the last alternative possibility to the *here* and *now*: without it, there is nothing more than a world made of tyrannical certainties that no one has any words to question anymore. The society of the spectacle depicted in *Fahrenheit 451* molds a human being unfit to speak anymore, a passive puppet with no past and no future, with no words and no memories, thereby deprived of his heart, soul, and mind. As a postmodern Don Quixote, Montag is able to project himself in an ancient world—that, with Anders, we could define as obsolete as humanity is—created through the memory of a whole library saved from fire. There, he realizes his utopian alternative to a world with no more alternatives and will survive the holocaust, together with humanity, since he will be able to remember those words that keep him alive.

Works Cited

Anders, Günther. *Die Antiquiertheit des Menschen*. Munich: Beck, 1956.

_____. "The World as Phantom and as Matrix." *Mass Culture: The Popular Arts in America*. Ed. Bernard Rosenberg and David Manning White. Glencoe, IL: Free Press, 1957. 14-24.

Anonymous. *One Thousand and One Nights*. Trans. John Payne. 1901. *Project Gutenberg*. Project Gutenberg Literary Archive Foundation, 30 July 2003. 19 Sept. 2013. <http://www.gutenberg.org/cache/epub/8655/pg8655.html>.

Borges, Jorge Luis. "El Milagro Secreto." 1943. *Ficciones*. Bogotá: Oveja Negra, 1997. 139-47.

_____. "Magias Parciales del Quijote." 1960. *Otras Inquisiciones*. Madrid: Alianza, 1976. 52-55.

Bradbury, Ray. *Fahrenheit 451*. 1953. New York: Del Rey, 1991.

Cervantes, Miguel De. *Don Quijote de la Mancha*. 1605, 1615. Madrid: Ediciones Cátedra, 1991.

Debord, Guy. *The Society of the Spectacle*. 1967. Trans. Donald Nicholson-Smith. New York: Zone, 1994.

Dick, Philip K. *The Man in the High Castle*. 1962. London: Vintage, 1992.

_____. "We Can Remember It for You Wholesale." 1966. *Selected Stories of Philip K. Dick*. New York: Houghton Mifflin, 2013. 325-46.

Foucault, Michel. "Intervista a Michel Foucault." *Microfisica del Potere: Interventi Politici*. Torino: Einaudi, 1977. 3-28.

Hawthorne, Nathaniel. "Earth's Holocaust." 1844. *Project Gutenberg*. Project Gutenberg Literary Archive Foundation, 6 Sept. 2003. 19 Sept. 2013. <http://www.gutenberg.org/files/9231/9231-h/9231-h.htm>.

Huxley, Aldous. *Brave New World*. 1932. London: Vintage, 2004.

Marin, Louis. Utopics: *Spatial Play*. Trans. Robert A. Vollrath. Atlantic Highlands, NJ: Humanities, 1984.

McLuhan, Marshall. *The Mechanical Bride: Folklore of Industrial Man*. 1951. London: Duckworth, 2011.

Morson, Saul. *The Boundaries of Genre: Dostoevsky's Diary of a Writer and the Traditions of Literary Utopia*. Austin: U of Texas P, 1981.

Moylan, Tom. *Demand the Impossible: Science Fiction and the Utopian Imagination*. London: Methuen, 1986.

Orwell, George. *1984*. 1949. New York: Signet, 1950.

Zamyatin, Yevgeny. *Noi*. 1921. Milan: Feltrinelli, 1984.

The Argument about Memory in *Fahrenheit 451* _____

Anna McHugh

Most readers of *Fahrenheit 451* would agree that the idea of memory, both as a cognitive and ethical faculty and as a collective asset of the community, is important to the plot and politics of the novel. Montag's apotheosis in the final pages is a result of his willing, even joyful, integration with a memorized text—he becomes the Book of Ecclesiastes. The Book Men, who memorize the best of human wisdom and wait for the post-apocalypse when their memorized libraries will rebuild a new world, embody Bradbury's argument in favor of a return to a pre-modern memory praxis[1] and ethos. Integrating the Book of Revelation into its own textual structure, the novel ends with a gesture to the rich intertext, which memory makes possible, and which Bradbury's novel exalts and enlarges.

That the final part of the novel is rich in tropes, motifs, and metaphors of traditional memory praxis is no surprise. As a scaffold around which to build a post-apocalyptic world, and a remedy for the depleted, skeptical aesthetics and intellectual practice of the 1950s, the final part of *Fahrenheit 451* draws deeply on a corpus of texts and thinking about the cultivation of memory. Part Three thus sketches a solution, based on memory, to the protagonist's problem—our problem, too, if we think of literary dystopias as concentrations of the worst contemporary social trends and the protagonist's subjectivity as evidence of how they affect individuals. But if the last part offers a solution based on memory, it is because the problem is posed as one of memory, too. I suggest that issues of individual memory—work and the value placed on memory by the novel's social and cultural institutions—significantly inform its dystopian character. Bradbury projects a future America by drawing on contemporary trends which degraded the role of memory in individual and communal life. Memory-rich episodes show it being effaced as a formative power in an individual's ethical character and a neuropsychological faculty, which stores and provides affectively-tagged information and through which we make sense of our world. This essay will examine episodes from the novel's three parts to trace the argument about memory and to explore Bradbury's understanding of it.

"The Hearth and the Salamander" lays out the problem: Montag's world expunges the life of the mind and oppresses those who pursue intellectual activities or items. Critical examinations of the novel have located its dystopian character in this vulgar, repressive society, and some have commented on how it extrapolates social and political trends of the late 1940s and early 1950s, or how the science fiction genre responds to perceived threats to its own interest group.[2] Certainly the extrapolation of technological trends and the cultural tenor of the early 1950s is fairly clear. We can see almost immediately how the text articulates contemporary crises: about styles of academic thought and the politics of academic expression; about accepted views about the intellect's role in governing and using affect and the propriety of allowing individuals to exercise control over this by self-administered chemicals; and about the extent to which appropriating canonical texts (in the manner of pre-modern thought) hindered or helped the drive towards existential authenticity. What has not been explored, as far as I am aware, is the *way* that Bradbury characterizes the repression of thought, of reading, and of oratory, as a repression of memory.

"The Sieve and the Sand" proposes an initial solution to the problem of effaced and degraded memory, in the form of Faber and the mimetic mentorship which he offers Montag. This nascent solution also draws on a lexis and discourse of pre-modern memory praxis, but plot developments show that it is a faulty solution. It attempts to advance Montag and others to a stage of ethical and cognitive development without the foundation of elementary memory-work which he undertakes in "Burning Bright."

Several episodes in "The Hearth and the Salamander" use the lexis or imagery of pre-modern memory texts to show how those "higher-order thinking skills" which the society seems most zealous to efface are those which draw most on memory. In order, these are Mildred's overdose; Clarisse's description of the school day; the altered history in *The Firemen of America*; the burning of the old woman; the failure of Millie and Guy's autobiographical memory by forgetting how they met; and Captain Beatty's long *apologia* for the state of his world. Even a nodding acquaintance with pre-modern memory and intellectual culture, described in studies like those of Frances Yates and Mary Carruthers, will probably reveal other episodes. To examine all of these episodes is beyond the scope of this essay; I will explore Millie's overdose, Clarisse's description of schooling, and the burning of the old woman as evidence of the first part of the novel's argument about memory.

The lexis with which Mildred's accidental overdose is described is rich in references to memory and past time. I think the positioning of this depressing episode at the start of the novel states the problem with which Montag simultaneously grapples: how are healthy interior and civic lives possible when the memory, as the basis of ethical excellence and civic potential, is subjugated? Mildred is treated by two technicians and a portable stomach-pump, which replaces the chemical swamp with fresh blood and serum. "Old time" stored in Mildred's physical memory is one of the elements discarded by the pumps: "One of them slid down into your stomach like a black cobra down an echoing well looking for all the old water and the old time gathered there" (22). The operators reduce their task to a kind of neuropsychological garbage disposal, the extreme end of the pre-modern understanding of memory as a somatically-located faculty. They "took up their load of machine and tube, their case of liquid melancholy and the slow dark sludge of nameless stuff, and strolled out the door" (23). Mildred obliterates consciousness because it is the fuel of memory; she expunges her physical memory because the material within it is unhappy. Despite an abundance of vivid sensory experiences each day, her disoriented affect means that she experiences them negatively, and the resulting memories are melancholic. Although technology has developed to the point where massive transfusion is possible—the first, unreliable hospital blood banks having been initiated in America in the 1940s—it is not possible to transfuse "someone else's flesh and brain and memory."

With the Dial-a-Pump operators and their revelation of how frequent these overdoses are, Bradbury argues the consequences of cultural antagonism to memory. It is significant, I think, that so many of the tropes of the 1950s are present in the episode. Mildred's dependence on unidentified sedatives evokes the increasing problem of barbiturate dependence in the 1950s, particularly by younger women, whose enthusiastic use of amphetamines and barbiturates led to the pills' nickname, "mother's little helpers" (Metzl). Barbiturate use in the pre-benzodiazepine period was such that, in the United States alone, production of these drugs reached, in 1955, the quantity necessary for the treatment of 10 million people throughout an entire year (Lopez-Munoz, Ucha-Udabe, and Alamo 336). While Bradbury's novel was being written, the Durham-Humphrey Amendment (1951) to the Food, Drug, and Cosmetics Act (1938) divided medicines into two categories as a reaction to this problem: prescription and over-the-counter. By 1952 and 1956, the Narcotics Expert Committee of the World Health Organization recommended that barbiturates should only be available on prescription. The novel's salient overdose episode argues that sedative abuse is the individual's response to a culture hostile to memory and the cultivation of thought.

Cultural hostility to critical thought is revealed by structures of formal education. Schooling is "an hour of TV class, an hour of basketball or baseball or running, another hour of transcription history or painting pictures...we never ask questions...they just run the answers at you, bing, bing, bing, and us sitting there for four more hours of film-teacher. That's not social to me at all" (37). Schools of the future exploit the television's effect of "quick and wide spreading of current and often emotionally charged information which is designed and destined to be forgotten at the instant of its reception" (Möckel-Rieke 9). History, the curriculum's *laudator temporis acte*, is reduced to rote transcription, a *reductio ad absurdam*, a simulation of memory. As a curricular subject, History—the narrative of actual events and speculation about their causes, derived from meditative acts of reading and questioning other representations of the past, and composing new material about events—is purposely rendered impotent.

It is significant, I think, that Clarisse objects explicitly to the lost social nature of learning, for it shows Bradbury's ideal of learning as a hermeneutical dialogue with two minds engaged in drawing out and re-forming the matter shaped between them. In the *Metaphysics*, Aristotle points out that "experience is formed of many memories" (I.i.), but by *memories* he means itemized results of the mind working on data, either sensory or semiotic, and shaping it into knowledge by applying questions and heuristics as a way of "coming to terms" with it. Communication between people is the ideal way to commence this process, but in TV class the communication is monodirectional, and the resulting *materiel* transmitted to the student remains data rather than knowledge. In fact, the social element of learning is so valuable to memory that even books only represent the voice of a person whom time has rendered inaccessible. In the *Phaedrus* Socrates reminds his listeners that writing is only of value as a reminder, but that it can't be properly questioned because it has no power to listen—it can only repeat itself (274D-275A).[3]

The relative dismissal of memory as a goal of pedagogy was reflected in the now-famous Bloom's Taxonomy, written in 1956 by a group of educators who sought to clarify the goals of learning and taxonomize the tasks by which they were achieved. Although the group hoped to achieve a pedagogical unity between Cognitive, Affective, and Psychomotor "domains," the taxonomy is, even after its revision in 2000, frequently understood as a hierarchy, which places "remembering" at the bottom and "creating" at the top. While this echoes the Classical insistence on a solid base of texts grasped in and by the memory and then manipulated as a means of producing new compositions, poor restatements of the Taxonomy[4] transmitted the idea of memory as the lowest order thinking skill and the one dismissed fastest by students hoping to hone their "critical thinking skills." Certainly, Bloom's Taxonomy reflects modernity's view of memory as a "mere" ability to reproduce accurately rote-remembered data, and as separate from the Romantic notion of a Work inspired by *ingenium* rather than an orderly intellectual process.

Bradbury's depiction of schools driven by technology and sport joins previous speculative works, which expressed skepticism at technology's relevance and ethical role in the classroom or the library. In her survey of how books and libraries appear in futuristic texts, Katherine Pennavaria shows how, from the late nineteenth century, science fiction routinely showed adulterated or merely artefactual texts being transmitted through increasingly tyrannical or sinister technology. Doctored or high-tech texts can only produce a simulacrum of the process of basic understanding (what pre-modern culture would have called *lectio*) and meditative reading (*meditatio*), for there is nothing *behind* these texts. There is a resulting erosion of citizens' ability to think critically, discern misinformation, avoid irrelevance, and compose new texts. The faculty of individual and communal discernment was under particular threat during the 1950s as the House Un-American Activities Committee (HUAC) sought an unprecedented level of censorship. The American Library Association's 1953 statement "The Freedom to Read" argued that the ordinary individual's exercise of "critical judgment" was the bulwark against government-sponsored suppression (Preamble). Bradbury shows an educational system that works to erode the faculty of critical judgment by systematically eroding students' experience of, or hunger for "the extended discussion that serious thought requires...[and] the accumulation of knowledge and ideas into organized collections" (ALA, Preamble). Clarisse's poignant objection shows a natural preference for human interlocutors in the face of redundant, transparent technology. Credible, meaningful memory is an integration of the human (the true, the authentic) and the literary (the beautiful, the worthy). Bradbury argues that this synthesis is contained in the authentic, memory-feeding text, not a thin and inauthentic technological medium.

Where formal schooling fails to stymie intellectual growth, other mechanisms of social control work more punitively against it. The burning of the old woman in Part One remains one of twentieth-century fiction's most poignant representations of cultural biblioclasm. The old woman meets the Firemen with a quotation from *Foxe's Booke of Martyrs*: "Play the man, Master Ridley; we shall this day light such a candle, by God's grace, in England, as I trust shall never be put out" (43). By appropriating Hugh Latimer's words, the old woman evidences her reading and the ethical use of this reading. She has integrated Latimer's words so completely into her memory that this speech act both reveals her attitude to the current context, and conflates it with Hugh Latimer's. The two contexts are brought to bear on the atemporal *res*—oppression of the innocent—of which they are only temporal instances. In her analysis of people using others' literary words *in extremis*, Mary Carruthers remarks on the profound integration between affect, ethical awareness, and re-collective memory, which is required to perform this. The point at which a reader "speaks again," another's words shows that "the student of the text, having digested it by re-experiencing it in memory, has become not its interpreter, but its new author, or re-author" (210). Once again, the relevance of Aristotle's comment about knowledge being composed of the memories of others is evident in Bradbury's novel. Carruthers comments that:

> A modern woman would be very uncomfortable to think that she was facing the world with a self constructed out of bits and pieces of great authors of the past, yet I think in large part that is exactly what a medieval self or *character* was. Saying this does not, I think, exclude a conception of individuality, for every person had domesticated and familiarized these *communes loci* [commonplaces], these pieces of public memory. (224)

Latimer's remark is no longer a piece of public memory, and the woman's speech act reveals both the depth of her own reading and the threadbare nature of the public memory to which she (re-)marks. The woman has hardly lost her own individuality—though I think her deliberate anonymity makes her situation more poignant and sinister—by conflating her identity with Hugh Latimer's through this act of memory. Rather she shows that the ethical situation remains the same, and argues that their speech acts constitute appropriate ethical responses to it. Her display of memorative skill points out that "rhetoric does not normalize an occasion, it occasionalizes a norm" (Carruthers 225).

The burning scene draws a straight line from the HUAC's witch-hunts, which began in earnest in 1947, to a future where the government works "to remove or limit access to reading materials, to censor content in schools, to label 'controversial' views, to distribute lists of 'objectionable' books or authors, and to purge libraries" (ALA, Preamble). Certainly, Nazi book-burning primarily informed Bradbury's novel (Bradbury 179), but American cultural suspicion of free expression had grown as a result of movement against Communists in the late 1940s.[5] As the number of texts deemed subversive grew, thanks to the surreal "Aesopian language thesis" advanced by Louis Budenz[6], the likelihood of a world where "the older academic styles have been driven out completely" (Bell 404) and where old women burn with their books, increased.

Captain Beatty's long *apologia* about his society deserves its own study. Beatty's *apologia* is at once a refutation of the very memory arts, which compose it, and a polished example of the rhetorical strategy, which draws on them. It responds epigramatically to contemporary events that suppressed "[a]uthors, full of evil thoughts" (64) and where "the word 'intellectual,' of course, became the swear word it deserved to be" (66) throughout the years of HUAC. The speech demonstrates many tropes and strategies that beginning orators were taught by rhetorical-instruction manuals such as the *Rhetorica ad Herrenium*, Quintillian's *Institutio oratoria*, Cassiodorus' *Institutiones* and Geoffrey of Vinsauf's *Poetria Nova*. These invariably drew on a full and ordered memory, which manipulated texts to produce new compositions. Beatty's *apologia* is a wonderful set-piece, full of paratactic hyperbole, where auxesis functions like a madly-wound zoetrope zooming through the twentieth-century. Many of Beatty's epigrams are worthy of their own essay, and Beatty himself deserves more critical attention than he has had, for he represents a new kind of anti-hero in American literature, a figure torn between the old, civilized, conservative tyranny, which enforces absolute ideals, and the closeted existentialism that proves too hard to maintain in the face of disapproval.

Millie's overdose is the first of several episodes that show how Montag's society ruthlessly cripples the idea and function of memory and how this impairs the life of individuals and the community. Each episode explores the failure of some aspect crucial to the use and function of formal memory. The novel's second part, "The Sieve and the Sand," responds to this state of affairs by suggesting a lifeline of recovery in the relationship between Montag and Faber, but uses several catastrophes to argue that a foundation of textual acquisition and memory training must be laid first. Readers can examine for themselves how Guy and Millie's argument reveals Montag's growing use of a formal memory "filing system," the *topoi* or *loci* that order the items of memory and provide the framework, through which we live.

The Montags have forgotten how they met; Guy points out to Millie that her degraded sense of autobiography is not simply a cognitive failure of memory-capacity. It is an ethical failing because she has failed to digest, store, and make relevant her experiences. This cuts her off from her own past, and the wider ethical past composed of others' similar experiences. "Maybe the books can get us half out of the cave" (81), Montag says, alluding to the Platonic darkness in which everything we see is a misapprehension of flickering, deceptive images. Montag is becoming aware of the connections between his experiences and the language that books can give to them, the *voces paginarum*, which allow him to recognize his own maturing sense of self in the words and experiences of others. Beyond that, he is becoming aware of a greater truth, a *res*, of which all experiences— his own and others'—are merely instances. Faber, whom Montag recalls in an argument with Mildred, draws the distinction between the meaning (the *res*) and the representation (the words); in the novel's second part, Montag hungers for the things themselves.

It seems touching that Montag, hungering for the meaning and intellectual richness that he believes books hold, rushes off to seek a *person* who can make sense of things for him. Faber outlines for Montag the three elements required for ethical development, without which society has become degraded. These correspond well to the three stages of moral development, which Hugh of St.

Victor describes in his allegorical work on the "ark of studies which one builds board by board in one's memory" (Carruthers 202-3). Moving through these stages, our relationship to the wisdom we read changes from merely correct (*rectus*), to ethically useful (*utilis*), and eventually becomes morally and intellectually habitual (*necessarius*). Faber's bitter speech illuminates how far the world and even devoted readers like himself, have drifted from this, but the speech also offers a faint hope of recuperation.

The first element a reader requires is quality of information, which Faber defines as highly textured representations of life—the same highly textured, striking representations vital to making memorable, stable *phantasia*, the mental images that encode information and experience. By ruminating upon this "fibrous" mental matter, the cultivated memory can analyze situations' ethical characters according to the *topoi* firmly fixed in their mind. By comparing and considering experiences against an ethical paradigm located in memory, we become aware of the world around us as a shadow of a finer one and can react to it in ethically appropriate ways, as the old woman does with her speech-act. High-definition mental representations, developed as the brain moves through the reading experience, engage the inner eye of the mind with their dimension, immediacy, and volume (as the televisors do) but possess moral *auctoritas* because they are deeply rooted.

The second element is leisure to digest these materials and to integrate them into one's developing moral character. When Martianus Capella remarks that *meditatio*, the depth-work of thoughtful reading, is better done at night time, because there is silence and a lack of distracting stimuli (Stahl and Johnson V.539, lns. 22-23), he is only touching the tip of the concentration—what Thomas Aquinas called *sollicitudo* or "worrying" at something—needed to integrate texts into the mind. When Faber refers to *leisure*, he means a slowing of the pace at which the entire culture works—"a hundred miles an hour, at a clip where you can't think of anything else but the danger" (92)—and a return to the solitude and mindfulness that so threatens Montag's world. A leisure of the mind and heart is required for thoughtful reading; if the heart is somewhere else, it is not open to being augmented by great texts.

Finally, Faber argues, the reader requires the right to carry out action based on what he has become from reading the text. Texts codify and communicate ethical wisdom, and it is absurd to expect that the intelligent reader can absorb them in isolation from his ethical context, or cease to become more potent in ethical excellence as a result of reading them.

Faber gives Montag a tiny two-way radio by which he can listen to Montag's conversations and help him to negotiate Beatty's traps. This is a witty literal rendering of the traditional *"voces paginarum,"* the "voices of the pages" (Balogh), which the cultivated intellect commits to memory and uses prudently to negotiate life. On the one hand, Faber uses the radio to comfort Montag in his sleeplessness, keeping him company as wisdom should. On the other, this "prosthetic memory" foregrounds Montag's own paltry stock of wisdom and his relative defenselessness against Beatty. David Seed compares "Montag being addressed on the one side by Beatty and on the other by Faber [to] a morality play" (234), but I think Bradbury employs this memory-prosthetic to show that any attempt to cheat the long, painstaking process of acquiring knowledge and integrating it into one's conscious mind is doomed to failure.

This evokes the distaste which met one of the great commercial projects of American 1950s: the Great Books series of Robert Hutchins and Mortimer J. Adler. The unique selling point of this project was Adler's "Syntopicon," a kind of index-cum-concordance, which filleted all 443 Great Books into an alphabetized list of Great Ideas. These Great Ideas and the list-form which ordered them are like an assembly-line version of the memory arts familiar to students of pre-modern memory culture. *The New Yorker*'s scathing review, published in 1952, explained:

> [A]n idea is a vague object that takes on protean shapes, never the same for any two people...every man makes his own Syntopicon, God forbid, and this one is Dr. Adler's, not mine or yours. ...the only one of the authors who wrote with Dr. Adler's 2,987 topics in mind was

Dr. Adler. And it is wrong practically because the reader's mental compartmentation doesn't correspond to Dr. Adler's. (Macdonald)

Nor does Montag's correspond to Faber's, and though comforting to have in Montag's ear, Faber's wisdom cannot be integrated wholesale into Montag's memory. Like the old woman who appropriates Latimer's words, the texts embedded in memory must be given voice by Montag, who will re-speak them as his increasingly-honed ethical mind recommends them.

The radio, and the reading of "Dover Beach" that Faber hears through it, develop the novel's argument in favor of a culture of memory by elaborating on the *wrong* way of going about it. There is no fast-track, no technological scaffold on which wisdom can be built, only the painstaking acquisition of good content, which orders the memory palace even as it builds it. As the American Library Association notes, there is no point in book-lovers forcing their own ideas on others: "they do not foster education by imposing as mentors the patterns of their own thought" (Proposition 2). Montag attempts to shock his wife's friends into an epiphany by reading aloud Arnold's "Dover Beach", but instead provokes only hysteria and rejection. Mildred excuses it as "a sample to show you how mixed-up things were, so none of us will ever have to bother our little old heads about that junk again" (107). Mrs. Phelps bursts into tears. Mrs. Bowles storms out. The episode evinces the cognitive dissonance in unprepared minds confronted with a *res*, for which they have no structure. Carruthers points out that historically, tears were regarded as a better reaction to a text than laughter, since laughter implies a critical distance, while tears result from affective—and so more profoundly cognitive—engagement with the material (209), but it is clear that emotions must be correctly disposed *before* the text is encountered. The point is that none of the women can see the benefit of the text; it is merely an unpleasant and embarrassing cultural experience that reinforces how much more appealing their own way of life seems. In the same year that Bradbury's novel was published, Irwin Kahn argued that the "war of words" in the fight against Communism was going against America, and that "to convince people of anything one must show (and do more than show) how the people, themselves, personally and individually, will benefit." The novel's second part suggests a remedy for the intellectual desert, but the protagonists' mistakes remind them that authentic wisdom is integrative; it cannot be grafted onto an immature intellectual structure like a prosthesis.

At the end of the second part, Captain Beatty abuses his copious memory for texts, revealing the difference between intellectual and ethical immaturity. Under the guise of recounting a dream, Beatty assembles a florilegium of quotations demonstrating the *catena* (chain) principle of recollection, where one item recalls another by some organizing principle such as opposition, agreement, precedence, even rhyme. Beatty argues that there are inconsistencies in the intertext and his *sic et non* style reveals the principles of division and categorization, which organize his plenitudinous memory. The drive toward mental and textual division and depletion characterizes the American 1950s: ideas and categories are clearly exhausted and, under extra-mural pressure, the secular academic becomes desolate and cynical, an adept manipulator or political ventriloquist, of texts. Recalling the 1950s, Daniel Bell could almost have been describing Captain Beatty when he writes that "[o]ne simply turns to the ideological vending machine, and out comes the prepared formula. And when these beliefs are suffused with apocalyptic fervor, ideas become weapons, and with dreadful results" (405). Beatty's suicide-by-fireman ends the novel's depiction of the absence of memory in a culture and its cost. Montag, Faber, and Beatty err in their attempts to address it, and the novel's final movement argues that only a return to traditional memory *praxis* can save it.

The first two parts of the novel, I have argued, state its problem as one of memory and locate its solution in a return to the *ethos* and *praxis* of pre-modern memory culture. The second part confirms that the cognitive route to wisdom is through careful use of a cultivated and plenitudinous memory, but the narrative turns also reveal Bradbury's conservatism—there is no shortcut, and part of the joy of memory-work lies in the elementary exercises, which are the first steps on the *via memorativa*. The railroad, which leads Montag to

---

the Book Men, is a wonderful allegory of this structured intellectual trail, which begins with the slow acquisition of texts and the building of a memory palace within the heart. Aristotle reminds those who engage in structured recollection, that in every sequence the thinker must find the *arche* or starting point (*On the Soul* 451b 18), just as Montag locates the railways tracks beneath his feet.

The Book Men's stories of destroyed academic careers, which evoke the cost of HUAC and the McCarthy era to American scholarly enquiry[7], do not deter them from storing up the best of human wisdom and knowledge by rote memorizing the texts. They "have photographic memories, but spend a lifetime learning how to block off the things that are really in there....we've got the method down to where we can recall anything that's been read once" (158). The Book Men are the final part of the novel's argument about memory: memory is the link between conceiving of good and doing it, and those who exercise their memories in a structured way, engaging fruitfully with texts, can do so both for practical utility, like Cicero's friend Lucullus (*On Academic* 3-4), and for ethical excellence, as in the *Rhetorica ad Herrenium*. Although most pre-modern writers noted that rote memory can be very fragile[8], the Book Men's memorizing endeavor is valuable and necessary. Their patience and plenitude reflects the pre-modern understanding of "perfecting the *res*," the matter under discussion, as an ongoing, meditative, and communal task. By embedding the text within a person who "re-speaks" anew each time, the text comes with its own human commentary, the 'embodied paratext', who can help the listener make sense of it. Answering Clarisse's complaint about the lack of "social" learning, the new world will wrap text, heuristic, and hermeneutic equipment up in one human body. This resolves in part Socrates' reservations about books as meaninglessly repetitious and ensures that the work of interpretation and transmission is a humane and socially-located one. Certainly, there is a risk of a gap or "slippage" between what is remembered and the thing itself, as there is a slight misfit between the words and the idea of the text, but recuperation is at the heart of human endeavor.

In his *Partitiones Oratoriae*, Cicero describes memory as "the sister of writing" (*Orations* VII), which explains the hostility towards books and memory in Montag's world. Those who consume books rather than goods are far less controllable, in part because they recognize the character of bad governments and reckon out how long they will have to endure them. They are not static subjects who possess externally-located goods, but subjectivities who remember and, in remembering, also feel and think and judge. Unlike Millie's televisor, when texts are "activated," they change the ethical—we might say the quantum—state of the user. The reader *qua* reader, becomes integrated with the text. Although Granger says, "We're nothing more than dust-jackets for books" (160), this is an ethical, not existential, statement. A strong sense of person and personal history anchors and makes relevant the human-text relationship, and it is one within which governments are usually unwelcome. These readers are the "well-qualified citizens" (Borges 358), whom one academic noted in 1951, were becoming timid and fearful for their own safety and whose fate Bradbury depicts in his novel.

Bradbury drew on this climate to depict a social problem of memory and to test what solutions the technology and tenor of his age came up with. The forest in which the Book Men live is a kind of *silva rhetoricae*, the wood of beautiful speech, in which learning waits for the shockwaves to pass before emerging. I think that this place and the activity of memory that occurs within it is only the last part of *Fahrenheit 451*'s long discussion about the value of prudence, humility, contemplation, method, and perseverance. The praxis which puts these virtues into action is memory-work; although painstaking and full of reversals, the reader who uses his memory "never gets so discouraged or disgusted that he gives up doing it all over again, because he knows very well it is important and *worth* the doing" (161).

Notes

1. For the purpose of this essay, 'memory praxis' refers to those formal exercises, which were part of an individual's rhetorical, ethical, and spiritual

training from around the time of Cicero until their reworking in the light of early eighteenth-century medical knowledge about the brain.

2. See, for example, Klein, Suvin, and Lecorps; and Seed.

3. See also Derrida.

4. Bloom himself reputedly said that it was "[o]ne of the most widely cited yet least read books in American education" ("Reflections" 9).

5. The FBI Subversive Squad used Angela Calomiris to pose as a Communist for seven years from 1942-49 and then asked her to testify before Judge Harold Medina at the trial of eleven Communists charged with plotting to overthrow the U.S. government. Far from focusing on her knowledge of subversive actions, Calomiris' testimony was primarily about Party members' reading habits.

6. For a brief account of this, see Filreis (307).

7. For more on this, see Schrecker.

8. From Quintillian to Chaucer, rote memory is has not been regarded as valuable in itself—a trick which even a parrot can perform has no basis in specifically human excellence. The *Rhetorica ad Herrenium* reserves rote memorization only for children and as a kind of limbering up. See *Rhetorica* III.24).

Works Cited

American Library Association. "The Freedom to Read Statement." 25 May 1953. <http://www.ala.org/advocacy/intfreedom/statementspols/freedomreadstatement> 13 Sept. 2013.

Aristotle. *Metaphysics*. Trans. H. Tredennick. Cambridge, MA: Harvard UP, 1969-1975.

_____. *On the Soul, Parva Naturalia, On Breath*. Trans. W.S. Hett. Cambridge, MA: Harvard UP, 1957.

Balogh, Josef. "'Voces Paginarum': Beiträge zur Geschichte des lauten Lessens und Schreibens." *Philologus* 82 (1927): 84-109, 202-240.

Bell, Daniel. *The End of Ideology*. Harvard: Harvard UP, 1988.

Bloom, Benjamin S. "Reflections on the Development and Use of the Taxonomy." Ed. Lorin W. Anderson and Lauren A. Sosniak. *Bloom's Taxonomy: A Forty-Year Retrospective*. Chicago: NSSE, 1994.

_____. *Taxonomy of Educational Objectives Handbook I: The Cognitive Domain*. New York: McKay, 1956.

Borges, Jorge Luis. "On the Cult of Books." 1951. *Selected Non-Fictions*. Ed. Eliot Weinberger. New York: Viking, 1999. 358-62.

Bradbury, Ray. *Fahrenheit 451*. 1953. London: Harper, 2004.

Calomiris, Angela. *Red Masquerade: Undercover for the F.B.I.* Philadelphia: Lippincott, 1950.

Carruthers, Mary. *The Book of Memory: A Study of Memory in Medieval Culture*, 2nd ed. Cambridge: Cambridge UP, 2008.

Cicero, Marcus Tullius. *On Academic Scepticism*. Ed. and trans. Charles Brittain. Indianapolis: Hackett, 2006.

_____. *The Orations of Marcus Tullius Cicero*. Trans. Charles D. Yonge. London: Bell, 1921.

_____. *Rhetorica ad Herennium*. Ed. and trans. Harry Caplan. Cambridge MA: Harvard UP, 1954.

Derrida, Jacques. "Plato's Pharmacy." *Dissemination*. Trans. B. Johnson. Chicago: U of Chicago P, 1981. 61-172.

Filreis, Alan. "Words with 'All the Effects of Force': Cold-War Interpretation." *American Quarterly* 39 (1987): 306-12.

Kahn, Irwin. "We're Being Worsted in the War of Words." *The Daily Pennsylvanian* 6 Oct. 1952. <www.writing.edu/~alfilreis/50s/war-of-words.html> 1 Aug. 2013.

Klein, Gerard, D. Suvin, and Leila Lecorps. "Discontent in American Science Fiction." *Science Fiction Studies* 4 (1977): 3-13.

Lopez-Munoz, Francisco, Ronaldo Ucha-Udabe, and Cecilio Alamo. "The History of Barbiturates a Century after Their Clinical Introduction." *Neuropsychiatric Disease and Treatment* 1 (2005): 329-343.

Macdonald, Dwight. "The Book-of-the-Millennium Club." *The New Yorker* 29 Nov. 1952: 11-29.

Metzl, Jonathan. "'Mother's Little Helper': The Crisis of Psychoanalysis and the Miltown Resolution." *Gender and History* 15 (2003): 240-267.

Möckel-Rieke, Hannah. "Media and Cultural Memory." *Amerikastudien/ American Studies* 43 (1998): 5-17.

Pennavaria, Katherine. "Representation of Books and Libraries in Depictions of the Future." *Libraries and Culture* 37 (2002): 229-248.

Plato. *Phaedrus*. Trans. H. N. Fowler. London: Heinemann, 1914.

Schrecker, Ellen W. *No Ivory Tower: McCarthyism and the Universities*. New York: Oxford UP, 1986.

Seed, David. "The Flight from the Good Life: *Fahrenheit 451* in the Context of Postwar American Dystopias." *Journal of American Studies* 28 (1994): 225-240.

Stahl, W.H. and R. Johnson. *Martianus Capella and the Seven Liberal Arts*. New York: Columbia UP, 1977.

Yates, Frances. *The Art of Memory*. London: Routledge, 1966.

If We Own It, We Can Destroy It: *Fahrenheit 451* and Intellectual Property

Aaron Barlow

Whose book is it? Does it belong to the author? Does it belong to the publisher? Does it belong to the purchaser? Or does it ultimately belong to the public, to the society that underwrote it in the first place? In some countries, it belongs to a state monopoly, or, as in Ray Bradbury's *Fahrenheit 451*, state ownership might be established through withdrawal of the right of possession (book-burning). Today, questions of ownership are complicated: *Content* becomes more important than the physical book, becoming "Intellectual Property" (IP). Proponents of the IP concept are often strident: "Creative property owners must be accorded the same rights and protection resident in all other property owners in the nation," said Jack Valenti, head of the Motion Picture Association of America, to Congress in 1982 (Lessig, *Free Culture* 117).

Valenti meant it. He spearheaded lobbying that led to enactment of the Digital Millennium Copyright Act of 1998, an expansion of already wide IP ownership rights established through the Copyright Act of 1976. Even so, it did not go quite as far as Valenti might have wished—extending the term of protection to forever minus a day—but it moved IP much more strongly into authorial and corporate control. There are other, more expansive models, though, some much older and one even ensconced in the United States Constitution (much to Valenti's dismay). Bradbury, at the end of *Fahrenheit 451*, presents one of these.

At extremes, we see things most clearly, a fact that science fiction writers often take advantage of. One extreme of IP holds ownership so close that no one but the owner can legitimately even *see* the book without the owner's (the State's) permission. Such a model seems to be where Valenti and the Digital Millennium Copyright Act (DMCA) would have us heading. The other extreme shows ownership so loose that it becomes not ownership at all, but part of the commons. Both are shown in *Fahrenheit 451*.

People who try to "liberate" texts and give them to "everyone" under this tradition are often called "pirates" today by supporters of the ownership position. Bradbury's pirates have so internalized the books they read that the books are quite literally part of them. Ownership rests neither with author nor state but in a commons represented by "readers" (reciters, really), sharers, not owners. The commons is a tool for human survival and should be respected, Bradbury claims, above mere ownership.

Twice in *Fahrenheit 451*, Bradbury puts books—and, by extension, their content— explicitly within the context of property and even of ownership, something implied in the beginning of the novel, as the right of the State. A book found anywhere else than in authorized State hands, we learn, is *prima facie* proof of theft. In the first of these two instances, when Guy Montag muses about how best to deal with his supervisor, Captain Beatty, he muses:

> "I don't think he knows which book I stole. But how do I choose a substitute? Do I turn in Mr. Jefferson? Mr. Thoreau? Which is least valuable? If I pick a substitute and Beatty does know which book I stole, he'll guess we've an entire library here!" (72)

Beatty has told Montag that he may keep a book for a day but nothing more. The "theft" will be ignored if Montag returns the book. Montag's conundrum is that he has stolen a number of books and does not know which book Beatty thinks he has, opening up a new can of worms should he choose wrong. Their exchange hints at a slightly different way of looking at books and the rules of society than is generally associated with the novel, conflating books and ideas at least at the start.

Fahrenheit 451 is not usually seen as a work raising questions of ownership. Yet when books become simple property, as Valenti would like, their content does, too, and book burning becomes less odious. If done by the "legitimate" owners, it is no more a problem than destruction of any other personal property. Bradbury rejects this, seeing a special status for the book, one more important than ownership. He recognizes what Kembrew McLeod, a communications professor and media activist, would write half a century later:

> When so many of our cultural experiences are commercial transactions, and so much of our culture is privately owned, we are in danger of being banished to a world that is not our own. It's a place where culture becomes something that is alien, and a primary cause of that alienation is the way intellectual-property laws are enforced. This leaves us very little breathing room to reshape and react to the popular culture that surrounds us. (332)

Bradbury was seeing this long before DMCA. Though what has happened in the intervening years is not the State ownership that Bradbury feared, the privatization of IP has had something of the same effect. The danger that McLeod sees, after all, is not really all that far from what Bradbury describes in his novel.

What may appear simple dichotomies, however, are actually quite a bit more complicated. James Gleick describes the early years of information in human hands (the base from which IP rises):

> The information produced and consumed by humankind used to vanish—that was the norm, the default. The sights, the sounds, the songs, the spoken word just melted away. Marks on stone, parchment, and paper were the special case. It did not occur to Sophocles' audiences that it would be sad for his plays to be lost; they enjoyed the show. Now expectations have inverted. Everything may be recorded and preserved, at least potentially. (396-97)

And everything may be owned. By virtue of contemporary American copyright law, almost all IP *is* owned once published.

This was not always the case. Gleick is expanding upon Walter Ong, who writes that "[i]n an oral culture, knowledge, once acquired, had to be constantly repeated or it would be lost" (23). Bradbury grasped this and understood it as the basis for the developing commons—and the surviving commons that he shows in *Fahrenheit*

451. Ong goes on to claim that the first move from oral culture, the development of writing, was also a restructuring of consciousness: "Without writing, the literate mind would not and could not think as it does" (77). This is another point Bradbury intuitively grasped, as is clear in the conversation between Montag, his wife, and the other housewives. Yet it is only with the ascent of what Ong names "literacy culture" that ownership of words, IP, and copyright become even a possibility—and this only once those marks on stone, parchment, and paper had given way to impressed ink and mass production. IP, in other words, is a concept derived from technology. It stems from societal/governmental attempts to deal with an entirely new (and evolving) way of dealing with information. IP is conventional, not natural, based on cultural agreements hashed out over time.

In the normal course of events, the right of possession of books includes an implicit "right of first sale," and has since the first copyright laws. This is implicit in the purchase of physical books and other artifacts associated with copyright. That is, the physical object itself is, once sold, completely the property of the buyer... with questions of ownership of the contents, the IP, laid to one side. That buyer, the new owner, can do whatever he or she wants with the object—including keeping it or even burning it. In the world of the novel, this right does not exist—or, more accurately, it exists only for the State. Possession of a book by anyone else becomes possession of stolen property. Ultimately, the "rebels" find the only way around this is to separate the book from its contents, something they do through the process of memorization.

As we have seen, much of the reason for the relatively new accent on IP, with recognition that ownership does not simply rest with the physical object, stems from problems surrounding, to use Walter Benjamin's phrase, "The Work of Art in the Age of Mechanical Reproduction." In his 1936 essay of that title, Benjamin points out that, for reproducible art, "changes of ownership are subject to a tradition which must be traced from the situation of the original" (571). IP ownership, unlike that of unique physical objects, is not an issue of simple possession but rests on cultural foundations and societal permissions. It is this fact that, as we will see, allows Bradbury to set up the most hopeful aspect of his novel's ending.

Bradbury confirms the fact of State ownership of IP in a second instance, through a conversation between Montag and Professor Faber, whom Montag hopes can lead him to a book-loving underground:

> His gaze returned unsteadily to Montag, who was now seated with the book in his lap. "The book— where did you—?"
> "I stole it."
> Faber, for the first time, raised his eyes and looked directly into Montag's face. "You're brave." (77)

This particular "theft," again, is only of the physical artifact, and it only is this, we see in the novel, that the State can control absolutely—though it tries to control content as well, as can be seen in Montag's answer to the question, "Do you ever read any of the books you burn?": "He laughed. 'That's against the law!'" (5).

As we learn later, the "rebels" also understand that there is a difference between artifact and content: the physical artifact is no longer even significant to them, but the creative and intellectual output carried is. In other words, it is the words themselves, the content, which they care about. Relying on memory, they have gotten rid of the culpatory evidence of the one type of theft and are assuming by their actions a free public domain of words and ideas in oral form. As Faber says, "It's not books you need, it's some of the things that once were in books" (78). He goes on to make the real point of Bradbury's own argument: "The magic is only in what books say, how they stitched the patches of the universe together into one garment for us" (79). This is the warp and woof of the argument for the importance of the commons, an argument not seen much today: "The things you're looking for, Montag, are in the world, but the only way the average chap will ever see ninety-nine percent of them is in a book" (82). Without a commons, our experiences are meager, at best. With the commons, we all fly.

It is never quite so simple. Other considerations, besides the right of the commons, need to be taken into account. For the purposes of his novel, Bradbury elides them, but they do remain important and color how we read the novel. Henry Mitchell explains that:

> The dialectic of intellectual property rights is driven by the interaction of three conceptions: a pragmatic or economic point of view, a view that focuses on the property rights of creators, and a view that focuses on the uncircumscribed nature of ideas and the inherently communal nature of the creative process. The first point of view is the typical ideology of legislators, the second that of authors and publishers, and the third that of "users." (13)

In *Fahrenheit 451*, only two of the constituencies are presented: the pragmatic (the State, in this case) and the communal. The role of the author—and the rights of the author—are necessarily ignored.

When copyright was established in England at the end of the first decade of the 18th century, its intent was protection for writers and publishers for a limited time, giving incentive for production of new work. It did not establish content as property or, as we call it now, IP. It allowed authors to apply for copyright protection for 14 years, renewable by the author for another 14. Copyright was not automatic and could only be applied for or extended by a living writer—the rights to the work, if assigned someone else, reverted back to the author after 14 years. The United States Constitution, some eighty years later, followed a similar line of thinking. Although it made no specifications—that would come in a law passed soon after the Constitution was ratified, one based on the British model—Article I, Section 8 proclaimed the government's right "[t]o promote the Progress of Science and useful Arts, by securing for limited Times to Authors and Inventors the exclusive Right to their respective Writings and Discoveries." This right is clearly different from property rights: it is granted for a specific purpose and for a limited time—the clause Valenti was trying to get around by a copyright term of forever minus a day. Neither of these conditions applies to any legal definition of the rights to other "property." James Madison

---

wrote that, through this section, "The public good fully coincides... with the claims of individuals" (*Federalist* 261). Though that may have been true to the Founding Fathers, it has not remained the case. The claims of individuals have taken precedence; in *Fahrenheit 451*, the claims of individuals have been superseded by those of the State, but the effect is the same, the diminution of the public good.

The limits of copyright, early on, were clearly marked. It had to be applied for, it lasted only a set time, it pertained to content as particular sequences of words, and it covered, in terms of physical manifestations, only first sale. A writer could forego copyright completely simply by not applying for it, could let it lapse, could not sue under copyright statutes for unauthorized use of ideas (that was covered by other laws), and could not control what happened to the book once sold. Today, all published works are covered by copyright. Its limits (in legal terms) are not disposable. It is beginning to cover close paraphrase, and electronic copies are not considered the possessions of the purchaser in the way physical books still are (that is, rights to them can be withdrawn). The content of my Kindle Fire is so constituted that Amazon can revoke my access without my leave—the irony of the product name becomes clear when seen against *Fahrenheit 451*.

That Amazon has the capability to do this, if not the desire, was shown in 2009, when copies of George Orwell's *Animal Farm* were pulled without announcement:

> In a move that angered customers and generated waves of online pique, Amazon remotely deleted some digital editions of the books from the Kindle devices of readers who had bought them.
> An Amazon spokesman, Drew Herdener, said in an e-mail message that the books were added to the Kindle store by a company that did not have rights to them, using a self-service function. "When we were notified of this by the rights holder, we removed the illegal copies from our systems and from customers' devices, and refunded customers," he said.
> Amazon effectively acknowledged that the deletions were a bad idea. "We are changing our systems so that in the future we will not

remove books from customers' devices in these circumstances," Mr. Herdener said. (Stone B1)

Though Amazon says it will not do this again, the fact remains that it can—something that could not be done with physical books except, of course, in the fictional world of *Fahrenheit 451.*

At the time copyright first was formalized, there really was no other vehicle of mass reproduction of art or intellectual "content" other than print. The only mass art possible was produced on paper through presses. Only in the 19th century (photography) and the 20th (film, sound recordings, etc.) were other vehicles for mass art developed. This led to a generalized conception of the book not being part of mass art and not being kitsch or the less valuable "low" art—certainly not to the same degree. Bradbury makes this type of distinction: The electronic entertainment in the Montag home has no connection to the books Montag burns, though today both are treated as equally valuable under the law—even as identical. In the novel, both are "owned" by the State, but only one has value, intellectually or culturally. This is a mindset of distinction that was reaching its height—though it was also being challenged—when Bradbury was writing *Fahrenheit 451.* Like most people, Bradbury did not then see an artistic or intellectual value in the electronic arts and certainly not in those produced by the State. In this, he differs from Benjamin and others, including Marshall McLuhan, who did not see a difference in medium as a necessary difference in value—a point of view that would gain strength over the coming decades.

Avant-garde and kitsch, paradoxically, always have been tied together, as Noël Carroll points out in his discussion of mass art (170-71). Though Bradbury's books are certainly *not* those of the avant-garde, his yoking (through comparison, if nothing else) of the electronic kitsch that pervades the home and the real and thoughtful works of art and intellect that are kept from it shows an elitist attitude toward art common to his time. After all, he did not need to bring the electronic kitsch into the book. That he did may seem a little ironic for a writer in a genre that, in the 1950s, had little "highbrow" respect, but it certainly served the purposes of *Fahrenheit 451.*

The mass art, "low" art, or kitsch that Bradbury shows can be owned by the State without objection. It is not television shows (or even their scripts) that need protection by the commons, but a certain type and level of books. This explicit division is emphasized by the ending of the novel, when the city is destroyed but the best of the books, the carriers of "real" culture (the commons) are not. There is no sense of loss regarding electronic media or mass art (or even science fiction, which is never mentioned in the novel). In this, Bradbury not only is reflecting a major assumption of his time, but is exhibiting the one great weakness of his book. How, we might ask, are we to determine what belongs in the commons and what can be safely discarded?

The very real power of *Fahrenheit 451*, on the other hand, arises from the contrast between the controlled world of property—in this case, State property—and that of the nascent commons building spontaneously outside of the city of the novel. When Montag first encounters it, Bradbury describes this world in terms of hands held to the warmth of a fire and faces seen only through the motion of its light. For Montag, this is a new sense of fire: "He had never thought in his life that it could give as well as take" (139). This is a fire as the center of community, as something all contribute to and gain from— not fire, as Montag has known it, as nothing more than an expression of an ownership divide: "This is mine, and you cannot partake in it." It is also fire that brings people together, taking the anger from the individual ("When we were separate individuals, all we had was rage" [143]) and turning it into the power of the community.

There is a further aspect of what Montag is seeing, one that relates to a point Benjamin makes. Referring specifically to copies, Benjamin writes that:

> technical reproduction can put the copy of the original into situations that would be out of reach for the original itself. Above all, it enables the original to meet the beholder halfway, be it in the form of a photography or a phonograph record. The cathedral leaves its locale to be received in the studio of a lover of art; the choral production,

performed in an auditorium or in the open air, resounds in the drawing room. (571)

By the same token, it allows the reader to reach the book halfway, something that will become apparent as the "rebels" begin to explain their "rebellion" to Montag. They have discovered, in the words of Benjamin, that the "authenticity of a thing is the essence of all that is transmissible from its beginning, ranging from its substantive duration to its testimony to the history which it has experienced" (571)—"transmissible," of course, being the key. After all, as Benjamin goes on to say, the "uniqueness of a work of art is inseparable from its being imbedded in the fabric of tradition" (572).

Ultimately, "the work of art reproduced becomes the work of art designed for reproducibility" (Benjamin 572). That is, its very nature destines it for the commons and limits rights of ownership. One of the "rebels," Granger, explains to Montag that we are all of us what we read: "We are all bits and pieces of history and literature and international law, Byron, Tom Paine, Machiavelli or Christ, it's here" (145). He explains how *this* commons arose: "It wasn't planned, at first. Each man had a book he wanted to remember, and did" (146). *That* is how the literature of a culture—its traditions—is born, not through individual control and ownership. Granger explains to Montag that this carries from generation to generation: "Grandfather's been dead for all these years, but if you lifted my skull, by God, in the convolutions of my brain you'd find the big ridges of his thumbprint. He touched me" (150).

Questions of property are questions of the relationship between the individual and the society. In an absolute libertarian situation such as Ayn Rand might envision, the need of the individual is the ace of trumps, more powerful than every other card in the deck. At the other extreme, that of the commons, no card has a value higher than any other. Granger tells Montag,

"[H]old onto one thought: You're not important. You're not anything. Someday the load we're carrying with us may help someone. ....
We're going to meet a lot of lonely people in the next week and the

next month and the next year. And when they ask us what we're doing, you can say, We're remembering." (156-57)

What they have does not belong to them, but is held in trust.

As I have said, Bradbury never ventures to speculate on the right of the author. He moves discussion to books written by people no longer able to assert their own rights of ownership, that is, to authors long dead. Yet there are loads of ownership issues here. Were the rights of Emily Dickinson, who chose to secret away most of her poetry rather than to publish it, abrogated by publication after she had died? Now in the public domain, the poems belong to "us." Should they? There is a difference between property and published property, a difference codified, for the United States, by the Constitution, as we have seen. What about something published completely without permission? Or, what if someone writes a great novel and decides to destroy it rather than publish it? Certainly we can burn our own manuscripts, but how does that affect the commons and *its* rights?

Bradbury does not address much of this. What he *is* reminding us is that there is something other than ownership important to intellectual and artistic endeavor, that the future lies in the commons that will survive even the war that destroys the city of his novel. He is arguing that, as Lawrence Lessig writes, the commons:

> produce something of value. They are a resource for decentralized innovation. They create the opportunity for individuals to draw upon resources without connections, permission, or access granted by others. They are environments that commit themselves to being open. Individuals and corporations draw upon the value created by this openness. They transform that value into other value, which they then consume privately. (*Future* 85)

This is Bradbury's key point: The commons creates abundance, while close ownership is stultifying and, ultimately, destructive.

There are other questions rising from our readings of *Fahrenheit 451*. In the digital age, when anyone can publish and do so almost immediately, where do those works stand once published? Should an author be able to withdraw publication, in effect burning all of her or his work? If I have a copy of something you wrote, do I have a permanent right of possession? As we have seen with Amazon.com, the answer (for the moment, at least) is no. Should it be? Though Bradbury never intended to address such questions, we certainly are faced with them today. Fortunately, *Fahrenheit 451* provides us with a basis for discussion. Although thanks to DMCA, the novel itself will remain under copyright protection for years to come, the discussions it engenders are already in the public domain—or are, at least, public.

And that, of course, was Bradbury's main intent.

Works Cited

Benjamin, Walter. "The Work of Art in the Age of Mechanical Reproduction." Trans. Harry Zohn. *Modernism: An Anthology of Sources and Documents.* Eds. Jane Goldman, Vassiliki Kolocotroni, and Olga Taxidou. Chicago: U of Chicago P, 1998. 570-77.

Bradbury, Ray. *Fahrenheit 451.* 1953. New York: Simon and Schuster, 2012.

Carroll, Noël. *A Philosophy of Mass Art.* Oxford: Clarendon, 1998.

Gleick, James. *The Information: A History, a Theory, a Flood.* New York: Pantheon, 2011.

Hamilton, Alexander, James Madison, and John Jay. *The Federalist Papers.* 1788. New York: Bantam, 1982.

Lessig, Lawrence. *Free Culture: The Nature and Future of Creativity.* London: Penguin, 2005.

_____. *The Future of Ideas: The Fate of the Commons in a Connected World.* New York: Random House, 2001.

McLeod, Kembrew. *Freedom of Expression®: Resistance and Repression in the Age of Intellectual Property.* Minneapolis: U of Minnesota P, 2007.

Mitchell, Henry C. *The Intellectual Commons: Toward an Ecology of Intellectual Property.* Lanham, MD: Lexington, 2005.

Ong, Walter J. *Orality and Literacy: The Technologizing of the Word.* London: Methuen, 1982.

Stone, Brad. "Amazon Erases Orwell Books from Kindle." *The New York Times.* 18 July 2009. B1.

Bradbury, Technology, and the Future of Reading _____

Ádám T. Bogár and Rebeka Sára Szigethy

"Okay, don't think. Nobody think. No ideas. No theories. No nothing."
— Douglas Adams, *The Hitchhiker's Guide to the Galaxy*

In 1953, Ray Bradbury had a vision on the disappearance of books and on the way this disappearance would happen. Moreover, his vision maps the consequences such a disappearance of books— or, better still, the outlawing of reading itself—may have on the sets of relationships between self and world, as well as between self and other selves. As we sit here now, in late 2013, we still are surrounded by a plethora of printed books. Reading can be done without limitations (in most cases, at least, although certainly there are exceptions[1]), and books are widely available and accessible. One difference, however, is the e-book reader, which manufacturers, some users, and certain environmentalists hope are gradually replacing the printed book. The question is, will this process of replacement trigger any changes in reading, be it the reading of a book, of the world, or of the emotions of ourselves? Will this change the relationships between self and book, between self and world, between self and other selves?

In the beginning of Part I of *Fahrenheit 451*, a conversation takes place between fireman Guy Montag and his young and somewhat eccentric neighbor, Clarisse McClellan. This conversation reveals interesting characteristics of the respective different stances, which Montag and Clarisse take toward the world surrounding them. Clarisse, "seventeen and insane" (Bradbury 5), is immersive: she has a comment, a note, a thought, or an observation ready on anything and everything around her, be it a two-hundred-foot-long billboard, a driver not knowing how grass is more than a "green blur" (6), a man in the moon, or the morning dew on the grass (6). She is looking and paying attention to everything and everywhere: she admittedly "love[s] to watch people too much" (6), yet this attitude is by no means limited to people alone. A teenage whirlwind, she rushes from

---

one idea to another, from one question to another, from one topic to another, but nevertheless, she takes her time to consider every utterance she makes, every thought she puts into words. Although she behaves in a seemingly unheedful way, her observations prove her to be a very attentive, apprehensive, and imaginative. Her stature is fleeting and dynamic—it is even inappropriate to call it a stature, a word implying staticness, as dynamism is the key aspect of Clarisse's relationship with the world.

In contrast, Montag seems to be the exact opposite of Clarisse. Always hasty to answer, he comes through as an inattentive person, who deploys a nervous laugh every time a question catches him off guard, which is exactly what happens after almost all of Clarisse's questions and comments. The Montag we see in this scene is a man leaning forward, looking forward, never turning his head toward anything, never looking at anything long enough to engage with it. He, unlike Clarisse, is a static figure, who could well be pictured in a sitting position, leaning slightly forward with a stiff neck, staring close in front of himself. This, incidentally, is something similar to a stereotypical stature taken up while reading. Montag's behavior draws an image of him in a reading position, while he is described as unimaginative and inattentive—that is, lacking exactly the skills necessary for reading. The apparently distracted and disorganized behavior of Clarisse is in fact an embodiment of impulsiveness, imagination, and dynamism, an array of faculties employed during, and needed for, reading. Montag embodies the act of reading inattentively, while Clarisse's very behavior is a reading, an intense reading of life itself.[2] Montag's body position metaphor surfaces at various points throughout the novel, which are to be reflected upon in due course.

The novel describes how Montag, a proud starter of fires employed by the country's totalitarian government, becomes an underground book-preserver, operating outside the law. His attitude toward books and towards reading changes radically: he goes from book-burner to book-learner, and his conversation with Clarisse, mentioned above, is catalytic in this process. Montag begins to question his profession, his country's government, his happiness, and, ultimately, his life as a whole. His frustration is triggered by his talk with Clarisse, but it is also attributable to the confluence of a number of factors that undermine and demolish his established faith and trust in the State:

> [Montag's] doubts about the government he is serving accumulate through the latest suicide attempt by Montag's wife, Mildred (and her casual acceptance of this attempt after she is resuscitated); through his witnessing of a book-hoarding woman who chose to ignite her own home rather than flee in the face of the firemen's flamethrowers; through the government's systematic elimination of Clarisse; through his own growing need to read and understand books. (Hoskinson 129)

Montag becomes the enemy of the State, a topic commonly mentioned in Bradbury criticism.[3] Many see the culmination of the "confrontation of Individual vs. State" (Hoskinson 129) in the scene involving Montag and Fire Chief Beatty, after Montag was ordered to burn his own home to purge it of anti-State matter, that is, of books. Montag, somewhat sarcastically aligning with Beatty's statement that, if "a problem gets too burdensome, then into the furnace with it" (Bradbury 109), burns the Captain to death, thus getting rid of the burning problem (pun irresistible) Beatty meant for him.

Montag's limping, half-paralytic escape from his own burnt-down house is a symbolic splitting-up between him and the society sustaining the system. Beatty represents an imminent and direct threat for Montag: he intends to arrest Montag, and besides this, he has discovered Montag's relationship with Faber, a former university professor and fellow book-preserver, who thus also has been rushed into danger. Beatty is a threatening force at another level as well, for he uses his extensive knowledge of literature, philosophy, rhetoric, and history to defend the ideology of the system he serves and sustains. For Montag, Beatty is the most hazardous enemy that can be imagined, yet later he realizes that Beatty's psychological warfare against him had one sole purpose: to enrage and upset Montag to such an extent that Montag would kill Beatty in the end.[4]

Montag's escape is also the next stage of the body-position metaphor. In the beginning of the novel, we saw Montag in a stereotypical reading position, looking close in front of himself, which is in sharp contrast to the vibrant, upright, head-up position of Clarisse, with her reading-the-world position. After killing Beatty, Montag becomes ultimately detached from the society of ignorance, and from the body position he has taken previously. He is walking with a heavy limp, which is what happens when one stands up and takes the first steps with legs still numb from sitting for a long, long time. Montag at last manages to stand up and walk.

The third and final stage of Montag's body metaphor arrives when the city is bombed:

> "Look!" cried Montag.
> And the war began and ended in that instant.
> …. Montag saw the flirt of a great metal fist over the far city and he knew the scream of the jets that would follow, would say, after the deed, *disintegrate, leave no stone on another, perish. Die.*
> Montag held the bombs in the sky for a single moment, with his mind and his hands reaching helplessly up at them. ….
> …. Montag crushed himself down, squeezing himself small, eyes tight. ….
> Montag, lying there, eyes gritted shut with dust, a fine wet cement of dust in his now shut mouth, gasping and crying, now thought again, I remember, I remember, I remember something else. What is it? Yes, yes, part of the Ecclesiastes and Revelation. (151–53)

In this extended scene, Montag is forced—and manages—to raise his head and open his eyes to the reality of the world. The dust of reality fills his eyes, and this hurts, as reality is cruel and piercing. Reality is war: During the whole timeline of the novel's plot, we can grasp bits of information on a war that is going on in the background. War is neglected and ignored by the public. It is not considered something crazy and violent that is to be opposed, since, as Montag's wife Mildred and her friends exclaim, "'It's always someone else's husband dies, they say'" and " 'I've heard that, too. I've never known any dead man killed in a war. Killed jumping off buildings, yes, like Gloria's husband last week, but from wars? No'" (91). Montag realizes that war is as far from this naive concept as possible. He stands up, recognizes the harshness but at the same time also the authenticity of life, and although this experience literally sweeps him off his feet, along with it comes a very important event: he remembers. He remembers where he first met his wife Mildred, and even more importantly, he remembers a section from the Bible he previously tried and failed to memorize. The past becomes acknowledged, memories come to life: he begins his journey to reading the world in the way Clarisse did.

In the society of *Fahrenheit 451*, conversations become empty. It is not even justifiable to call them conversations, since a conversation requires two (or more) parties with at least slightly different views, different ideas, different experiences, and different opinions. In the world of *Fahrenheit 451*, however, it is difference that is meant to be eradicated, thus rendering conversations impossible. If people have no new, original, or personal ideas or opinions, then people can have nothing new, nothing original, nothing of their own to say, and if we consider conversation and discussion the engine of social life, then without new, original, and personal ideas, social life itself becomes empty. This process is exemplified by the concept of the "living-room," consisting of a chair in the middle, plus three or four TV-walls, which provide the experience of a quasi-immersive virtual reality, filled entirely with soap operas and other forms of distraction. The room for living is, in fact, a room for the avoidance of living and of the living. Although "there are these people named Bob and Ruth and Helen" (Bradbury 18), questions like "Who are these people? Who's that man and who's that woman? Are they husband and wife, are they divorced, engaged, what?" (43) clearly offer themselves. These soap operas are works of fiction, even if simplistic and meaningless ones, and as such, are "about non-existent people" (59), about the non-living, and their sole purpose is to distract people's attention from the lives of other people. Yes, the people in *Fahrenheit 451* do have lives, but the perpetual stream of broadcast distraction obscures them, in a way similar to Aldous Huxley's *Brave New World*:

In *Brave New World* non-stop distractions of the most fascinating nature…are deliberately used as instruments of policy, for the purpose of preventing people from paying too much attention to the realities of the social and political situation. A society, most of whose members spend a great deal of their time…in the irrelevant other worlds of sport and soap opera…will find it hard to resist the encroachments of those who would manipulate and control it. (Huxley 37, qtd. in Seed 228)

People without anything to say or think become empty, and ultimately they lose their own selves. Selves are constructed by, and made of, memories. Memories are imprints and preservers of the past, and the essence of books in a way is to contain and record the past. Jorge Luis Borges writes in one of his essays, "Fire, in one of Bernard Shaw's comedies, threatens the library at Alexandria; someone exclaims that the memory of mankind will burn, and Caesar replies: 'A shameful memory. Let it burn'" (Borges 358). This is similar to what is done in *Fahrenheit 451*, where memories of the past are considered problems that get too burdensome; consequently, "into the furnace with it" (Bradbury 109). The society of *Fahrenheit 451* is a stagnant one where no progress is made, since progress requires the acknowledgement of things past. Books, in Emerson's words, are "the best type of influence of the past" (56). Books are burned, thus the past is burned, and the possibility of social progress dissolves into thin air, along with the smoke from the flames.

The reaction of the group of "old Harvard degrees" (Bradbury 126), former academics, is to preserve books by memorizing them, or rather, by becoming identical with the books, by becoming the books:

"I am Plato's *Republic*. Like to read Marcus Aurelius? Mr. Simmons is Marcus."….
"I want you to meet Jonathan Swift, the author of that evil political book, *Gulliver's Travels*! And this other fellow is Charles Darwin, and this one is Schopenhauer, and this one is Einstein, and this one here at my elbow is Mr. Albert Schweitzer, a very kind philosopher indeed. Here we all are, Montag. Aristophanes and Mahatma Gandhi and Gautama Buddha and Confucius and Thomas Love Peacock

and Thomas Jefferson and Mr. Lincoln, if you please. We are also Matthew, Mark, Luke, and John." (144–45)

Although these ex-professors are portrayed as the trustees of culture and difference, it is questionable whether they can regain their own selves in the process of becoming books. It is also important to ask: is it a good idea in the world of *Fahrenheit 451* to become a book?

In the novel's world, all people are books in a sense, mostly books that are not read, or if read, then not reflected upon. Montag is a rare exception to this as Clarisse reads him and even takes some pleasure in this reading. Montag's "let's talk" (92) to his wife and her guests is a pleading for reflection, for discussion, for opinions that would stir the still water of everyday dullness. Reading itself cannot provide revelation, only the conversation that results from it: it is reflection that counts, not only reading. The 'interactive innovation' of living-room plays—that is, the mindless approval of what one is told—kills exactly the essence, the heart-and-soul of conversation: unpredictability and the free formulation of one's own opinion.

In the future of *Fahrenheit 451*, books and reading are not available to, and are forbidden for, the general public. In our contemporary real world, however, all books, opinions, connotations, and allusions are readily accessible; one may make notes about them and also may comment on them immediately. Questions offer themselves: To what extent can we exploit our possibilities? Will and can such an extended, almost universal access replace personal conversation? In other words, will it hinder or assist personal interaction?

It may hinder personal relationships because many may be led to think that communication is not necessary, since one may tell everything one wants to via chat, e-mail, or Google Talk as well; face-to-face interaction may be easily replaced by P2P. Enhanced and increasing online presence and connectedness, however, also may enrich and assist communication. One may contact and communicate with people who would be otherwise physically out of reach—feedback, ideas, opinions, and suggestions from all around the world can be received in an extended blink of an eye. If we narrow it down to reading only, then it can be said that, with the help of the Internet, reading can become a collective action, with all the advantages and drawbacks that come with it. It is easy to imagine a futuristic e-application: Using a brain implant, one could display a real-time streaming flash video as blog post or a Facebook status message, where others could follow exactly what one is reading, see the page and the letters, trace the reader's eyes as they move along the lines, and comment on what they (the 'secondary readers') and the person who is actually reading (the 'primary reader') see in real-time.

Such a collective reading may seem futuristic, but e-book reader applications like Readmill[5] already provide such features: "Readmill aims to fulfill the potential of networked reading. Readers can underline and comment on a text to their heart's content, then open up those comments for discussion among a growing community of passionate readers" (Walter par. 5). Readmill goes even further, as it allows "authors to claim ownership of their books, and interact with readers in the margins of the text. So not only could I and my anonymous commentator debate the feminist critique of *The Silence of the Lambs* but, should he feel so inspired, Thomas Harris himself could respond, in a conversation directly related to the text itself" (Walter par. 6). In fact, collective and collaborative reading used to be the standard for centuries: "Modern reading is a silent, solitary, and rapid activity. Ancient reading was usually oral, either aloud, in groups, or individually, in a muffled voice" (Saenger 1).[6]

The above-mentioned digital collective reading extended almost universal access to our reality. It is the hypertext. It is networked literature. It is networked reading. As Michael Heim claims, hypertext is "a mode of interacting with texts, not a specific tool for a single purpose" (29-30). He also points out an inherent characteristic of the hypertext, namely that:

hypertext unsettles the logical tracking of the mind. .... [O]ur linear perception loses track of the series of discernible movements. A hypertext connects things at the speed of a flash of intuition. The interaction with hypertext resembles movement beyond the speed of light. …. The jump, not the step, is the characteristic movement in hypertext. (31)

The books that are most often cited as the precursors of hypertext are *Ulysses* and *Finnegan's Wake* by James Joyce, but all books in general contain allusions, references, and connotations that may or may not be recognized or taken note of by the reader. Within the realm of print media, however, if one wants to find out what, for example, the phrase *"epi oinopa ponton"* (Joyce 5) in *Ulysses* refers to, then one must look up the meaning of the phrase in a Greek-English dictionary, find the phrase among the example sentences therein, then consult the relevant sections on Homer's *Odyssey*, where the phrase appears originally (Thornton 12).

Somewhat similarly, e-books may contain links to other sources. However, as they are read mostly on devices with Internet access, all information pertaining to what is read is readily available within the same interface, in which the e-book itself is read. To see what *"epi oinopa ponton"* means in context, one only has to do a simple Google search and get results including references, analyses, blog posts, annotations, explanations, theories, essays, translation memory entries, forum posts, and even videos and pictures in only 0.13 seconds. What e-book reader devices provide is ubiquitous reading and access, and since many of these devices are capable of displaying images and videos and playing music as well, it becomes possible to read, watch, and listen simultaneously. The e-book reader opens up a whole world to reader, a world similar, in a sense, to the world "read" by Clarisse.

The e-book format, besides its obvious advantages, nevertheless has a number of issues. One of these is a technically less, yet psychologically more, important one: the issue of ownership. Is it possible to own an e-book? And if not, then is it enough to have the perpetual possibility to read them without owning them?

The virtual world of the Internet and of electronic communication is often considered a parallel one that cannot be fully reached, in which one cannot actually participate, and the same holds for e-books. E-book reader devices are named, and indeed become, the "reader" instead of the human agent: it is the device that establishes direct connection with the e-book, rendering the human agent a second-order reader. Due to the "in-betweenness" (Floridi 111) of technology, books really are accessed, not read. The e-book reader is an example of second-order technologies that are "relating users no longer to nature but to other technologies, that is, they are technologies whose affordances are other technologies" (Floridi 112). Moreover, the book is about to cease being a singular thing, becoming instead a process:

> The primary shift is one of thinking of the book as a process rather than artifact. We are moving from the culture of the book to the culture of booking. Our focus is no longer on the book, the noun, but on booking, the verb—on that continuous process of thinking, writing, editing, writing, sharing, editing, screening, writing, screening, sharing, thinking, writing—and so on that incidentally throws off books. Books, even e-books, are by-products of the booking process. (Kelly, "Booking" par. 6)

The very nature of e-books renders them unownable, since an e-book is infinitely replicable, with the contents of all copies being exactly the same as those of the "original." This is the conclusion to which Kevin Kelly comes:

> In the long run (next 10-20 years) we won't pay for individual books any more than we'll pay for individual songs or movies. All will be streamed in paid subscription services; you'll just "borrow" what you want. That defuses the current anxiety to produce a container for e-books that can be owned. E-books won't be owned. They'll be accessed. ("Become" par. 30)

Another issue that could be cited is concern about the books' loss of identity. In the case of electronic formats, books are virtual and uniform. They all become scrollable texts seen and read through a flat interface (a monitor, display, etc.), which means that, in a sense, books lose their identities (smell, touch, etc.).[7] Print books are different from one another: their communication with readers, their touch, smell, thickness, weight, and other physical properties are their "non-verbal traits." E-books are read *through*, and thus *mediated by*, the display of an e-book reader or a computer screen. Such a mediation unavoidably entails the uniformization of books, which essentially means that books lose a considerable portion of their identity: their "non-verbal traits" are gone. Physically, a PDF version of *The Complete Poetry & Prose of William Blake*, if ripped of its file name caption, looks exactly the same as a PDF of Allen Ginsberg's *Collected Poems 1947-1997* or of Aldous Huxley's *Brave New World*. In the case of print books, the difference is clearly apparent, even if the author's name and the title of the book are made unrecognizable (see Figs. 1 and 2).

These and other issues notwithstanding, e-books are here to stay, and the future of reading and reflection is most likely collective, networked, and virtual:

> Reading becomes more social. We can share not just the titles of books we are reading, but our reactions and notes as we read them. Today, we can highlight a passage. Tomorrow we will be able to link passages. We can add a link from a phrase in the book we are reading to a contrasting phrase in another book we've read; from a word in a passage to an obscure dictionary, from a scene in a book to a similar scene in a movie. (All these tricks will require tools for finding relevant passages.) We might subscribe to the marginalia feed from someone we respect, so we get not only their reading list, but their marginalia—highlights, notes, questions, musings. (Kelly, "Become" par. 21)

This is where we are now. But what if technological progress will grow faster? If the rate of technological progress accelerated exponentially, then an "intellectual runaway which is the essence of the Singularity" (Vinge 92) would occur, causing a series of paradigm changes that would make human beings more than human, even post-human. The phrase "technological singularity" was coined by mathematician and speculative fiction writer Vernor Vinge in the 1980s, with "the imminent creation by technology of entities with greater than human intelligence" (89) being the main cause of this change. In Vinge's view, superhuman intelligence also may be achieved through human-machine interfaces (HMIs) so highly sophisticated that "that users may reasonably be considered superhumanly intelligent" (89), and e-book readers may be seen as a possible substrate for the development of such HMIs. Isaac Asimov has described one such interface in his 1986 novel *Foundation and Earth*, when Golan Trevize, the novel's central character, is navigating his space ship and receives extensive amounts of information about his surroundings, and basically about anything, through a computer interface: "He thrust his hands out, right, left, and placed them on the outlines upon the desk. At once, he had the illusion of another pair of hands holding his. His senses extended..." (30-31). When connected to the computer of his vessel, Trevize becomes infinitely more intelligent and possesses more information on the world than he—or for that matter, anyone else—does otherwise. When online, Trevize may be considered a superhumanly intelligent agent.

As noted above, anyone with a WiFi-capable e-book reader may gain access to (vaguely put) the ever-current totality of human knowledge, and thus may be regarded to possess superhuman intelligence. The interfaces of today's e-book readers, however sophisticated they may seem, fall utterly short in terms of the intimacy of interfaces mentioned by Vinge (89). With a sufficiently intimate HMI, a posthuman being eventually may experience the mode of reading literature seen in Kurt Vonnegut's *Slaughterhouse-Five*:

> "We s read them [clumps of symbols] all at once, not one after the other. .... There is no beginning, no middle, no end, no suspense, no moral, no causes, no effects. What we love in our books are the depths of many marvelous moments seen all at once." (76)

Through, or rather *by*, such an intimate HMI, reading may lose its characteristic linearity—that is, reading word after word, sentence after sentence, page after page, etc.—and become non-linear. In such a post-human setting, the entirety of knowledge would become readable. Knowledge is information, and if the world represents information, then reading information means reading the world. If the entirety of knowledge is readable, then so is the whole world itself. This would become an elevated (dis-)embodiment of Clarisse's way of reading the world in *Fahrenheit 451*.

Computer scientist and inventor Ray Kurzweil contends that this singularity is imminent: in his view, the transition to singularity is happening in this very moment as well, and it consist of six stages, or as he calls them, "epochs." The sixth epoch, which Kurzweil names "The Universe Wakes Up" (35), reflects the idea that "intelligence, derived from its biological origins in human brains and its technological origins in human ingenuity, will begin to saturate the matter and energy in its midst" (35). This latter idea resembles Asimov's concept of Galaxia, "a super-superorganism embracing all the swarm of the Milky Way" (*Foundation* 4), as well as those described in his 1956 short story entitled "The Last Question." The story's plot involves a question put—"as a result of a five-dollar bet over highballs" (Asimov, "Question" 234)—to an early supercomputer called Multivac about "how can the net amount of entropy of the universe be massively decreased" (237). Multivac prints out its response, "INSUFFICIENT DATA FOR MEANINGFUL ANSWER" (237), and the short story revisits the status of the response throughout eons of human and post-human history. The penultimate state described in the story is when "Man, mentally, was one. He consisted of a trillion, trillion, trillion ageless bodies, each in its place, each resting quiet and incorruptible, each cared for by perfect automatons, equally incorruptible, while the minds of all the bodies freely melted one into the other, indistinguishable" (244), and finally, Man fuses with the Cosmic AC, a hyperspace-dwelling descendant of Multivac, "in a manner that was somehow not a loss but a gain" (245). The mental totality of humankind becomes one with an infinitely-greater-than-human intelligence, which is quite similar to the scenario Kurzweil describes, only described about 50 years earlier. It is not necessarily correct, and the idea may even become an object of ridicule later, but the important thing is that thinking results in further thinking, one idea leads to another, and fantasies may later on serve as the basis of real-world applications and events. This is what Timothy McGettigan calls "problematic reasoning":

> Instead of starting with facts, a problematic begins with a dream and then backtracks by inventing the facts that transform the dream into a reality. .... Crazy as it may seem, today's fantasies are often tomorrow's realities. In other words, fantasies represent a navigational star upon which to focus aspirations, and human reason—via the magic of problematic—often invents the necessary facts to transform fantasies into redefined realities. .... For those who are not convinced that zany pop culture fantasies can have any real impact on the production of scientific facts, then recall that the first nuclear submarine in the US fleet was named for Jules Verne's Nautilus. Or, if that's not wacky enough, note that Martin Cooper claims that he was inspired to invent the cell phone after watching Captain Kirk use his communicator on *Star Trek*. (213) Speculative fiction has been, and most probably will continue to be, an important source of inspiration for science[8] and for real life in general. This is precisely what it can provide for the building of the future of reading as well. One thing speculative fiction may contribute to this project is a whole host of fantasies, ideas, dreams, and visions concerning reading; another one is its very existence. As long as speculative fiction and, more generally, books are read, there will always be a "faithful less-than-1-percent minority stick[ing] to the books. .... The book may be ancient, but it is also the ultimate, and the reader will never be seduced away from it. They will remain a minority, but they will *remain*" (Asimov, "Ancient" 271).

Notes

1. See, for example, yearly lists of banned books compiled by the American Library Association at http://www.ala.org/bbooks/bannedbooksweek/ideasandresources/freedownloads#lists.

2. "The world, according to Mallarmé, exists for a book; according to Bloy, we are the versicles or words or letters of a magic book, and that incessant book is the only thing in the world: more exactly, it is the world" (Borges 362).

3. In fact, a significant portion of *Fahrenheit 451* criticism is concerned with issues of totalitarian rule, censorship, and government oppression. Bradbury

himself, however, claimed that this is, in fact, a misinterpretation of his novel: "Bradbury, a man living in the creative and industrial center of reality TV and one-hour dramas, says it is, in fact, a story about how television destroys interest in reading literature. 'Television gives you the dates of Napoleon, but not who he was,' Bradbury says..." (Johnston pars. 9–10). The threat that reading may become outdated and eventually disappear was the main idea he meant to call attention to in his novel.

4. Beatty's death wish is understandable to a certain extent, since such a society cannot be considered a preferable one for a well-read person like him, who has his own opinions and ideas; from this point of view, Beatty is radically different from most of his contemporaries. At the same time, however, the method of suicide Beatty chooses, that is, stampeding another person into killing him and thus into becoming an outcast, may precisely exemplify the uncaring attitude of the novel's whole society. Yet, his behavior may also be read in another way, namely that Beatty stampedes Montag into being an outcast precisely for Montag's sake, so that Montag is forced to detach himself from the society of ignorance.

5. See http://readmill.com

6. The Bible provides a characteristic episode depicting reading out loud in the story of Philip the Evangelist and the Ethiopian eunuch:

7. and, behold, a man of Ethiopia, an eunuch of great authority under Candace queen of the Ethiopians, who had the charge of all her treasure, and had come to Jerusalem for to worship, was returning, and sitting in his chariot read Esaias the prophet. Then the Spirit said unto Philip, Go near, and join thyself to this chariot. And Philip ran thither to him, and *heard him read the prophet Esaias*, and said, Understandest thou what thou readest? (Authorized King James Version, Acts 8:27-30, emphasis added)

8. This was of concern for Bradbury himself. He opposed the release of his works as e-books: he said that "e-books 'smell like burned fuel', telling the *New York Times* in 2009 that 'the internet is a big distraction'" (Flood par. 2). This is why it was a considerable feat by the publishing house Simon and Schuster to convince him to consent to the publication of the e-book version of *Fahrenheit 451* in late 2011.

9. For example, out of the thirty cited and consulted references in the bibliography section of Vinge's paper, ten are works of speculative fiction by authors like Asimov, Frank Herbert, Poul Anderson, Greg Bear, and Vinge himself (Vinge 94).

Works Cited

Asimov, Isaac. *Foundation and Earth*. 1986. New York: Bantam, 2004.

_____. "The Ancient and the Ultimate." *Journal of Reading* 17.4 (January 1974): 264-71. *JSTOR*. 5 Oct. 2013.

_____. "The Last Question." *Robot Dreams: Remembering Tomorrow*. New York: Ace Books, 1990. 234-46.

Authorized King James Bible. Oxford: Oxford U P, 2008. *BibleGateway.com*. 5 October 2013.

Borges, Jorge Luis. "On the Cult of Books." 1951. *Selected Non-Fictions*. Ed. Eliot Weinberger. New York: Viking, 1999. 358-62.

Bradbury, Ray. *Fahrenheit 451*. 1953. New York: Simon and Schuster, 2013.

Emerson, Ralph Waldo. "The American Scholar." *Essays & Lectures (The Library of America)*. Ed. Joel Porte. New York: Library of America, 1983. 50-71.

Flood, Alison. "*Fahrenheit 451* E-book Published as Ray Bradbury Gives in to Digital Era." *The Guardian*. 30 Nov. 2011. <http://www.theguardian.com/ books/2011/nov/30/fahrenheit-451-e-book-ray-bradbury> 5 Oct. 2013.

Floridi, Luciano. "Technology's In-Betweeness." *Philosophy & Technology* 26.2 (2013): 111-15. *SpringerLink*. 5 Oct. 2013.

Heim, Michael. *The Metaphysics of Virtual Reality*. New York: Oxford UP, 1993.

Hoskinson, Kevin. "Ray Bradbury's Cold War Novels." *Ray Bradbury*. Ed. Harold Bloom. New York: Infobase, 2001. 125-39. Bloom's Modern Critical Views Ser.

Johnston, Amy E. Boyle. "Ray Bradbury: *Fahrenheit 451* Misinterpreted." *The LA Weekly*. 30 May 2007. <http://www.laweekly.com/2007-05-31/news/ ray-bradbury-fahrenheit-451-misinterpreted/> 5 Oct. 2013.

Joyce, James. *Ulysses: The 1922 Text*. Oxford: Oxford UP, 2008.

Kelly, Kevin. "Post-Artifact Booking." *The Technium*. 9 June 2011. <http://www. kk.org/thetechnium/archives/2011/06/post-artifact_b.php> 5 Oct. 2013.

_____. "What Books Will Become." *The Technium*. 15 Apr. 2011. <http://www. kk.org/thetechnium/archives/2011/04/what_books_will.php> 5 Oct. 2013.

Kurzweil, Ray. *The Singularity Is Near: When Humans Transcend Biology*. New York: Viking, 2005.

McGettigan, Timothy. "Holy Megabucks, Batman! The Astounding Popularity of Superhero Movies." *The Reasoner* 5.12 (Dec. 2011): 212-13. 5 Oct. 2013.

Saenger, Paul. *Space Between Words: The Origins of Silent Reading*. Stanford, CA: Stanford UP Press, 1997.

Seed, David. "The Flight from the Good Life: *Fahrenheit 451* in the Context of Postwar Dystopias." *Journal of American Studies* 28 (1994): 225-240.

Thornton, Weldon. *Allusions in* Ulysses*: An Annotated List*. Chapel Hill, NC: U of North Carolina P, 1968.

Vinge, Vernor. "The Coming Technological Singularity: How to Survive in the Post-Human Era." *Whole Earth Review* 81 (Winter 1993): 88-95.

Vonnegut, Kurt. *Slaughterhouse-Five, or the Children's Crusade*. New York: Delacorte, 1969.

Walter, Damien. "Who Owns the Networked Future of Reading?" *The Guardian*. 23 Aug. 2013. <http://www.theguardian.com/books/2013/aug/23/reading-networked-future-readmill-app> 5 Oct. 2013.

Figures

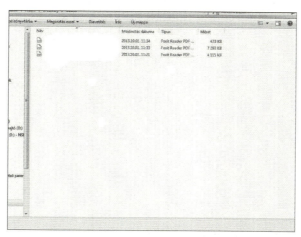

Figure 1. A screenshot of a folder containing PDF versions of *The Complete Poetry & Prose of William Blake*, *Collected Poems 1947-1997* by Allen Ginsberg, and *Brave New World*.

Figure 2. Hard-copy versions of *The Complete Poetry & Prose of William Blake*, *Collected Poems 1947-1997* by Allen Ginsberg, and *Brave New World* on a bookshelf.

RESOURCES

Chronology of Ray Bradbury's Life _____

1920	22 August, Ray Douglas Bradbury is born in Waukegan, Illinois.
1926-1933	Bradbury family moves back and forth between Waukegan and Tucson.
1931	Bradbury begins writing stories on rolls of butcher paper.
1934	Family moves to Los Angeles.
1936	18 August, first poem published: "In Memory to Will Rogers," in *Waukegan News-Sun*.
1938	January, first story published: "Hollerbochen's Dilemma," in Forrest Ackerman's fanzine *Imagination!*
1939-1940	Writes and publishes fanzine *Futuria Fantasia*.
1941	August, first paid story: "Pendulum", with Henry Haase, in *Super Science Stories*.
1944	Writes second half of *Lorelei of the Red Mist* for Leigh Brackett.
1947	*Dark Carnival* published by Arkham House.
1947	Marries Marguerite McClure.
1947	Receives O. Henry Award, Best First-Published Story, for "Homecoming" in *Mademoiselle*.
1948	Receives O. Henry Award, Third prize, for "Powerhouse" in *Charm*.
1949	Susan, first of four daughters, is born.
1950	*The Martian Chronicles* is published by Doubleday.

1950	October, review of *The Martian Chronicles* by Christopher Isherwood appears in *Tomorrow*.
1951	February, "The Fireman" published in *Galaxy*.
1951	*The Illustrated Man* is published by Doubleday.
1951	Ramona, second of four daughters, is born.
1953	*The Golden Apples of the Sun* is published by Doubleday.
1953	Film *It Came from Outer Space*, directed by Jack Arnold, is released.
1953	Film *The Beast from 20,000 Fathoms*, based on "The Fog Horn" and directed by Eugène Lourié, is released.
1953	*Fahrenheit 451* is published by Ballantine.
1953-1954	Bradbury works on John Huston's film *Moby Dick* in Ireland.
1955	*The October Country* is published by Ballantine.
1955	Bettina, third of four daughters, is born.
1956	Film *Moby Dick*, directed by John Huston, is released.
1957	*Dandelion Wine* is published by Doubleday.
1958	Alexandra, fourth of four daughters, is born.
1959	*A Medicine for Melancholy* is published by Doubleday.
1962	*R is for Rocket* is published by Doubleday.
1962	*Something Wicked This Way Comes* is published by Simon & Schuster.
1964	*The Machineries of Joy* is published by Simon & Schuster.
1964	*The Anthem Sprinters* is published by Dial.

1966	Film version of *Fahrenheit 451*, directed by François Truffant, is released.
1966	*S is for Space* is published by Doubleday.
1966	*Twice 22* is published by Doubleday
1969	*I Sing the Body Electric!* is published by Knopf
1969	Film version of *The Illustrated Man*, directed by Jack Smight, is released.
1971	Lunar feature is named 'Dandelion Crater' after Bradbury's novel *Dandelion Wine* by Apollo 15 astronauts.
1972	*The Halloween Tree* is published by Knopf.
1973	*When Elephants Last in the Dooryard Bloomed* is published by Knopf.
1976	*Long after Midnight* is published by Knopf.
1977	Bradbury receives World Fantasy Award, Life Achievement.
1980	Bradbury receives Gandalf Grand Master Award from World Science Fiction Society.
1980	*The Stories of Ray Bradbury* is published by Knopf.
1983	Bradbury receives Prometheus Award, Hall of Fame, from Libertarian Futurist Society.
1985	*Death is a Lonely Business* is published by Knopf.
1988	*The Toynbee Convector* is published by Knopf.
1988	Bradbury receives Bram Stoker Lifetime Achievement Award from Horror Writers Association.
1989	Bradbury receives Damon Knight Memorial Grand Master Award from Science Fiction and Fantasy Writers of America.

1990	*A Graveyard for Lunatics* is published by Knopf.
1992	*Green Shadows, White Whale* is published by Knopf.
1992	Newly discovered asteroid is named 9766 Bradbury.
1994	Bradbury receives Daytime Emmy for screenplay of animated *The Halloween Tree*.
1996	*Quicker Than the Eye* is published by Avon.
1997	*Driving Blind* is published by Avon.
1999	Bradbury suffers stroke.
1999	Bradbury is inducted into Science Fiction and Fantasy Hall of Fame.
2000	Bradbury receives Medal for Distinguished Contribution to American Letters from National Book Foundation.
2001	*From the Dust Returned* is published by Morrow.
2002	*One More for the Road* is published by Morrow.
2002	*Let's All Kill Constance* is published by Morrow.
2002	Bradbury receives star on Hollywood Walk of Fame.
2003	Bradbury's wife dies.
2003	*Bradbury Stories* is published by Morrow.
2003	Bradbury receives honorary PhD from Woodbury University.
2004	Bradbury receives National Medal of Arts Award from National Endowment for the Arts.
2006	*Farewell Summer* is published by Morrow.
2007	Bradbury receives French Commander *Ordre des Arts et des Lettres* medal.

2007	Bradbury receives Arthur C. Clarke Special Award.
2008	Bradbury receives Rhysling Award, Grand Master Poet, from Science Fiction Poetry Association.
2009	Bradbury receives honorary PhD from Columbia College Chicago.
2012	Bradbury dies in Los Angeles on June 5.
2012	Curiosity Mars rover touchdown is named Bradbury Landing on August 22.

Works by Ray Bradbury

Novels, including Fix-Up Novels
The Martian Chronicles, 1950
Fahrenheit 451, 1953
Dandelion Wine, 1957
Something Wicked This Way Comes, 1962
The Halloween Tree, 1972
Death is a Lonely Business, 1985
A Graveyard for Lunatics, 1990
Green Shadows, White Whale, 1992
From the Dust Returned, 2001
Let's All Kill Constance, 2002
Farewell Summer, 2006

Story Collections
Dark Carnival, 1947
The Illustrated Man, 1951
The Golden Apples of the Sun, 1954
The October Country, 1955
A Medicine for Melancholy, 1959
R is for Rocket, 1961
The Machineries of Joy, 1964
S is for Space, 1966
Twice 22, 1966
I Sing the Body Electric!, 1969
Long After Midnight, 1976
The Stories of Ray Bradbury, 1980
The Toynbee Convector, 1988
Quicker than the Eye, 1996
Driving Blind, 1997
One More for the Road, 2002
Bradbury Stories, 2003

Poetry

When Elephants Last in the Dooryard Bloomed, 1973
Where Robot Mice and Robot Men Run Round in Robot Towns, 1977
The Haunted Computer and the Android Pope, 1981

Drama

The Anthem Sprinters and Other Antics, 1963
The Pedestrian, 1966
The Wonderful Ice Cream Suit and Other Plays, 1975
Pillar of Fire and Other Plays, 1975

Bibliography

Bloom, Harold, ed. *Ray Bradbury's* Fahrenheit 451.. Philadelphia: Chelsea, 2001. Modern Critical Interpretations Ser.

———, ed. *Ray Bradbury's* Fahrenheit 451, new ed. New York: Infobase, 2008. Bloom's Modern Critical Interpretations Ser.

Bould, Mark. "Burning Too: Consuming *Fahrenheit 451*." *Essays and Studies* 58 (2005): 96-122.

Bradbury, Ray. *Bradbury Speaks: Too Soon from the Cave, Too Far from the Stars*. New York: HarperCollins, 2005.

Brown, Joseph F. "'As the Constitution Says': Distinguishing Documents in Ray Bradbury's *Fahrenheit 451*." *The Explicator* 67 (2008): 55-58.

Connor, George E. "Spelunking with Ray Bradbury: The Allegory of the Cave in *Fahrenheit 451*." *Extrapolation* 45 (2004): 408-18.

De Koster, Katie, ed. *Readings on* Fahrenheit 451. San Diego: Greenhaven, 2009. Greenhaven Literary Companion Ser.

Eller, Jonathan R. *Becoming Ray Bradbury*. Urbana: U of Illinois P, 2011.

Eller, Jonathan R., and William F. Touponce. *Ray Bradbury: The Life of Fiction*. Kent, OH: Kent State UP, 2004.

Greenberg, Martin Harry, and Joseph D. Olander, eds. *Ray Bradbury*. New York: Taplinger, 1980. Writers of the 21st Century Ser.

Grossman, Kathryn M. "Woman as Temptress: The Way to (Br)Otherhood in Science Fiction Dystopias." *Women's Studies* 14 (1987): 135-45.

Guffey, George R. "Fahrenheit 451 and the 'Cubby-Hole' Editors of Ballantine Books." *Coordinates: Placing Science Fiction and Fantasy*. Eds. George E. Slusser, Eric S. Rabkin, and Robert Scholes. Carbondale: Southern Illinois UP, 1983. 99-106. Altenatives Ser.

Hoskinson, Kevin. "*The Martian Chronicles* and *Fahrenheit 451*: Ray Bradbury's Cold War Novels." *Extrapolation* 36 (1995): 345-59.

Huntington, John. "Utopian and Anti-Utopian Logic: H.G. Wells and His Successors." *Science-Fiction Studies* 9 (1982): 122-46.

Johnson, Wayne L. *Ray Bradbury*. New York: Ungar, 1980. Recognition Ser.

Laino, Guido. "Nature as an Alternative Space for Rebellion in Ray Bradbury's *Fahrenheit 451*." *Literary Landscapes, Landscape in Literature*. Eds. Michele Bottalico, Maria Teresa Chialant, and Eleonara Rao. Rome: Carocci, 2007. 152-64.

McGiveron, Rafeeq O. "Bradbury's *Fahrenheit 451*." *The Explicator* 54 (1996): 177-80.

_____. "'To Build a Mirror Factory': The Mirror and Self-Examination in Ray Bradbury's *Fahrenheit 451.*" *Critique: Studies in Contemporary Fiction* 39 (1998): 282-87.

_____. "'Do You Know the Legend of Hercules and Antaeus?' The Wilderness in Ray Bradbury's *Fahrenheit 451.*" *Extrapolation* 38 (1997): 102-9.

_____. "'They Got Me a Long Time Ago': The Sympathetic Villain in *Nineteen Eighty-Four*, *Brave New World*, and *Fahrenheit 451.*" *Critical Insights: Dystopia.* Ed. M. Keith Booker. Ispwich, MA: Salem, 2013. 125-41.

_____. "What 'Carried the Trick'? Mass Exploitation and the Decline of Thought in Ray Bradbury's *Fahrenheit 451.*" *Extrapolation* 37 (1996): 245-56.

McNelly, Willis E. "Ray Bradbury—Past, Present, and Future." *Ray Bradbury.* Martin Harry Greenberg and Joseph D. Olander. New York: Taplinger, 1980. 17-24.

McNelly, Willis E., and Keith Neilson. "*Fahrenheit 451.*" *Survey of Science Fiction Literature.* Vol. 2. Ed. Frank Magill. Englewood Cliffs, NJ: Salem, 1979. 749-55.

Mengeling, Marvin E. "The Machineries of Joy and Despair: Bradbury's Attitudes toward Science and Technology." *Ray Bradbury.* Martin Harry Greenberg and Joseph D. Olander. New York: Taplinger, 1980. 83-109.

Mogen, David. *Ray Bradbury.* Vol. 504. Boston: Twayne, 1986. Twayne's United States Authors Ser.

Moskowitz, Sam. *Seekers of Tomorrow: Masters of Modern Science Fiction.* Cleveland: World, 1966.

Nolan, William F. *The Ray Bradbury Companion.* Detroit: Gale, 1975.

Reid, Robin Anne. *Ray Bradbury: A Critical Companion.* Westport, CT: Greenwood, 2000. Critical Companions to Popular Contemporary Writers Ser.

Reilly, Robert. "The Art of Ray Bradbury." *Extrapolation* 13 (1971): 64-74.

Seed, David. "The Flight from the Good Life: *Fahrenheit 451* in the Context of Postwar Dystopias." *Journal of American Studies* 28 (1994): 225-240.

Sisario, Peter. "A Study of the Allusions in Bradbury's *Fahrenheit 451.*" *English Journal* Feb. (1970): 210+.

Slusser, George Edgar. *The Bradbury Chronicles.* Vol. 4. . San Bernadino: Borgo, 1977. Mitford Series, Popular Writers of Today.

Smolla, Rodney A. "The Life of the Mind and the Life of Meaning: Reflections on *Fahrenheit 451.*" *Michigan Law Review* 107 (2009): 895-912.

Spencer, Susan. "The Post-Apocalyptic Library: Oral and Literate Culture in *Fahrenheit 451* and *A Canticle for Leibowitz.*" *Extrapolation* 32 (1991): 331-42.

Touponce, William F. *Ray Bradbury and the Poetics of Reverie*. Vol. 2. 1981. Ann Arbor: UMI, 1984. Studies in Speculative Fiction Ser.

Touponce, William F., and Jonathan R. Eller, eds. *The Collected Stories of Ray Bradbury: A Critical Edition, 1938-1943*. Kent, OH: Kent State UP, 2011.

Watt, Donald. "Burning Bright: *Fahrenheit 451* as Symbolic Dystopia." *Ray Bradbury*. Martin Harry Greenberg and Joseph D. Olander. New York: Taplinger, 1980. 195-213.

Weller, Sam. *The Bradbury Chronicles: The Life of Ray Bradbury*. New York: Harper, 2005.

_____. *Listen to the Echoes: The Ray Bradbury Interviews*. New York: Melville, 2010.

Zipes, Jack. "Mass Degradation of Humanity and Massive Contradictions in Bradbury's Vision of Humanity in *Fahrenheit 451*." *No Place Else: Explorations in Utopian and Dystopian Fiction*. Eds. Eric S. Rabkin, Martin H. Greenberg, and Joseph D. Olander. Carbondale: Southern Illinois UP, 1983. 182-98. Alternatives Ser.

About the Editor

Rafeeq O. McGiveron holds a BA with Honors in English and History from Michigan State University (MSU), an MA in English and History from MSU, and an MA in English from Western Michigan University (WMU). Having taught literature and composition for many years at a number of schools, including MSU, WMU, and Lansing Community College, in positions that have allowed his scholarship to be driven by personal interest and the serendipity of the classroom rather than by necessity, he has published around 20 articles of literary criticism on the works of such authors as Ray Bradbury, Robert A. Heinlein, Aldous Huxley, Yevgeny Zamyatin, Robert Silverberg, Willa Cather, Amy Lowell, Sharon Olds, and Robert Yellen. Currently, he works as an academic advisor and an interdepartmental liaison at Lansing Community College, where he has served since 1992. He also dabbles in fiction, occasionally poetry, and mobile art, and like the woman at 11 North Elm Street, he would not willingly abandon his attic. His novel, *Student Body*, is forthcoming.

Contributors

Aaron Barlow is Associate Professor of English at New York City College of Technology (CUNY). He is also Faculty Editor of *Academe*, the magazine of the American Association of University Professors. He earned his PhD from the University of Iowa with a dissertation on the science-fiction writer Philip K. Dick but has turned his attention since to cultural studies. Books of his include explorations of film, the blogosphere, and cultural divisions within American society. His most recent title is *The Cult of Individualism: A History of an Enduring American Myth*. His longstanding interest in questions surrounding Intellectual Property and Academic Freedom have led him to reconsider the message of *Fahrenheit 451*, especially in terms of an age where books need not be publicly burned but, instead, can be "disappeared" quietly from digital environments.

Ádám T. Bogár is an independent scholar and editor, with an MA in English from Károli Gáspár University, Budapest (2012). He has published scholarly articles chiefly on Kurt Vonnegut and John Milton, including his most recent essay, "Can a Machine Be a Gentleman? Machine Ethics and Ethical Machines" in *Critical Insights: Kurt Vonnegut* (2013). He is currently co-editing a volume of essays on Vonnegut and trauma and was a member of the organizing committee of "The Arts of Attention" conference held in Budapest in September 2013.

Imola Bulgozdi earned her PhD at Eotvos Lorand University, Budapest (2010) for a dissertation focusing on the cultural embedding of the creative process and the resulting short stories of Katherine Anne Porter, Eudora Welty, Carson McCullers, and Flannery O'Connor. Her interest in Southern representations of women also branched off to the analysis of novel-to-film adaptations from a Cultural Studies perspective. Her publications include "Probing the Limits of the Self" in *Eudora Welty's Delta Wedding* (Rodopi, 2008), the forthcoming article "New Criticism and Southernness: A Case for Cultural Studies" in *The New Criticism: Formalist Literary Theory in America* (Cambridge Scholars Publishing), and "'Barbarian Heroing' and Its Parody: New Perspectives on Masculinity" in *Conan Meets the Academy* (2012), along with forthcoming articles "Artificial Intelligence and Gender Performativity in William Gibson's *Idoru*" (ID Press), "'Some Genetics

Are Passed on Via the Soul:' The Curious Case of Susan Sto-Helit" (McFarland), and "Spatiality in the Cyber-World of William Gibson" (University of Tel Aviv).

Jonathan R. Eller (BS, United States Air Force Academy, 1973; BA, University of Maryland, 1979; MA, 1981; PhD, 1985, Indiana University) is a Chancellor's Professor of English, Director of the Center for Ray Bradbury Studies, and Senior Textual Editor of the Institute for American Thought, a research component of Indiana University's School of Liberal Arts (IUPUI). He has edited or co-edited several limited press editions of Ray Bradbury's fiction, including *The Halloween Tree* (2005), *Dandelion Wine* (2007), and two collections of stories related to Bradbury's publication of *Fahrenheit 451* in 1953: *Match to Flame* (2006) and *A Pleasure to Burn* (2010). Eller's most recent book, *Becoming Ray Bradbury* (2011), centers on Bradbury's early life and development as a writer through the 1953 publication of *Fahrenheit 451*. He recently completed *Bradbury Unbound*, a companion volume focusing on the middle decades of Bradbury's career and his rise to cultural prominence. Professor Eller also prepared Simon & Schuster's recent sixtieth anniversary edition of *Fahrenheit 451*. Two of his books have been LOCUS Award finalists.

Wolf Forrest has been a freelance artist and writer for over thirty years. He sold his first cartoon to *Boy's Life* at 17, and his articles and illustrations have appeared in such diverse publications as *Cinefantastique*, *Midnight Marquee*, *The Asheville Citizen*, and *Backyard Bugwatching*. He has also contributed to Sky Harbor Airport's continuing art exhibitions like *Baseball Hits* and *Arizona Valentine*. He lives in Tucson, and his two cats stand guard over his ridiculously excessive collection of movies, toys, and books. He cites his maternal grandmother and her basket of blood-curdling tales as a primary influence. He is currently working on a pop-up book based on the 1922 film *Nosferatu*.

Timothy E. Kelley holds a BA in English and an MA in English/Creative Writing from Michigan State University, where he was awarded the Mildred B. Erickson Fellowship for Creative Writing. He has worked as a warehouseman, a painter, a carpenter, and—for one life-changing, 104-degree day—a watermelon picker in Falfurrias, Texas. He currently lives with his wife, Paula, in Lansing, Michigan, where he has taught writing at Lansing Community College since 2002. While seeking a publisher for his first book, a novella called *Solid Contact*, he continues his reading and writing and enjoys the natural wonders of his home state, where he wanders the forests and kayaks the lakes and rivers whenever he gets the chance.

Andrea Krafft is a PhD candidate in the department of English at the University of Florida, where she is writing her dissertation about the intersections of the fantastic and the domestic in American literature after World War II. Ray Bradbury is a central figure in this project, and she has presented her research at both the 2013 Popular Culture Association national conference and the International Conference on the Fantastic in the Arts. Her chapter, "Appliance Reliance: Domestic Technologies and the Depersonalization of Housework in Postwar American Speculative Fiction," will appear in *Home Sweat Home: Perspectives on Housework and Modern Domestic Relationships* (Scarecrow Press). Her other research interests include the Cold War, women's and gender studies, speculative fiction, humor writing, and magazine studies.

Guido Laino is an independent researcher working in Italy both as a critic and a creative artist. He received his PhD in American Literature from the University of Salerno and has worked mainly on postmodern forms of utopian and dystopian fiction. He has published more than twenty articles on Italian and international reviews and books. As for Bradbury's *Fahrenheit 451*, Laino has written "Destinazione 'Good Old Days': il viaggio nel tempo in *Fahrenheit 451*" (*Cuadernos de Literatura Inglesa y Norteamericana*, vol. 9) in 2006 and "Nature as an Alternative Space to Rebellion in Ray Bradbury's *Fahrenheit 451*" (*Literary Landscapes, Landscape in Literature*, Carocci Editore) in 2007.

Anna McHugh studied at the universities of Sydney and Oxford. Her first doctoral thesis (Sydney) was about memory in Chaucer's *Canterbury Tales*, and her second (Oxford) was about political literature in late-medieval Scotland. She was a postdoctoral fellow at the University of Oxford and now teaches high school in Sydney, Australia.

Phil Nichols teaches Video and Film Production in the Faculty of Arts at the University of Wolverhampton in the United Kingdom. He holds an MA in Screenwriting, is working on a Ph.D. on the screen works of Ray Bradbury, and is a Fellow of the Higher Education Academy. He serves on the Advisory Board of the Center for Ray Bradbury Studies (Indiana University) and the Editorial Board of *The New Ray Bradbury Review*. His previous writings on Bradbury have appeared in *The New Ray Bradbury Review* and *The Radio Journal* and in the books *Science Fiction Across Media*, *Visions of Mars*, and *When Genres Collide*. His website (www.bradburymedia.co.uk) catalogs and reviews Bradbury's work across all media and is the most extensive bibliography and filmography of Bradbury on the web.

Robin Anne Reid received her doctorate in English from the University of Washington in 1992 and has been teaching in the Literature and Languages Department, A&M University-Commerce, since 1993. Her areas of teaching are creative writing, critical theory, and marginalized literatures. Her scholarly interests include fan studies, speculative fiction, corpus stylistics, and adaptation studies. She published *Ray Bradbury: A Critical Companion* (2000) in Greenwood's Critical Companions to Popular Contemporary Writers series and was the editor of *The Encyclopedia of Women in Science Fiction and Fantasy* (Greenwood, 2008). Recent articles have appeared in *Style*, *Extrapolation*, and *English Language Notes*.

Garyn G. Roberts received his BBA in Marketing from the University of Wisconsin, Whitewater in 1981 and his MA in Popular Culture Studies and PhD in American Culture Studies (with emphases on English, History, and Sociology) from Bowling Green State University in 1983 and 1986, respectively. He has taught at Mankato State University, Michigan State University, and Northwestern Michigan College. Roberts is the author and editor of several books and a range of book chapters, articles, and literary dictionary entries. Subject matter of these includes, in part, dime novels, pulp magazines, 1950s science fiction invasion movies, pulp magazine editors Hugo Gernsback and Joseph T. Shaw, Jack London, Stephen King, Anne Rice, and Dean Kootz. In 1994, Roberts received an Edgar (Allan Poe) Award nomination in the "Best Critical/Biographical" category from the Mystery Writers of America for *Dick Tracy and American Culture: Morality and Mythology, Text and Context* (McFarland, 1993), and in 2013 he received a Munsey Award from PulpFest for his contributions to the field.

Joseph Michael Sommers is an Associate Professor of English at Central Michigan University, where he teaches courses in children's and young adult literature as well as courses in modern and contemporary Anglophone literature, visual narratives, and popular culture. He has published work on figures such as Gary Paulsen, Hunter Thompson, Denise Levertov, and Judy Blume. Recently, he has brought out chapters and articles on the culture of childhood in nineteenth-century lady's journalism, the maturation of Marvel Comics' characters in the Post 9/11 Moment, Hellboy amongst the Melungeon People, and, of course, *Twilight*. More recently, he brought out further work on Christopher Nolan's *The Dark Knight*, a revisionary examination of C. S. Lewis's *Narnia*, his first book-length collection of essays covering contemporary investigations into the work of Alan Moore, and a book on video game adaptation entitled *Game on, Hollywood!*

Rebeka Sára Szigethy holds an MA in Hungarian Language and Literature from Károli Gáspár University (2012) and Professional Certificates in Printmaking from Óbuda School of Fine Arts (2013) and in Journalism from Szeged University of Sciences (2003). In recent years, she has been concentrating on her artistic career and is the co-founder and core member of the 60% Fuji Art Group. Both her artistic practice and her research have been considering the similarities and differences between, and the intricacies of, the reading of texts and of images. She has also published scholarly essays and articles on William Blake, the sublime, Herman Melville, Hieronymus Bosch, and José Saramago, as well as works of short poetry, mainly haiku.

Index

Critical Insights